T0001027

"Monique Jenkinson is the Jane Goodall of drag."
—Justin Vivian Bond, trans-genre artist

FAUX QUEEN

A LIFE IN DRAG

MONIQUE JENKINSON

FAUX QUEEN
A LIFE IN DRAG

MONIQUE JENKINSON

AMBLE
PRESS
Ann Arbor
2022

Amble Press

Amble Press First Edition: January 2022

Print ISBN: 978-1-61294-221-6

Printed in the United States of America on acid-free paper.

Cover photo by Fontaine Weyman, 2008
Author photo by Robbie Sweeny, 2021
Cover design by TreeHouse Studio

This is a memoir. The events, places, and conversations are
portrayed to the best of the author's memory. While all the
stories in this book are true, the chronology of some events has
been compressed. When necessary, the names and identifying
characteristics of individuals and places
have been changed to maintain anonymity.

THE FOLLOWING MUSIC LYRICS
ARE REFERENCED IN THIS WORK:

"This is the time. And this is the record of the time."
Anderson, Laurie. "In the Air." Warner Bros. 1982.

"Well I went to school . . . Do it for the kids, yeah." Erlandson,
Eric/Hole/Love, Courtney/Pfaff, Kristen/Schemel, Patty.
"Rock Star." DGC. 1994.

"I'm gonna take my hips to a man who cares."
Harvey, PJ. "Sheela-Na-Gig." Too Pure. 1992.

"Sit back and enjoy the real McCoy."
Sioux, Siouxsie. "Monitor." Polydor. 1981.

"Why do we always come here? I guess we'll never know. It's
like a kind of torture to have to watch the show."
Henson, Jim/Pottle, Sam. "The Muppet Show Theme."
Arista Records. 1977.

"We could be married and then we'd be happy."
Asher, Tony/Love, Mike/Wilson, Brian. "Wouldn't It Be Nice."
Capitol Records. 1966.

"Will I miss the sky? Will I miss the clouds?
Will I miss the city lights?"
Ono, Yoko. "Will I." Capitol Records/EMI. 1995.

"Take a cruise to China, or a plane to Spain . . . Meet a
girl on a boat, meet a boy on a plane."
Oakey, Phillip/Wright, Phillip Adrian.
"The Things That Dreams
Are Made Of." Virgin. 1981.

"Fuck the mothers, kill the others."
Sioux, Siouxsie. "Night Shift." Polydor. 1981.

"I still have my hands, I still have my telephone,
I still have my allergies."
Monk, Meredith. "The Tale." ECM. 1980.

"You aren't never goin' anywhere."
Gordon, Kim/Moore, Thurston/Renaldo, Lee/Shelley, Steve.
"Tunic (Song for Karen)." DGC. 1990.

"I did go from wanting to be someone, now I'm drunk
and wearing flip-flops on Fifth Avenue."
Wainwright, Rufus. "Poses." Dreamworks. 2000.

"Keats and Yeats are on your side, while Wilde is on mine."
Morrissey/Marr, Johnny. "Cemetery Gates."
Rough Trade. 1986.

"Sometimes I've been to cryin' for unborn children that
might have made me complete."
Hirsch, Ken/Miller, Ron. "I've Never Been To Me."
Universal. 1982.

"Go out on the lawn! Put your swimsuit on!"
Brownstein, Carrie/Tucker, Corin.
"I'm Not Waiting." Chainsaw. 1996.

"When I think of those East End lights, muggy nights/The
curtains drawn in the little room downstairs."
John, Elton/Taupin, Bernie.
"Someone Saved My Life Tonight."
MCA Records. 1975.

For my blood family & my drag family.
For Mitzi, Tom, Marc & Kevin.

TABLE OF CONTENTS

FOREWORD
SLAY, ILLUSION

When I try to remember one of the first times I saw Fauxnique perform—around 2008, when San Francisco's drag subculture became my unofficial beat as a freelance alt weekly arts reporter—I see myself on a Sunday, walking into a bar in the Castro in the middle of the day. Near the door, in a little circle of bar floor space cleared for performance—the kind of improvised ritual performance space I've come to associate with that place and time—Fauxnique stands, making angular turns and gestures, reflected and reproduced in a video monitor while ominous, discordant music plays: Laurie Anderson's "From the Air."

I knew this song from my own misfit teenage years in the 90s spent seeking arty escape hatches from suburban life on Bainbridge Island, Washington: my queer friends and I, like Monique and hers not so long before us, ran to music for solace and for provocation, for some mirror, too, in which we might catch a reassuring glimpse of our own outcast inner lives, worshipping Nina Hagen and Yoko Ono and The Slits. Now Fauxnique was lip-synching, or maybe she wasn't:

This is the time. And this is the record of the time.

And I was there reveling in this postmodern glory because the search had, naturally, continued: into the clubs and bars of the Bay, dark and sticky rooms where generations of "art-damaged" seekers mixed and mingled, recognizing one another in, if nothing else, this shared mission of discovery and of love: love of music and, more often than not, of the women who made it; love of irreverence and of subversion; love of absurdity, of play, of making things, of *breaking* things, of casting spells, of glamour.

It all came together in drag. In those years in San Francisco, drag appeared to be enjoying a special moment, part of a long and continuing process of mutation. Drag was busy both celebrating and transcending itself: the drag scene there was also a performance art movement, one that predated and foreshadowed drag's storming the gates of popular culture.

Drag has always been here and it always will be: to slightly alter what Jeff Goldblum's Dr. Ian Malcolm says of life itself in *Jurassic Park:* drag finds a way. (Incidentally, Jeff Goldlbum appeared as a guest judge on *Rupaul's Drag Race* in 2020, where he got himself into hot water; questions he posed to one contestant, Jackie Cox, an Iranian Canadian, about Islam being "anti-homosexuality and anti-woman" led to outcry and argument online.) Who could have known that one of the ways it would find would be Fauxnique, the first "faux queen" winner of San Francisco's biggest drag pageant, which started as a parody of a drag pageant, doing, essentially, a conceptual dance number in the middle of the day, at a gay bar in the Castro, to a song from Laurie Anderson's *Big Science*?

👑 👑 👑

This book is the time, and this book is a record of the time. In it, Monique Jenkinson traces her artistic lineage from a childhood curiosity excited by "difficulty practices" (acting out Mary's sudden blindness in *Little House on the Prairie*, for example) to full-fledged, pageant-winning performer, guiding us through the cultural moments and movements that whirled through her imaginative world like weather systems: Punk, British New Wave, New Romantic, Goth. Meanwhile, too, the rigors of ballet, which shaped her artist's psyche and embodiment in indelible ways, fostering discipline on the one hand and dysmorphic perfectionism on the other—a complex inheritance that she would eventually fold into her work, integrating it into a creative metamorphosis that took place on the stages of San Francisco's drag clubs.

Chief among those stages was the eight-by-ten foot one at Trannyshack, the drag night where we undoubtedly first met. The name has since changed; among the many pleasures of this memoir is the way in which Monique reflects upon and examines the ever-changing deployment of language and identity in this and other respects, putting it into the context of a specific time, place, and personal history (or "herstory," as she would have it). This, too, forms part of the artist's archaeological examination of how she came to be:

> *When I entered the drag world, the word, though transgressive, was so generalized and casual a term of endearment that people used it almost as one would use "girl" today, that is, for pretty much everyone in the scene, myself included. It would be disingenuous for me to erase that moment and the words those generous people used as they welcomed me into their family.*

Faux Queen, too, is anything but disingenuous—a quality which got you nowhere at Trannyshack, unless you were making a self-aware (and self-destructing) spectacle out of it on stage. Instead, it approaches the task of memoir—the dance of memoir, the drag of memoir—in the same spirit that ruled over those Tuesday nights at the Stud (the bar that hosted "the 'shack"): honest, unflinching, and irreverent; funny, experimental, subversive, bold. Monique will explain to you, shortly, what a "faux queen" *is*, but only as the beginning of a much more capacious and complex conversation about what it might mean to be *queen, queer, female,* or *faux.* The drag world from which Fauxnique emerges contains multitudes, and even its multitudes contain multitudes: a "context for irreverence," as she puts it, where fluidity reigned (not to mention actual body fluids of every imaginable kind, incorporated into a cascade of three-minute performances).

All this to say that, while unfolding a personal history of artistic inquiry, feminism, and the metamorphosing self, and while capturing the artistic-efflorescence-through-drag taking place during a particular era of San Francisco's nightlife, *Faux Queen* also looks back at the people, the places, and the social and cultural forces that enabled, in Monique's life, that most vital, most quicksilver creative practice: play.

♛ ♛ ♛

I have a confession to make: I've never watched *Rupaul's Drag Race.* Okay, that's not entirely true—I watched a few episodes when it first came out, just to see how it was set up, but nothing since then. Competition for status saturates nearly every aspect of American life, and I have minimal interest in watching people compete—which is to say, *play to win*—in this particular way, whether it's in the arena of sports, modeling, fashion, or drag.

In a state of true play, you're not trying to prove yourself to anyone, which is why it so often opens up into the thrill of true freedom. Of course, discoveries made in play may then be taken and refined into extraordinary creations through the rigors of *work*—a process Monique depicts here with the seasoned artist's obsessive love of detail and specificity. But the fundamental energy of play is exploration for exploration's sake: finding something new to do, or a new way to do something old, and then doing it because it feels interesting or exciting (and, maybe, forbidden).

Play also happens, more often than not, with others; accomplices real or imaginary. Describing a museum event she orchestrated at which children created outfits for drag queens, Monique writes:

> *Kids with all kinds of gender expression were thrilled to play with living dolls who then proudly walked the runway in their kinder-craft creations. The event reaffirmed something I've known forever: drag queens and kids are like chocolate and peanut butter. We like to play dress-up and dream ourselves into fantastical ways of being. And anyone who has spent time with both a cranky two-year old and a messy queen can confirm that they are kindred creatures in more ways than one. As Margo Channing in All About Eve says of children, "they'd get drunk if they could."*

It's the *people* in Monique's story—the "messy queens," the people who met and played and fought and flourished around Trannyshack at the time—that remind us of the difference between those most remote, most spectacular specters of reality show drag stardom and our co-conspirators on the ground, in the bar, on the street, and backstage. From the middle of any discourse about what is *faux* and what is authentic, the creative friendship shines forth, moving and complex and undeniably human.

What drew me to drag in San Francisco was, believe it or not, its humanity. This world of illusion was made up of people moving through rooms, people with all their particular shapes, voices, and smells, their virtues and their foibles, their inner lives and their outer ones, their madness, their reason, their *realness*.

Drag pop culture, in this respect, can never hold a candle to it, preoccupied as it is—as so much of our popular culture is—with competitive hijinks edited and glossed and groomed to seamless surface perfection.

People, relationships, and works of art are imperfect. What's more, the best of them aren't afraid to be. The best of them are capable of laughing at themselves, knowing they are always works in progress. Monique Jenkinson knows this; her knowledge is hard-won and meaningful, and it's part of the reason she writes with such wise humor, knowing that the magic in all of it comes from the very imperfection that makes us so ridiculously and beautifully human. Through her own history—"herstory"—she bears witness to the authenticity of messy, complex, constant change.

If our day and age is marked in some major way by hand-wringing about what (existential) freedom really is and who really has it; I offer up, after reading *Faux Queen*, one fleeting, imperfect, improvised definition among many other simultaneous and perhaps even contradictory possibilities. Freedom is the courage to look at yourself and to see that you are fluid, not fixed; that you are changing, not concluded, and then, with a pure heart, with a heart full of wonder—no matter what else the world may say about your heart—to laugh.

Evan James
New York, New York
July 2021

WHAT'S
IN MY PURSE?

"Well, history has been made tonight.... It's been a long time coming. We'd like to introduce to you, Miss Trannyshack 2003. Fauxnique!"

This announcement is the reason I've written a book, the motivating event behind anyone's possible interest in my life. I was the first cisgender woman to win a pageant for drag queens. The inevitable question "How did that happen?" comes next. The multiple, wordy, roundabout answers fill the pages that follow.

♔ ♔ ♔

When I was eight, my mom, Mitzi, drove us the two hours from Modesto to San Francisco to join my dad, Tom, at a business dinner. I wore a dress of white linen piqué with a Peter Pan collar and big red pockets in the shape of tulips. Retro. Midcentury-little-girl drag. In 1979.

Upon meeting me, Bobby, the man we were dining with, squatted down to my level, looked straight at me, and said: "Love the dress. And those pockets, honey!" I didn't realize it at the time but I'd just met my first queen. In the surreal lingo of the era, he opened his mouth and a purse fell out.

And it was beautiful.

I replied, "Thank you," politely, as I had been taught. But I imagine saying "Bobby, honey yourself! I love your lavender snakeskin cowboy boots and your mauve polo shirt. Don't think for a second I didn't notice how they set off the sandy tones of your tidy mustache. Thank you. Thank you for getting it, for getting *me*."

I love gay men. I always have. When I am among gay men, I am among my people. That's the easiest way to say it. Not all gay men, not only gay men, but most, and mostly. The people with whom I share affinity—cultural, intellectual, philosophical—are gay men.

People have simplified this by saying "Oh, she's a gay man trapped in a woman's body!" but I never have. Even as I write the phrase "gay man" for the sake of convenience, I know that gay men are not a thing for me to distill into an easy category, an essence that I could trap in my body. Besides, though my life isn't a constant expression of unabashed liberty, rarely do I relate to the word "trapped." I live in the contemporary world of the queer, in which we subvert the binary and use "trouble" and "complicate" as verbs to act upon terms like "gay" and "man."

I would say my affinity with gay men is just perfectly natural, but of course I bristle at the word "natural" just like Oscar Wilde, my good Judy (that's old-time gay speak for "pal"). Nature is a concept I like to trouble and to complicate. Then there is the "nurture" part, which comes, as most nurture does, oh yes it does, from Mom. Mitzi instilled in me a system of cultural values that one might call Old School Gay, with an attendant love of all things associated with it: black-and-white movies full of swelling soundtracks and mid-Atlantic accents, the exuberant and wistful outpourings of musical theater (see Judy above), sophisticated fine design, and wicked, sometimes withering, humor.

The girl with the tulip pockets and sassy mother spent her

teen years aching to be taken seriously and trying to be good. Perfect, even. Conflictedness shaped my sense of self; pleasure was suspect. I'd be tempted to call my affliction "anhedonia," but there was a kind of hedonism, a fervor, to my state that bore the traces of what one might more accurately term Late-Stage Baroque Puritanism or perhaps Genetic Catholic Martyr Syndrome. But beneath that seriousness, and my desire for its affirmation, were strata of glitter, lava flows bubbling with glamour and delight.

Performing drag helped heal some of the most stubborn wounds of my angsty youth, inevitable psychic damage from formative years spent under the microscope of classical ballet training. My closest friends and I, many of them men who do drag, have recognized a common ground of intense scrutiny and high stakes between growing up a sissy boy and growing up a fledgling ballerina. Each of us strove to please, to diet or quiet ourselves down to fit into a damaged culture's idea of perfection. Thank God, or Goddess, or Goddex we failed and found each other.

I found acceptance where a layperson might assume I wouldn't: at a drag club, the infamous Trannyshack in San Francisco. Trigger warning and buyer beware! This word is now Problematic with a capital *P*. Or rather, a capital *T*. It is a big ol' purse full of problems, which we will examine.

Dear reader, if you don't want to see me dump out my purse, don't want to see the broken compact, the old Kleenex, the stubby eyeliner, the bloodstained dollar bill, the expired condom, the half-empty baggie of ketamine (where did that come from?), the stale gum and the tampon wrappers, this book may not be for you, even though you may be one of the people for whom I wrote it.

That is the well of sorrow under this work, my fear that the contents of my bag will truly offend you. But we might be a lot alike, you and I. Maybe you were a funny kid full of innocent glee who had to grow up and perform or represent something she didn't want to. A sensitive child begging to be taken seriously and carrying a burden too heavy for her little arms. From oversized dance duffel to gem-encrusted "it" bag, there are a few purses in this story. But it isn't about the purses. Nora Ephron did the purse to perfection and I thank her.

As a cisgender woman performing as a drag queen in a world of cisgender men doing the same, people ask me if I get accused of trespassing, when what they really want to ask is "Are drag queens as bitchy as they are on TV? Do they hate you?" By "drag queens" they mean "real drag queens." By "real drag queens" they mean men. I answer "no." Not in my world.

I conceived and birthed my drag persona in a warm pool of liberation and love surrounded by cheerleading drag doulas. Sure, there was the rare naysayer who questioned my presence while clutching her pearls and clucking about women treading on gay men's territory. She was not drag family, but usually a distant relative from out of town (even if by "out of town" I mean just across town). I was ushered into the San Francisco drag scene by queens who valued me for my talents as well as my quirks, who embraced and encouraged me. These queens understood deeply that I had been performing drag my entire life, that we all perform our genders to an extent, most of us in some form of drag at least some of the time. And even when those queens dragged the abject and ridiculous aspects of femininity, the loving intention of their humor was clear. I went from the club back into the world feeling valued, celebrated, and intellectually engaged.

The drag club gave me a release valve exactly when I needed it. I walked into that queer space mortally afraid of saying the wrong thing, and the generous people there clobbered my fear with laughter. They said all the wrong things in all the most wrong and most fearless ways and then put it all onstage, and somehow it felt right. We exorcised our demons and paraded them around. The demons were ugly and pretty, smart and stupid, evil and banal. Some demons were sexist, racist, capitalist, misogynist, xenophobic, homophobic, transphobic. Some were truly frightening and some redemptive, positively angelic. Despite, or perhaps as a result of all of the demons onstage, backstage was by and large a place of loving care.

Trannyshack was not perfect, but its timing in my life was. After the release valve came relief. Its atmosphere of anarchic joy undercut my attempt at cool-girl art-criticality and transformed me into a shameless, screaming fan. A stressed-out, serious young woman rediscovered that she was a funny girl. I was afraid nothing I had to say was relevant, so they gave me an audience. That audience and its performers validated me the way that Bobby had. They encouraged me to show my edges and underbelly, all my garish colors. Suddenly I had something valuable to offer. Maybe someday I would be "fierce."

We live in a fractious time when people who should be on the same team can't seem to stop hurting each other or claiming to be hurt by each other. Is this always what happens when we raise consciousness? We were raising consciousness then too, and people had been for decades. I must note this, not to undermine the here and now, but to remind us not to rewrite the intricacies of history.

A memoir is and is not a history. Histories are supposed to tell it like it is, or rather, like it was, but the telling must always force itself through the clumsy sieve of the teller's subjectivity. Memoir, unlike most histories, admits this clumsiness. My (her)story, because it is mine, will leave out some important perspectives. I cannot tell your story, yet my story may hold yours.

Every memoir is a subjective story, but also a story of subjectivity. Inasmuch as I acknowledge that, while you cannot possibly feel what I feel and I cannot possibly feel what you feel, I am going to make a hopeful little leap toward you. I will attempt what seems impossible right at this cultural moment: to come together in difference. This book is about difference. It is about being different, feeling different, and finding commonality. Radical acceptance in a radical space. Or, radical at the time. Every era tends to find its own radical and reject what came before. For me, that space was Trannyshack, in all its fierce, flawed glory.

There I found a spot to lay down my burden, my big heavy purse. I found not only kinship, but also a creative practice, a career path, and maybe even some kind of relevance. All the things serious people want. I gave over to artifice and found authenticity. I gave over to humor and found myself being taken seriously. I found my people. We thrived in irreverence and still committed ourselves to the project of coming together in difference. The unsafest of safe spaces helped us enact an impossible project: to get free.

IT'S LIKE A
KIND OF TORTURE TO HAVE
TO WATCH THE SHOW

I knew Kevin was going to end up being one of my favorite people ever. He and I had met and bonded on a tour to Chicago with a friend's dance company in 1997. After an epic kiki (drag lingo for deep talk) on the plane ride there and a sweaty night of dancing at a gay bar in Boystown, we were instant pals.

"Girl, you really need to come to Trannyshack," he said in the summer of 1998.

"Hmmm." I had replied. "I dunno. I love drag queens, but they scare me."

Kevin was the first person I heard mention Trannyshack, the infamous Tuesday night weekly at the Stud in San Francisco. A lot of my other friends from the dance world were queer, but not the kinds of queers who went to nightclubs. Like me, they were enmeshed in a culture built around morning technique class at least three times a week.

I was a dancer, but rarely did I go out dancing, especially not at midnight on a Tuesday!

After working most nights waiting tables I skipped the post-shift drinks that my twenty-something coworkers enjoyed. Instead, I got up in the morning, pulled on sweats, and lugged my ass to the dance studio, sometimes up an actual "steep and very narrow stairway," as the song from *A Chorus Line* goes. I couldn't imagine a Tuesday late night out, but if Kevin thought I needed to go to Trannyshack, he was probably right. He was right about a lot. I *had* always loved drag queens and the drag aesthetic. In college I discovered RuPaul, Wigstock, and the grand ball culture depicted in Jennie Livingston's *Paris Is Burning*. They had me at the word "work," as in "You betta work!" That I could relate to.

But, drag queens did also kind of scare me. Weren't they mean? Wouldn't they bristle at having women in their space? Would it not be a kind of appropriation, an invasion, for me to even show up at a drag club? Kevin reassured me this was nonsense.

"Don't worry, honey. It's totally fierce, but not scary. I mean, it's *kind of* scary, but in a fun way, a performance-arty way. And it's not a total sausage party either. Lots of women go. You're gonna love it."

"Okay, but I might not want to stay too late. Tomorrow's Cunningham class!"

"Whatever, Mary, I mean *Merce*. The show starts at midnight. See you there at a quarter till."

I rode my bike through the wet-cold windy night to the corner of Ninth and Harrison, and locked up at a parking meter. I found Kevin inside and we sidled up to the bar, a lopsided mess, sunken in the middle from rot caused by decades of beer puddles. This place was a landmark, its rotten bar a monument to the legacy of a forty-year nonstop bacchanal.

"A club soda for me," I said, reminding Kevin that I had *dance class in the morning*. Over the sound system, right after Propellerheads' "History Repeating (featuring Miss Shirley Bassey)," came a sound from childhood.

The opening theme to *The Muppet Show*.

"Why do we always come here? I guess we'll never know. It's like a kind of torture, to have to watch the show," the two crotchety old Muppets sang.

"Come on! Let's get closer to the stage," said Kev as he guided me away from the bar. "That means the show's starting."

I kinda already loved the show and it hadn't even started. What's not to love about drag queens who, at the outset of their show, admit their affinity with Muppets? We paddled through a sea of people. There were trans-femmes of all stripes from the imposing Miss Chocolate at the door to gals in sensible pumps and "daytime realness" to glam working girls. Then there were cute boys and baby dykes, big-bellied bears, genderfuck queers in messy wigs and just a smear of lipstick, and more than a few gay-boy/gal-pal combos like us. Everyone was pliant and friendly as we pushed past. When we found a good spot, the muscle queen in front of me stepped aside so I could squeeze forward to see better.

"Thanks so much! It's my first time."

"Werq!" he shouted, and raised his pint glass.

There was that word again: "work," but this time a sassy *e* and *q* were implied in his joyous, haphazard delivery. This wasn't the first time I had encountered this word as a cheer and an exclamation of encouragement, and it would be far from the last. It meant everything from "you'd better take this moment seriously" to "amen."

The show created some illusions of course, as drag shows must, but totally shattered others. This was not the bitchy would-be minstrel show of radical feminist lore, oh no my sisters. The week's theme was "Riot Grrrl," drag queens embodying the musical heroines of Generation X. My generation. The show opened with the hostess, Heklina—big-shouldered, barrel-chested, and named after an Icelandic volcano—lip-synching to PJ Harvey's "Sheela-Na-Gig." "I'm gonna take my hips to a man who cares." Heklina reclaimed her feminine power. I shed a joyous tear of kinship.

Next up was a beautiful gap-toothed monster named

Renttecca, after her place of employment (she worked at a first-generation startup called Renttech. *Don't overthink it, girl!).* She threatened to graze the ceiling as she took the stage with "Rock Star" by Hole.

"Well I went to school (oh). Well I went to school (haha)."

When we caught her stage-dive on the "Do it for the kids, yeah" outro, it was a testament to our punk-schooled capacity for cooperation that nobody was crushed. Renttecca's body thrashed in our hands like a giant squid in a net. As I grabbed her ankle to keep her aloft, I got a close-up of her huge foot in a low-heeled sandal, long toes hanging over the front edge (what in drag parlance is known as "serving shrimp") and I realized she must be 6'5" without them.

Then there was Lady Sergio, in her messy bob, baby barrette, and combat boots, flashing her armpit hair, looking for all the world like the coolest college girl circa 1992. Sergio's petiteness, Renttecca's hugeness, the simultaneous and undeniable presence of masculinity and femininity performed physical feats that theory could not. These queens' idolatry and embodiment of this specific femininity, the feminism of riot grrrls, moved me. And they did all of this while *lip-synching!*

The next time I went to the 'shack (love had fast-tracked the club and me to nickname-basis) was for a tribute to Siouxsie Sioux, of Siouxsie and the Banshees. This was the night that would reveal a portal to my future.

The opening guitar riff of Siouxsie's "Monitor" buzzed as static fuzzed on two old TV screens onstage. A panic-stricken, tattoo-covered young man stumbled across the stage, and after him, his predator, a woman with a beautiful face—pale, sharp, and furious—in a spiky black wig and a shoulder-padded blazer. She transformed with Kabuki precision from seductive to menacing on the swells of Siouxsie's banshee shrieks.

Ms. Ana Matronic had made her entrance.

She shoved the man to his knees and forced a flexible

vacuum tube, running from one of the screens, into his mouth. He simulated a horrific seizure, as if the information were entering not only his visual cortex, but also his visceral body. On the song's final refrain, "Sit back and enjoy the real McCoy," she pulled open her jacket to reveal her breasts through a clear vinyl bustier. She was a cisgender woman like me! Her action was an irresistible physical pun and also dared anyone present to doubt the validity of her right to do drag.

After her number was over, Ms. Ana and her backup boy returned to the stage to drag the TV sets away. She smirked at the audience, still in her thrall and cheering, as she lugged the sets offstage, as if this were a planned epilogue. Catching the diva in the act of striking her props, very real manual labor familiar to anyone who has self-produced a show, did nothing to dissolve her spell. Now not only did I love her as one can only love a performer, but I liked her.

Trannyshack was an alternate universe. If drag was a subversion of gender performance, this club was a subversion of drag. The show was not about "female impersonation" although it celebrated every type of drag performer, from those squarely in the glam queen center to those gleefully teetering on the edge between beauty and ugliness. These queens worshipped Siouxsie Sioux and Grace Jones more than Judy Garland and Barbra Streisand (but never to the exclusion of anyone). They redefined gender and its performance, stretching, expanding, exploding it. They opened a lexicon of drag that included the arty and esoteric, the frightening and abject, as well as the fierce and the fabulous. Raised on John Waters and Susan Sontag, Dolly Parton and Boy George, the audience as well as the performers were pop-culturally literate, counterculturally astute, and whip-smart. All were welcome here, the entire gender spectrum and constellation represented on the eight-by-ten-foot stage.

A note on that tiny stage. While picturing all of this magic, I want you to imagine you are in a sea of people taller than you, standing on tiptoe or shifting into the gaps between their bodies to see the action, performers visible only from the waist up because the stage is three feet high. If you're standing in the very front row, then you'd be looking up the performers' noses, smelling their makeup, feeling their breath, and likely being hit, by aim or accident, with whatever fluids they expel.

Ms. Ana's presence at the 'shack invoked my secret hope: that a cis woman could be welcome here, not only as spectator, but as participant. Would the queens actually let me join them? Perhaps I might not have to endure the torture of only watching the show, but could actually be a part of it. I had been performing since I was a child, and here I was trying to figure out how to be a drag queen. Who would give me permission?

"I think all you have to do is ask," said Kevin.

Could it really be that easy? They would let just anyone onstage?

"Wait, there's not, like, an audition or something?"

"Mo, it's Trannyshack, not the San Francisco Ballet."

I don't remember whether it was my idea or Kevin's to perform a duet, but it turned out to be a great strategy. Women may have been welcome at the 'shack, but cute boys and their perky butts got Heklina's attention the fastest. Our duet would also cement my and Kevin's relationship as drag co-enablers. As I fidgeted in his rickety rolling chair trying not to squeal, Kevin called Heklina. When she said yes, we could be in the show the Tuesday after the Miss Trannyshack Pageant, I almost flipped myself ass over teakettle.

We began to build our very first drag number (in drag, as in old-time vaudeville, performances are known as "numbers"). We thought it would be wise, being 'shack first-timers, to play by the most obvious translation of the drag rules and dress me as a boy, even though I really wanted to be a queen.

"We could be Mormon missionaries," I suggested.

I had dressed as a Mormon missionary the year before for

Halloween, but hadn't really thought of it as drag. I still had my navy-blue suit, my burgundy tie, and my name tag that read "Elder Mike Hunt."

"We need a twist. Maybe Mormon missionaries in love?" said Kevin. "It can be a Gay Marriage number, a political number. Oooh, let's use 'Wouldn't It Be Nice' by the Beach Boys." Around that time, the Beach Boys' *Pet Sounds* was enjoying a music nerd resurgence.

"That sounds ridiculous. I love it. Oh my god, we're gonna do Drag!"

Kevin went to Thrift Town, found a suit for himself and rigged it to tear away with two simple gestures to reveal a cute bridal negligee underneath. By the end of the number, we would both technically be in drag, satisfying Heklina's stated criteria for participation. He also made himself a missionary name-badge: "Elder Jack Mieoff."

We rehearsed in Kevin's studio apartment, perfecting our timing—his tear-away on the drum fills, then my unzipping his backpack and taking out a wig with an attached bridal veil and placing it lovingly on his head on the line, "We could be married (we could be married) and then we'd be happy (then we'd be happy)."

Kevin even used his genius design skills to craft two oversized "Books of Mormon" from poster board. My book opened to reveal a drawing of two bicycles on a dotted-line journey from Salt Lake City to San Francisco. Kevin's book revealed pages cut from gay porn mags featuring wholesome-looking guys engaged in various outdoorsy sex acts on logs and boulders. The drag gods are in the details.

On the night of the performance, we met each other at the club and entered backstage for the first time. "Backstage" at the Stud was not much—a curtained-off corner of the room with a banquette and slightly better lighting, crammed full of queens.

"Aw, look at you, dude!" said Kevin. I already knew my boy

drag was nearly passable. On Halloween, people had actually run away from me and my friend Jack thinking we were real missionaries when we tried to tell them the "good news." Since then I had been growing my pixie cut into a bob, but it was still short enough to slick back and pull off the requisite well-groomed, good-Mormon effect. And my 32Bs did not need much binding.

"I'm nervous," I said.

"I know, me too, but we're pros. We can take this audience," Kevin assured me.

Kay White had won the Miss Trannyshack Pageant the Sunday before, and her first duty as royalty was to act as co-hostess. She was one of my favorites. Sad-eyed and petite. With her signature side-parted frizzy wig and her penchant for Kraftwerk and opera. Kay evoked a kind of Weimar-era tragedy. Tonight, she appeared to still be drunk from Sunday. We had a hostess who could barely stand, let alone talk. Good omen? We landed somewhere in the middle of the lineup, right after Renttecca. Hopefully, whoever introduced us could manage to speak when the time came.

Before Renttecca came a ritual that the audience had learned to expect, but that still somehow seemed completely spontaneous. Heklina picked a cute boy out of the audience, the more innocent and straight-looking the better, and pulled him onstage. Then she flipped him around, knelt down, pulled down the back of his pants, buried her face between his butt-cheeks for five seconds and stood up with a giant, open-mouthed, not un-Muppet-like smile.

She always asked first, "Hi, what's your name? Chad? Chad, can I rim you?" None of us could tell if there was any true butt-licking going on, but from the looks on the guys' faces, it seemed that there was. It was all a little shocking to me, despite having lived in San Francisco for the better part of my twenties, which were almost over. But the shock was good for me. Bracing. This queer space was not for the timid. There had always been assimilationist gays, and true queers—the ones adhering to Harvey Milk's adage: "never blend in." After the depths of the AIDS crisis, it seemed that mainstream culture had a lot invested in turning away from the more transgressive displays of queerness. It made sense in a way. Assimilation into heteronormative culture was safer. This act was the ultra-transgressive opposite. It made Trannyshack a safe space for open queerness, but would surely freak out anyone not equipped to be there.

Scary in a good way, just like Kevin had said. It also displayed the prerogative of the drag queen to seize sexual power over the masculinist principle. I don't think Heklina was acting strategically with any of that in mind—I think she just loved burying her face in cute guys' butts. But by peppering her show with rimming, and constant references to it, Heklina marked her territory as undeniably queer. If you could hang with that, you were queer enough.

Renttecca's number consisted of her getting fake peed-on by a bunch of drag cops (or were they drag leathermen?) to the tune of "I'm Only Happy When It Rains." Good thing we added that dildo-dick blowjob at the end of our number, or we really would have seemed like a couple of goody-goodies.

I knew and loved the audience from having been a part of it for the past several months, and getting out in front of them was addictive in a way I totally expected. In my years of performing for contemporary dance audiences I relished the moments I could make them laugh, but those moments were usually few, and a little tinged with shame and suspicion. Artists were supposed to want complex responses from their audiences. To simply get a laugh is the provenance of the entertainer. In this space, on this stage, in front of this crowd, there was no shame in that.

And entertain, we did. Our Mormon missionaries-in-love

number drew massive cheers from the audience. We were a huge hit, especially with the surprisingly (or perhaps unsurprisingly) high percentage of traumatized former Mormons in the crowd.

Emboldened by success, I immediately called Heklina to book my second performance—a solo this time. She confirmed, which at that time consisted of her actually calling you on the actual telephone the Wednesday before the show saying: "Hi! It's me, Heklina. Just confirming you for next Tuesday." The theme was Cosmic Dream and I went into the new wave archives and dreamt up a number to the song "I Dream of Wires" by Gary Numan. I bought a copper-colored bobbed wig—my first— reminiscent of copper wire (this wig would convince me that I was a redhead in spirit and I've been dyeing my hair ever since).

My costume was black vinyl hot pants and a trompe l'oeil T-shirt painted on my torso in black liquid latex. I would portray a histrionic replicant who short-circuits, tearing away part of my second-skin top to reveal an "ERROR" message in digital font stenciled in Sharpie across my upper chest. New wave, sophisticated and, looking back on it, more than a little bit inspired by the robot-obsessed oeuvre of my new role model, Ana Matronic.

I arrived for the show and immediately got the feeling something was off. There were queens in Raggedy Ann and Tammy Faye Bakker wigs. One backup dancer wore a mouse mask, and Lady Sergio was focused on loading up a paper plate with Cheez Whiz. I found Heklina to give my music to the DJ.

"Hey honey, what's your drag name?"

"Glory Hologram. Pronounced *hole-o-gram*."

I had not yet settled on a drag name, thinking somehow that choosing one might jinx it, might make it all vanish in a puff of glitter just as magically as it had appeared. Now, under the gun, I chose a too-specific temporary name, one that referred to that night's futuristic theme and one of the dirtier traditions of gay culture.

"Okay, Glory, do you have your music?" I handed her a cassette (yes, a cassette) cued to the song. It was cassettes and phone calls in the early days.

"The theme is Cosmic Dream, isn't it?" I asked, eyes wide under the shade of a brand-new set of false lashes.

"Oh no!" Heklina said, taking note of my space-age drag—the silver accents of my makeup and my rubber top. "Hahahahahahahahaah! Oh no! I forgot to tell you. The theme has been changed. To CHEESE! Sorry, Glory! But whaddyagonnado? You'll be fine."

Cheese. And I was serving space age. *My first time out on my own would be my last.* The crowd would eat me alive like Lady Sergio would eat that Cheez Whiz, or Heklina ate ass. I took a deep breath and did what performers do. I went on. I *served* robot intensity. I *worked* replicant rage. And that blessed crowd gave back.

Had I done it? Earned their love? Was I in? I didn't want to just take up space on that stage; I wanted to find my way into that world, to be in conversation with it, to become one of the people I had observed and admired. I barely knew any of them, but I knew they were for me.

♔ ♔ ♔

Within the congenial mixed group at the 'shack were various intersecting circles. The trans women who were there to meet their admirers stayed up front near the door, occasionally watching the show. The "boys" were the ones who made the scene in the back. I don't mean to be so binary, but it did literally play out on opposite ends of the bar. None of my gay friends ever said, "I'm going to the Stud to meet some fine men." It was: "Oooh, girl, there are so many hot boys here tonight." Hot boys at the Stud were not literal boys—they were of age—but neither were they circuit queens or fussy twinks. They were smart, arty, fashion-forward, and up for a little mischief.

If you came for the show, you walked in, paid Miss Chocolate, and checked your coat with Teresa. As you headed toward the back, you passed the bar on your right, where you might stop to buy a drink from the sweet, even-keeled Kristo or farther down at the end toward the stage from the petite, whirring hummingbird that was Bernadette. Both of them poured with a heavy hand, lots of bang for your six bucks, so you had to pace yourself.

Gay boys packed themselves shoulder to shoulder every week to worship the queens onstage. But not to fuck them. By and large, drag queen charisma didn't translate to sexual magic. Even within that mixed, arty, cute, queer space, the dominant aesthetic in gay male sexual culture leaned toward "masc-for-masc." Whether due to its blatant femininity or its power to intimidate, for most gay men, drag tended to be a boner killer. Drag queens joked about this all the time and teased each other with it, wielding drag names the way kid siblings use intel on their mortified sisters. When a queen saw another queen out of drag chatting up a cute guy on the street, they would yell from bikes or out car windows from down the block: "Oh my God, look! It's Peaches Christ! The famous *drag queen!*" Gay men who were willing to date known drag queens were boyfriend material, but not all the men in that space were looking for boyfriends. This was before the advent of the hookup app, let alone the phenomenon of an app like Scruff expanding its notion of masculinity to include the category "Femme."

After the show, Putanesca and Precious Moments could not get out of their wigs and gowns fast enough, wiping off their makeup, pulling on jeans and T-shirts, not wasting a second of the time ticking away on the sexual trading floor of the club in those years before the apps. But their very means of wiping away their lady faces must have left a lingering whiff of the femme: the scent of Pond's cold cream and drugstore baby wipes.

Anyone looking for a fail-safe path to some easy and/ or anonymous dick decamped to The Hole in the Wall, The Powerhouse, or My Place. In so doing, they also cleared the necessary space on the floor for anyone who might have been there to dance. A healthy ecosystem.

Some stayed at the Stud to hook up, and maybe got lucky with out-of-town trade who had read about this singular scene; but by and large, the 'shack was a true clubhouse of familiar faces and good Judys. One might bring a date to the 'shack, which would be the equivalent of introducing them to the family, or showing them your record collection, or post-college me, sitting you in front of Sandra Bernhard's *Without You I'm Nothing* to see if you could hang.

♔ ♔ ♔

Shortly after the onset of my Trannyshack fandom, I noticed a poster announcing a contest. "The Annual Faux Queen Pageant: A Pageant for Drag Queens Trapped in Real Women's Bodies" hosted by a queen called Ruby Toosday. "Real women." *Problematic.*

When Ruby Toosday dreamed up the first Faux Queen pageant in 1995 (a year before Trannyshack was born) its participants had yet to be named as a group. The inaugural poster bore a hefty carnival sideshow descriptor. Brace yourselves, kids; it read: "The Fabulous She-Male Impersonator Contest! DQ's (Drag Queens) Trapped in RG's (Real Girls') Bodies!" Before I go any further, we'll discuss terminology.

As soon as Ruby Toosday printed her poster, the language changed, and has been changing ever since. Over the course of the two short weeks in 1995 between her pageant's conception and realization, Ruby Toosday dreamed up the moniker "faux queen." Though her language around it would continue to evolve—"she-male" and "real girl" fell swiftly out of use—Ruby's intention in creating the Faux Queen pageant was right on. She had seen her girlfriends, fabulous femmes who held their own as drag performers, on the receiving end of discrimination and rejection from the drag queen community at large. It bummed her out and so she made a place for them to turn it out. In the decades since, the Faux Queen pageant and spaces like it have welcomed cis women, trans women, and nonbinary people to parade their femininities.

After seeing Ms. Ana for the first time at the 'shack and dipping my toe into that little corner of the drag scene, the Faux Queen pageant appeared like an enchanted bridge across its depths. I signed up to compete.

Without much effort, I realized a concept for my Faux Queen pageant number. I would dramatize a version of my first drag club experience, one shared by a lot of people in those spaces, of struggling to view the show over the crowd of tall men and queens. Into that I would fold a sort of Cinderella story, to the song "Unpretty" by TLC, the hitmakers of 1999. It involved a theme and practice that would become the foundation of my future drag work, the onstage transformation, and would culminate in my drag queen transformation. Who doesn't love a makeover montage? I ensnared Kevin and his boyfriend Karl as the helpful fairy drag mothers who would take me under their wings and literally elevate me. They had recently attended a film screening in drag, so they were game and warmed up.

"Ooh, fun! I get to break out my drag name again," said Karl.

"And that would be?"

"Brianna Cracker."

"A classy snack," I replied. "What about you?" I turned to Kevin.

"Pleased to meet you. I'm Celine Solution."

This would be Kevin's second time in drag, and he would find what so many other queens discover early on. As soon as he arrived at my place as Celine he exclaimed, "I look like my sister!

But not as pretty."

Having seen pictures of Kevin's sister, glam with her backdrop of massive, long brown curls, I had to agree. But I thought Celine was pretty enough, with most of her face space taken up by what Kevin always called his "great big eyeballs." Kevin's big hazel eyes would've been at home in old Hollywood. Bette Davis eyes. Buster Keaton eyes. The kind in which you see a little white below the iris. The window to the soul flung open.

"These brows are a couple of bitches." The eyes were gorgeous, but Kev's brow-taming skill was in its infancy. Later, he learned the magic to make those wiry caterpillars disappear.

"Well, most queens end up looking like their mothers, so I think she's doing pretty well," said Karl as Brianna.

Brianna was actually pretty, Karl's refined features and high cheekbones lending themselves easily to the feminization project. She was almost, to use a word we would hear a lot that night, "fishy."

We arrived at the club on the late side, working under the assumption that everyone else would be on drag time (about twenty to thirty minutes late). We were wrong. Contestants would perform in the order they arrived.

"What's your name, honey?" asked Ruby Toosday as I screeched to a halt in front of her.

After some waffling, I had settled on a drag name. It had the right amount of queer cachet, spoke self-deprecatingly to the vestige of the good girl that died hard in me and hinted at female anatomy.

"Glory Holesome," I answered "And this is Celine—"

"Get in there, Glory! You almost missed the cutoff." No time for pleasantries.

"Oh."

"You're number thirteen."

"Out of thirteen?"

"Yup. You're last."

Who knew there were even thirteen "drag queens trapped in women's bodies" in all of San Francisco? But here we were. Among the others were Anita Cocktail, Windy Plains, and Crickett Bardot. I didn't realize it at the time, but we all stood on the invisible shoulders of many "drag queens trapped in women's bodies," all the women whose personae made it possible to think of femininity as performance. There were Mae West and Marilyn Monroe, the latter categorized (or diagnosed?) as a drag queen by Gloria Steinem. Fayette and Sweet Pam of The Cockettes were drag queens despite resistance from a few narrow-minded members of their freaky 1960s tribe. Dolly Parton, Cher, and Charo from my 1970s youth were certainly drag queens in spirit if not in name. And my idol Sandra Bernhard had upended and reclaimed the requirements of femininity in her own sophisticated way, as if vandalizing it with a Dior lipstick. Having this category "faux queen" opened my mind to welcome the fact that all these women, artists whose feminine performance belies a full, intellectual knowledge of itself, taught me how to be a drag queen.

The judges included one of the first official faux queens and Klubstitute kid Bea Dazzler (who took the helm of the Faux Queen pageant years ago and runs it today); Leigh Crow, also known then as Elvis Herselvis; and one of my favorite performers of all time, drag king Rusty Hips. I was excited to show them my stuff, and nervous. We arrived in the crowded dressing room and realized there was really nowhere for me to get settled. I now regretted my main prop, a ladder, which I thought would be a super cute addition: *Everyone loves a ladder number!* The last to arrive in a crowded dressing room, I was now the asshole with the ladder. Luckily we had our looks sorted out, just some minor fluffing to do, and could squeeze the ladder into a corner to use as a makeshift vanity.

Crickett Bardot was adorable in 1920s flapper drag, her eyes almost as big as Betty Boop's but not quite as big as Kevin/

Celine's. She had two backup boys too, in vintage gangster drag, who looked vaguely familiar, and as soon as one of them opened his mouth and went "HahahahaHA!" I knew he was Heklina. Right away I realized that the other one, who was futzing with Crickett's long string of pearls, making sure it swung just right, was Putanesca, boy version. *Whoa*, it was unsettling. Those two superstar queens must have loved Crickett a lot to deign to be her out-of-drag backup dancers. Spotting out-of-drag queens would grow into a joyous and often jarring hobby for me, Kevin, and Karl for years to come.

Crickett's number was "My Name Is Tallulah," from the delightfully disturbing 1976 movie *Bugsy Malone*, a gangster film with an all-child cast. The song, with vocals by an adult pretending to be a child, lip-synched in the film by thirteen-year-old Jodie Foster, was a perfect choice for Crickett, who has a childlike voice herself, high but not squeaky, with a touch of vocal fry. She fully charmed the audience and the judges.

Four years later, Crickett, in full drag and nine months pregnant with her daughter Sasha, hosted a mother-themed night at the 'shack. Eighteen months after that, Crickett brought Sasha, in a wiglet and little white bedazzled bell-bottom jumpsuit by Mr. David, to a Charo look-alike contest at the Stud. Charo herself showed up to judge and deemed Sasha the obvious winner.

Charo, by the way, was one of the most delightful celebrities I've ever met. She didn't bat an eye at the makeshift backstage area of our beloved dive bar, kiki-ing and cha-cha-ing with all of us as if there was nowhere on earth she would rather have been. She was also a *total* drag queen, jumping in and teasing Heklina as if she was one of us.

"Heklina, your mouth is so be-yoo-tee-ful. I want to know, *where* has this mouth been?"

"Hahahahahaha! Oh Charo, you do NOT want to know where this mouth has been."

"No. Rrreally. I *want to KNOW!*"

Back at the 1999 Faux Queen pageant…with the appearance of each contestant, I watched the decline of my chances, my potential splash getting smaller and smaller. Though there were judges present, the winner would be determined by how much the audience tipped each performer. By the time I stepped into the spotlight the crowd would be out of money and probably too drunk to care. This was indeed the case, and the judges were drunk, too.

I take the stage to perform my number. I begin in a dowdy shift over a beaded eighties party dress and a messy wig with pigtails. I fake-pine for the spotlight, craning to see and climbing up on my ladder for a better view, treating the stage as a fake audience and the audience as a fake show. The ladder turns out to be a good move because it helps me to be seen, overcoming the issue of nightclub sight lines. Celine and Brianna save the day, replacing my pigtail wig with the wavy red bob I love so much, stuffing my disco dress with drag boobs—the cut-off feet of old pantyhose, stuffed with birdseed and knotted—and teaching me how to over-enunciate my lip-synch to the repeated "Ooh-ooh, ooh, ooh, ooh-ooh" part of the song. By the end of my number, I am a drag queen!

"We love you, Glory!" slurred the tipsy but still functioning Leigh Crow from the judges' table. This hearty outburst of sweetness from none other than Elvis Herselvis boosted my spirit, but the audience might as well have turned their pockets inside out and made a sad face. My late-entry performance garnered hardly any dollars, and thus I did not place. Nevertheless, standing up there on that stage at the end of the show with all of those sisters was a feel-good moment.

The clear winner was Windy Plains, who had appeared like a tornado and smashed the competition with a camp Americana number chock-full of multiple reveals. She was also a loveable Miss Congeniality backstage and totally looked like a real drag queen. She snatched her crown with a Miss USA smile.

The last-place prize, a tradition that started with the first Faux Queen pageant in 1995, was the "Too Fish" award, not for the worst performance, but for the one who looked too effortlessly femme. The conceit was right in line with what I had been discovering: becoming a drag queen took as much labor for women as it did for men. A drag queen is not a "female impersonator" but another creature entirely. The lucky recipient of the Too Fish award was festooned with a frozen, plastic-wrapped flounder on a chain.

I stood by gamely while all of the names were called and all of the awards bestowed, even "Miss Also Ran."

"Waaaiiittt!" Leigh Crow bellowed. "We luuurrrrved Glory Holesome so much, so we made up a special category!"

"What's the category?" yelled Ruby.

"We dunno. But wewannagiversumthin!" *Miss Better Late Than Never?* I thought.

I was touched that the judges had seen me through the haze and hubbub, and made this special effort. My clubland Cinderella story had worked on them, and for that I received a curling iron, my first since high school. *Sisterhood is powerful,* I thought. *Thank you for this femme power tool!*

👑 👑 👑

Phatima was moving to New York and the 'shack was hosting her going-away party. Phatima teetered at the dazzling pinnacle of drag while simultaneously plumbing its swampy dregs. A big queen who embraced her fat as an avant-garde accessory, she worked a genderfuck look, often with no wig on her bald head, face painted to perfection. She once constructed pointe shoes out of duct tape and balanced her glorious heft on her toes like a pro. I loved her.

Phatima's performance art experimentation liberated me to do something I had always wanted to do: a drag salute to Yoko

Ono's "Cut Piece." In the context of dance this would have been too earnest. Derivative. Suspect. In this context, however, the audience, a special combo of savvy and generous, would welcome it. Before entering this space, I had never wanted to get naked in performance. Nudity was all around me in the experiments of contemporary dance, but seemed kind of an easy choice, a shortcut to edgy legitimacy. Here it seemed essential. My "Cut Piece," like Yoko's, would end in nudity and expose the power of vulnerability.

Kevin, now known as Falsetta Knockers, wore my Nana's old wool tweed skirt suit, glasses, and a gray-streaked wig—Art Curator Realness.

She carries me out and sets me on a high stool. In stillness I lip-synch Yoko's words "Will I miss the sky? Will I miss the clouds? Will I miss the city lights?" Then, to the hard guitar strains of her song "New York Woman," Falsetta cuts off my clothes piece by piece, my wig, even my jewelry. I'd have been happy if three people in the audience caught the reference, but I've transmitted something, even if it is mostly the fact that I am brazen enough to expose myself. Though being caught naked in front of a crowd is the stuff of literal nightmares for some, I am not as terrified as I thought I'd be. Having Kevin up here with me helps, as does the intention of the queerdo audience, which is to enjoy some arty drag, not to ogle a naked lady. This reinforces something I already knew about myself: when I'm onstage, in the moment, I feel invincible.

The night of my Yoko Ono tribute, I met two queens I admired, major players in my new drag milieu. The first, Peaches Christ, horror movie queen extraordinaire, San Francisco's answer to Elvira and John Waters rolled into one, saw me backstage right before I went on. I would say she raised her eyebrows as she looked at me, but they were always in that state, drawn-on halfway up her forehead. "Your makeup. Looks. Kind of. Like *mine*." She sucked in her cheeks and nodded, a gesture that for all I knew could have signaled approval, or silently affirmed a plan to kill me later.

After the show, Peaches introduced me to the second major player, Vinsantos, aka the "Macabre Snob," a goth queen known for pyrotechnics. Peaches, with her penchant for blood and gore, and Vinsantos, with his images of death and destruction, were two peas in a poison pod. Vinsantos looked me up and down.

"Who . . . is this?"

"This is Glory Holesome. Glory Holesome, this is Vinsantos," said Peaches.

"I can't even look at you right now," said Vinsantos, staring at me. He turned to Peaches, and in unison they nodded and said, "Fierce," as if it were a prophecy of doom.

Two weeks later at the 'shack I saw Peaches again, this time with Heklina.

"Have you met Glory Holesome?" asked Heklina.

"Yeah," said Peaches. "The kid's good."

"The kid's too good," Heklina replied.

"The kid GOES!" they chanted in perfect unison, and commenced cackling. The possibility that these two queens had invoked lines from *Valley of the Dolls* to insinuate that I could be ousted for being too good was better than any award.

I was a drag queen.

LET'S
PRETEND

I. Every Day Is Halloween

When I was a tiny baby, my parents put a wig on my head and took a picture. It has always been one of my favorite pictures of me. I kind of look like an old lady in a nursing home. Not thrilled, not angry, just staring off into Goddess-knows-where. This is before social media made a parenting staple out of photographing one's children in wigs. The wig is blondish-red and the curls overdone. It must have belonged to my mother or maybe a grandmother, from the late 1960s moment when white women still wore wigs in unabashed pursuit of fashion. The year I was born, the same year as Carole King's *Tapestry* and *Ms. Magazine*, was a year of natural hair, loose clothes, and earnestness.

I've told the story of my infant self in that wig when explaining drag mothers. A drag mother is the queen who teaches you how to be one. She teaches you how to put on your eyelashes and eye makeup, how to "beat your face" as they say. "Beat your face" sounds so violent, but that is how the queens say it. Like a lot of drag queen language and humor, the term is a practice of camp that reclaims and transforms pain, in this case the alarming suggestion of battery. "Beating one's face" refers to the vigorous action of the powder puff, tamping the powder into the pores and sending clouds into the air. Beating your face is honest, time-consuming, highly skilled labor.

Eventually, I would grow from the wisdom of many spiritual drag mothers, fairy godmothers, and goddessmothers, but my primal drag mother is Mitzi: my own biological mother who, on my ninth birthday, put me and the rest of the girls at my slumber party in full Studio 54 sparkly disco glam face. This was the first time I saw my face fully made up and thought *Yes. This.* My mother is my drag mother. However, it is a little more complicated than that . . .

One night in 2009, after my cabaret show *Faux Real*, the drag queen Juanita More! told me she happened to be sitting, out of drag, next to my dad in the theater. If you ever happen to be sitting next to Juanita More! out of drag, you would never think "famous drag queen." If you ever happen to be sitting next to my dad in the theater, or in a waiting room or on a plane, he will smile, introduce himself with a firm handshake ("Tom Jenkinson!"), and you will leave with a new friend. So when I started in with my wig-on-the-baby story from the stage, my dad leaned over to his new friend, whom he assumed was just some nice man in a very nice sweater, and whispered, "I put that wig on her head."

My dad had also dressed me up as Raggedy Ann when I was two—for no reason. He was in charge of me one Saturday while my mom was out and wanted to surprise her. So really both of my parents made me the drag queen I am. And as a drag queen I basically do what I have done since I was little. Many a drag queen gets her start on Halloween, but I got a head start. I'm glad my parents were not into pageants. That could have been a slippery slope for all of us.

The Halloween I was two, my parents dressed me up as a geisha. When I say "geisha," I wish I meant true Kabuki with black lacquered wig, layers of kimono, and white face paint finished with tiny red lips, but my young and thrifty parents used what they had on hand. My geisha look was all Pier 1 Imports bricolage. Though my robe was originally Japanese, it was not a real kimono, but what was called a "happi coat" made of red rayon. I wore it until it faded and ripped, making it a shirt after I was too big to wear it as a robe. The slippers were Chinese, brown vinyl with a circular gold bat symbol on them. I wore those until my heel hung off the end like Cinderella's stepsisters trying on the glass slippers: "serving biscuit" (if long drag queen toes hanging off the front of a too-small sandal is "serving shrimp," the heel flesh hanging off the back of a too-small mule is its doughy counterpart). Of course, a chopstick stuck into my tiny bun of wispy toddler hair completed the look. There is a photo of me, already an excellent poseur, standing with my little arms outstretched to display the flowing sleeves.

The whole situation is what we would now call "highly problematic." Clueless cultural appropriation by white people in the name of Halloween fun. But at the time, the seventies, while there was certainly consciousness around racism and anti-racism, we had yet to examine the racial implications inherent in a white couple dressing their blond daughter up as a pan-Asian geisha for Halloween. We had not yet learned that culture is not a costume. Edward Said had not yet written *Orientalism*. And there was still David Carradine in "yellowface" playing a Kung Fu master on TV.

In the 1970s and into the 1980s cultural appropriation in fashion was how white people showed they were down, by rejecting the uncool trappings of whiteness. I know I am not the only seventies kid with a picture of my infant self in the arms of a dashiki-clad white mom.

In second grade I was Little Miss Muffet for Halloween. I went for realness, full-on character creation. Again, my mom made the costume. It was never lost on me how lucky I was to have a mother/drag mother who had the time and resources to make such great costumes. This one was a little calico dress and pinafore, with a mop cap and bloomers, which I got lots of use out of later in playing *Little House on the Prairie*. As accessories, I carried around our wooden salad serving bowl and its matching big wooden spoon from which dangled a rubber spider on an elastic band. I really wanted to carry around a tuffet, but it would have been overkill.

If you look up "Little Miss Muffet costume" now, you come up with the full range. There's everything from an adorable costume for a baby with a cuddly spider attached to the dress to a Sexy Little Miss Muffet costume for a grown-up, also with a cuddly spider attached to the dress. This costume was a breakthrough moment for me because of the props. They necessitated an enactment, a performance, the commitment of presence. The drag gods are in the details: the dangling, jumping rubber spider was paramount. My spider was not cuddly. The other details were the big bowl and spoon. An important lesson in detail I learned then, from my mother no doubt, which would serve me later as a drag queen was about scale. Scale in a Halloween costume, as in drag, needs to be cartoonish. A normal-sized bowl and spoon would not have done the job.

Two Halloweens later I donned a news cap, knickers, suspenders, and argyle socks to imagine myself as a Depression-era shoeshine boy. Getting bolder and more committed with my props, I carried my dad's cumbersome old-timey wooden shoeshine kit and hung a cardboard sign from a string around my neck that read: "Shoeshine 5 cents," the first *S* in *shoeshine* purposely written backward to make it look janky and kid-made. As an only child, children were not familiar creatures to me, but I imagined my Depression-era shoeshine boy might not be an ace speller. I was a kid, and yet I had to consciously make sure my sign looked like it was made by a kid. I was a kid imitating a kid. I was in drag.

As an adult I would see an episode of *The Simpsons* in which Bart is expelled from school and proposes to make his way as a nineteenth-century Cockney bootblack ("Shine your boots, guv'nah?") and feel like my child self was seen, even if in hindsight by TV writers. They had Bart riffing on Dickens as I was riffing on *Our Gang* (a 1930s short film series, which was in heavy rotation on Sunday mornings in the 1970s) and the smash hit musical *Annie*. *Our Gang* was complicated, subversive. It engaged all the expected stereotypes of its time, while modeling integration, shocking for that same era. *Annie* was less subversive, but if its fantasy of political harmony had come true, the Reagan eighties might have been less brutal.

Millions of little girls aspired to play Annie, everyone's favorite destitute-yet-eternally-hopeful orphan, but apparently I also needed to play with gender. I remember being annoyed when someone called me "shoeshine girl," that they refused to make the leap in gender perception. It couldn't have been that hard considering that until I was four, unless I was wearing a dress, strangers usually thought I was a boy. The shoeshine boy costume with its reference to the Great Depression and child labor, not to mention its heavy prop, was a way for me to try on hardship. I now see it as a kind of difficulty practice, a way to build character. I began to *identify* with difficulty. My exasperated mom put it more concisely: "Why do you always have to do everything the hard way?"

In sixth grade, age ten, I dressed up as *Private Benjamin* for Halloween. I was too young to see the movie, which had come out the year before in 1980, but I loved the poster: an image of Goldie Hawn in a helmet with mascara running down her face. Hawn gives an Oscar-nominated performance as a young woman whose goal in life is to marry a rich man, but who, after her husband dies of a heart attack on their wedding night, gets duped into joining the Army. Her shallow, sexist parents come to rescue her from basic training, but she stays as an act of rebellion, and by building resilience also begins to build a meaningful life on her own.

This costume choice picked up where the Depression-era shoeshine boy left off—an enactment of hardship, and a demonstration of a budding awareness of my own privilege. I saw myself as a wimpy girl who needed to go to boot camp and toughen up. Around age nine we become self-aware in relation to the world, and that is when we (hopefully) begin to develop a sense of social justice. Indeed, around this time I began to obsess about the randomness of my good fortune and the unfairness and cruelty of the world. My parents had already hammered into my brain how lucky I was. But the costume also felt campy, as if I had already perceived my relative privilege through a filter of humor. I was camping my privilege. I was in on the joke. When I think of my ten-year-old self playing Goldie Hawn playing a rich princess who finds herself in the army, I think of myself as a little drag queen.

The *Private Benjamin* costume failed. Not only was I the youngest kid in class, but I was also the new girl. This costume announced my lack of interest in being understood or accepted by my peers. It was my first niche art performance, kind of a big "fuck you." But mostly I just really liked that poster image of Goldie Hawn in fatigues with muddy rivers of mascara running down her cheeks: glamour in the face of hardship. Not only did the costume proclaim my wish to be an adult and my compulsion to make life difficult for myself—choosing it instead of something easier, more relatable—but it also spoke to how I began to intentionally make things difficult for myself just by *being* myself.

Around this time I was taken to see David Lynch's *The Elephant Man*. I don't know whose parents thought that was a good idea, but the film wrecked me. It also helped form a good part of my ethical self. I was in chaos for weeks and could not make any sense of a world in which people could be so cruel to someone so unfortunate. Of course, the writing of the protagonist Joseph Merrick, and his portrayal by the great John Hurt as a sensitive aesthete made it all the more painful. I think it may also have subliminally imparted the idea that it is nobler to be ridiculed than to be a Philistine, and that all sensitive souls could somehow find, like Merrick finds in his fictionalized friendship with actress Madge Kendal, someone to understand them.

In seventh grade I was Joan Crawford from *Mommie Dearest*. Or rather, Joan Crawford as played by Faye Dunaway. I had just read the book and the movie had come out the previous summer. I wore my mom's blue chenille bathrobe, to which I pinned a monogram cursive "JC" cut out of pink construction paper. I spray-painted my hair with black hair paint and pulled it back with a hair band I made out of an old T-shirt sleeve. I slathered my face in green clay masque, grabbed a wire hanger, and got on the bus to school, where exactly one person, a teacher, got what I was doing with my costume. If my social mind was a scale and making friends of my classmates was on one side and alienating them with my aesthetic choices was on the other, the *Mommie Dearest* costume added the weight of an anvil to the latter. Better to be ridiculed than to deprive myself of a Joan Crawford fantasy. I chose my queerest costume at the time when kids were at their meanest.

In eighth grade, undaunted, I dressed as Boy George, corralling a stable of drag icons. I have two pictures of that day. In one, I am standing with my friend Susan who is dressed as kind of an ethereal goth Isadora Duncan—Greek sandals with straps up the ankles, teased hair, and a chiffon wrap. In Susan I had finally found a kindred spirit. Later, she and I would spend hours together mooning over Duran Duran. The second photo is a closer shot of me in front of my locker. Over my shoulder you can see a poster of A Flock of Seagulls and a picture of Rupert Everett in a promo shot from *Another Country* torn from *The*

Face, the British magazine my mom used to let me buy as a treat from Wax Trax, the cool record store in Boulder. My Boy George outfit is a combo of Express and Esprit, all of it found on sale. I am wearing two oversize button-down shirtdresses layered over each other, one a bright madras plaid and one turquoise. Under that is a pair of white baggy pants and orange baggy socks with clear, buckle-up jelly shoes. On my head is a cheap Halloween witch wig that my mom and I have braided with colorful rags and string in imitation of Boy George's look from the "Karma Chameleon" video. My head is wrapped in the cut-off hem of the extra-large T-shirt, which I am wearing under the big shirts. To top it off I have perched a wide-brimmed rust-colored felt hat on the back of my head. I am wearing every color of eye shadow I could find in my mom's makeup collection.

This was not so much costume as emulation, one that bled into my life and the expression of myself. Unlike Miss Muffett or Private Benjamin or Joan Crawford, I really wanted to *be* Boy George. I wanted to be that beautiful, talented, brave, and witty in the face of hate. I wanted to do something that stirred up that much controversy. I would have dressed as Boy George every day if my mom had permitted me to wear that much makeup to school on any day besides Halloween. She let me wear whatever clothes I wanted, but her Southern Catholic upbringing had her draw a strict line between a "trashy" amount of makeup and what she still calls "looking polished." Mitzi, for her part, wore a full face every day: foundation, concealer, eyeliner, several shades of brown or navy shadow, blush, lip-liner and lipstick. She kept her makeup in a huge basket, and products spilled over into every drawer in her bathroom. "For that natural look," she used to joke. When I first saw a picture of the French-Canadian actress Geneviève Bujold, I was struck by how much she looked like my mother in the morning before she put on her face.

Like my mother, Boy George also created glamour, and he was one of the most dazzling creatures I had ever seen. This act of creation, this will toward beauty was of special significance because he, like me, had kind of a big nose and light eyes. I liked my eyes, and drew attention to them with an approximation of George's colorful eye shadow. I hated my nose though, and I studied closely the way Boy George shaded and worked his until it blended harmoniously with the rest of his gorgeous drag face.

The next year I sang my praises of Boy George in an essay for a contest put on by the Optimist Club. The winning essay was one written by a girl about her sibling with Down syndrome, a generous soul and an accomplished athlete who transformed all of the lives they encountered. There was no contest. After that kid's story I felt totally shallow for offering up a faux-rasta club kid and future drug addict as the object of my Optimist admiration. But I love that my parents had no qualms about my making my case for Boy George in an attempt to win scholarship money from a bunch of old conservative Christian do-gooders (do-gooders in many ways I am sure, but we should note, probably anti-gay). Tom and Mitzi just sent me up to that podium to fangirl out with no chance to win, to go on about how brave, witty and talented Boy George was, about how he was "himself." When I was in junior high "be yourself" was our mantra, a phrase that would become cliché a few years later and empty out more of its meaning with each successive year. But "be yourself" was how I and so many of my future friends got through days of merciless taunting at the hands of stupid boys and scary mean-girls. Boy George was my beacon, visible all the way from American suburbia.

I began to dress for life the way I dressed for Halloween. By ninth grade, on any given weekday, I would come downstairs in whatever look I had concocted for school—Bookish Beatnik, Zen Peasant, Victorian Vampire Victim, Punjabi Princess, Warhol Superstar—and my mother would sigh, "Must it always be a costume?" Yes! Life is a party deserving nothing less. As I dressed for Halloween and then for school, I didn't think of it as part of my training as a performer, but that is what it was. The rigors and intricacies of costume, the Study of character through the lens of dress, the interrogation of the difference between appropriation and celebration, these were to become integral parts of my art practice.

Halloween was drag school.

II. Dress-Up

In the hall closet lived my mom's old sunshine yellow vinyl suitcase, bulging with treasure. It was like something Carol Brady might have carried as she entered that fabulous modern house after her honeymoon with Mike to start their famous blended family, *The Brady Bunch*. When I opened its straining latches, a jumble of hand-me-down goodies popped out like a jack-in-the-box: sparkly sequin sweaters, silky nightgowns and filmy negligées, Halloween costumes, random pieces of seventies polyester daywear, a flouncy crinoline, a sexy black Liz Taylor slip, tangled necklaces, mismatched clip-on earrings, and a wavy brown fall that my mom had worn a decade earlier.

Whatever game I happened to be playing was also always dress-up. I might choose a sequined minidress and fall for climbing the backyard pepper tree, a white crocheted vest and skirt number for chasing cats with Anthony from next door, or my black cat costume for playing kickball in the driveway. Drag has never held me back from action.

Off-limits as street-play attire were the garments that had adorned my mother on three of her most special occasions: First Communion, prom, and wedding. These did not live wadded up in the yellow suitcase but hung formally, wrapped in plastic and stuffed with tissue, in the back of her closet. The prom dress was a muted butter yellow, her color. She knew her colors long before that book *Color Me Beautiful* came out in the eighties to dictate everyone's palette. She is, as one might guess from the prom dress and suitcase, an Autumn, the yellow shades a complement to the warm undertone of her always-tan, Italian-American, Southern California skin. The prom dress, the suitcase, our living room shag carpet, and our kitchen cabinets: all variations on golden (never lemon chiffon or sherbet; those were for Summers).

The golden yellow prom dress was matte taffeta, a simple strapless column à la Jackie Kennedy, with whom my mom was of a type: slight, well proportioned, and muscular, with a smart, worldly beauty. The style of Jackie and Mitzi, respectively a political wife and military daughter, said, "I can rise to any occasion, I can look put-together in any situation in any part of the world. I can meet anyone." My mom's wedding dress was Jackie-worthy too, another stiff column adorned only by a short-sleeved lace overlay with twenty-two buttons down the back. As an Autumn, a vanilla cream-colored gown would have flattered her best, but in 1965 anything but stark white would have flown in the face of propriety. The accompanying veil had a flat, square bow, geometric, not too girly, that sat on top of her neat little bubble flip hairstyle.

The prom and wedding gowns evoked an enduring elegance that would inform my future evening wear choices, but it was that frilly organza First Communion outfit that ensnared me then. This was a white dress and an actual veil made expressly for a child, not a child playing dress-up in an adult-sized gown. Kiddie bridal couture. I tried the dress all the way on only once before I grew out of it, already bigger at four than my mother had been at six. I begged her for one of my own, in my size.

"What's First Communion?" It sounded kind of scary.

"It means you have to be Catholic."

"What's Cath'lic?"

"Grandma's Catholic. And the little girls we see coming out of church all dressed up. They're Catholic. They're having their First Communions."

Oh, those girls! They were the most beautiful girls I had

ever seen in person. The little Latina girls I glimpsed whenever we drove into LA coming out of the big churches with their impeccably dressed parents. I coveted their frothy dresses, lacy socks, and patent leather Mary Janes, hair in perfect ringlets. And their veils! They weren't playing dress-up for some pretend event, but dressing for serious spiritual business. That was First Communion. Now I really wanted one.

"Catholic kids have to get baptized and go to church and Sunday school and pray." My parents' Catholic damage was so thorough that it put them off even having me baptized.

"Why do they have to go to school on Sundays? Are they being punished?"

"You could say that. But for no reason at all!" her voice all sarcastic sunshine. "That's how I grew up. Going to Sunday school and being told I was a sinner."

"What's a sinner?"

With her frilly starched First Communion dress my mother had been given a morbid fear of God, which seemed to have curtailed any sense of childish liberation she might have enjoyed. She believed fervently at first and even collected saint cards ("like they were baseball cards" she said). But her skepticism had come to fruition by young adulthood. My dad was irreverent from the get-go, kicked out of Catholic prep school after getting caught smoking in his sports car during afternoon prayers by Brother Whoever-He-Was, telling him to "beat it."

I really just wanted the dress, but I wasn't willing to go to school on Sunday for it, to eat a weird dry wafer and be told I was bad for no reason. Then as now I was kind of a poseur. Really, knowing what we know now, give or take some honest charitable work, the pomp and frippery are really the only good parts of the Catholic church. Now, drag is as holy as communion to me. Dress-up is the portal to the spiritual, a way to get at the thing from the outside in.

III. Oh, Mary

"Pigs in Spaaaaace!" It happened so fast. No sooner had it been snatched from my hand than I watched my Muppets lunchbox launch over the playground fence. *Stupid boys.* I cried as I trudged across the wet grass to retrieve it, hoping it would stay safe later in my fourth-grade classroom cubby. I sat at my desk and daydreamed about a way to transport myself to another time and place. While other little girls were playing Charlie's Angels and fighting over who got to be sexy Jill as portrayed by Farrah Fawcett with her famous feathered hair, I had another role model in mind.

I daydreamed a world in which my lunchbox would not be ridiculed, where I would walk down a dirt road to a one-room schoolhouse, my lunch (like everyone else's) in a tin pail, my books swinging by a sturdy leather strap. I would sashay proudly in my homemade calico dress, high-necked and nipped in at the waist, my bonnet shielding my face from the relentless prairie sun. My eyelet lace petticoat would swish around my shiny high-button boots (which required a special instrument to fasten). After school I would do my chores and then read by the fire after a meal of hearty stew eaten from a wooden bowl. I would take a bath in a tin tub in the middle of the kitchen and then run a brush through my long hair for a hundred strokes before climbing into my featherbed.

Then I would wake up feeling feverish. Ma would cover my burning brow with cold compresses. Laura would tell a joke to distract me as I shivered, freezing cold again, under the heaviness of the homemade quilt, its colorful geometric pattern now turning psychedelic. I would drift away, weaker and weaker, into a daze of terrible hallucinations. What was I seeing? Circles! Pinwheels! Could I see? Darkness! Darkness! "Ma? Ma! I can't see! Where are you? What's happening? I can't see!"

I would keep my eyes closed and try to find my way from my

bed to my door without knocking anything over, dramatizing my frantic search around my room with jazzy-mime hands: bed, bedside table, lamp, desk, 1-2-3-4-5 steps to the door … I would stare into the middle distance, training myself to simultaneously widen and relax my eyes, imagining the light entering them with no effect, while gently palpating the contours of my playmate's facial features.

"Pa, is that you?"

That was where my reveries delivered me, concocting a favorite childhood game: Mary Ingalls going blind from scarlet fever.

I had no idea how difficult life actually was for girls in the era of the Ingalls family, let alone one with a disability. On the TV show we referred to as "Little House," Mary grows into a young woman of exemplary poise and wisdom beyond her years. She finds true love and, with her handsome husband, opens a school for the blind and lives with dignity and purpose. Feisty Laura Ingalls was the storyteller and protagonist of the *Little House on the Prairie* books, but it was through Mary's sightless being that I fabricated the sensations of life on the imaginary frontier.

I did not come into contact with the cruelty of the elements in Modesto, California, in a house with running water, central heating, wall-to-wall carpeting, and a pool. My best friend Kristi and I walked six blocks to school down freshly paved sidewalks that sloped gently into the smooth asphalt, without even the steep curbs and crumbling cement erupting in tree roots that I had had to watch out for while playing in my old neighborhood in San Pedro. Sometimes there was so much fog you couldn't see six feet ahead, but that just meant we could play Marco Polo on dry land without having to shut our eyes, again imagining blindness. While winter rarely dipped below the forties, summer in Modesto often peaked at 110 degrees, but the pool solved that problem. My greatest hardship was negotiating one of those blazing summers with a broken arm, paddling with my left while keeping my shriveled and cast-encased right arm hovering above the water, wrapped in a plastic bread bag with a rubber band around it.

The closest I ever came to disaster was a mid-sized earthquake. I stood at the top of the stairs when the shaking started, the lighting fixture in the high-ceilinged entryway swaying back and forth like a pendulum, the pool sloshing around like a big shallow bowl of water, but there was no damage, no consequence.

Kids use play to create all kinds of challenges for themselves: can I jump over that? How far can I throw this? Easy is boring. But why did I play at being blind Mary? It was a childish experiment in challenge and sensation, but I also wanted to be like Mary Ingalls. I envied her stoicism, her capability in the face of her disability. Unlike Mary, I was a needy and high-strung little kid, overly sensitive and prone to crying at every little thing well beyond the age kids are expected to cry. I'm sure that's why the boys aimed their aggression at me and my lunchbox. I was an easy and responsive target, their own challenge: "I'll bet she'll get upset if . . ."

When I came home crying over their playground teasing, my mom told me to try to toughen up. She suggested I would be less upset if I played a sport instead of *Little House on the Prairie.* I remember thinking *why can't my Little House play make me tough? Aren't I practicing pioneer resourcefulness? Am I not literally building character?* Through Mary I could imagine my sensitivity channeled and tempered by resilience, a resilience hard-won by baking in the hot prairie sun and freezing in the cold prairie winters, a resilience that dragged you out of bed before dawn on a subzero morning to milk the cow before heading off to school, only to be bullied en route by that shrill Nellie Oleson. In truth, setting aside her sociopathic brattiness but considering her material stability, my friends and I had a lot more in common with Nellie than with anyone else on that prairie.

When I was in sixth grade, we moved to Broomfield, Colorado, a landscape not unlike the *Little House* prairie. I was the new girl and, at ten, the youngest kid in the class. I decided this was the moment to try my hand at choreography, and created my very first dance, a ballet solo, for the school talent show. My costume was a purple leotard to which Mitzi had lovingly sewn several long, asymmetrical pieces of multicolored pastel chiffon. Carla, the only kid who deigned to befriend me, accompanied me on piano. The song was "Through the Eyes of Love" from the movie *Ice Castles*, in which a small-town athlete overcomes unimaginable odds after being tragically blinded in a figure-skating accident. Another blind girl story, this one a romantic tale of triumph and hubris. The main character, Lexie, finds wild success-on-ice after being discovered by a big-time coach, leaving her old life (including her faithful boyfriend, played by dreamy Robby Benson) in the dust. Her accident is the crash after flying too close to the sun, its aftermath a life lesson in humility. At the end of the movie Lexie makes her comeback after a grueling course of rehab and takes to the ice again at great risk, still partially blind, and wows the audience who thinks she has fully recovered. After a routine of spins and leaps she reveals her disability only when she trips over the victory roses that litter the ice.

For me, as the new girl in sixth grade, stepping out onto the slippery linoleum stage in a sour-smelling room that served as both cafeteria and auditorium did not feel like a rose-strewn victory. But it did feel like flying too close to the sun, pure hubris to put myself in front of an audience of people from whom I was completely alienated. My family's move to Colorado felt like a preemptive crash, after which I had nothing to lose. At this new school, the kids looked at me as if I were an alien. Even my teacher treated me with condescension and suspicion. For what, I had no idea—teachers usually loved me. I was not a girl with a disability, but I was definitely an outsider. Everyone can look at their childhood and glean some sort of alienation—everyone is "special"—but that's not the same as realizing that you're the kind of person who will probably have a hard time no matter what. I felt a tension between wanting to be understood and wanting to express my uniqueness, between wanting to fit in and knowing that perhaps I never could. My particular way of being different shimmered at the intersection of choice and essence.

With that ballet solo, I made a choice guided by some divination from the depths of my tween soul never to blend in. Instead of blending in, I leaned in, leaned into sticking out. I leaned in with my teased hair when the rest of the girls wore theirs lank and feathered, leaned in with my ruffled miniskirts and Peter Pan boots against the tide of tight jeans, baseball shirts and sneakers. I looked toward the fantasyland of my distant future and committed to hurl myself at it as soon and fast as I could. I saw the obstacles between me and that future, popping up like the dizzying spirals and malevolent flowers on the *Alice in Wonderland* ride of my childhood Disneyland trips. I leaned in harder with my *Private Benjamin* costume.

In playing at the extraordinary, obstacle-filled lives of Mary and Lexie, practicing the difficult, I may have been girding myself for what I knew was coming: I would be the weird kid, the arty kid, the one who walked her own unavoidable path. I could have chosen to blend in, making my life easier in the short term, but that would have been an act of suppression. And, I think, somewhere in me lay the sense that my life would be richer in the long term if I didn't.

IV. Fairy Fancies

"I think I might be depressed," I suggested to my parents from the backseat on the drive home from Nana's house the night after Christmas when I was six. Despite the Barbie bonanza, despite the stocking and belly full of goodies, with the high point of the year being over, there was no other state I could imagine.

My mom turned around in the passenger seat, alarmed and amused, wondering where I had learned the d-word.

"If Christmas happened every day, you'd have nothing to look forward to."

On that deflated evening, her crucial life lesson was lost on me, the idea of ever again having something to look forward to, preposterous. Barbie's motor home was cold comfort. As evening turned into night, I squinted and blurred my eyes so that the headlights of the cars in front of us and in the opposite lane looked like white and red fairies, Christmas ice fairies gliding and sparkling down the iceless freeway from San Diego back up to San Pedro. I wished I could be one of them and I pretended that I was. Gliding and gliding in an endless cavalcade of brightness.

Later that year I asked my parents if I could please be sent away to boarding school. In Switzerland. Perhaps I had just seen *The Sound of Music* or read some story about a newly orphaned English ingénue being shipped off to a drafty old stone house on a moor. I don't think my mom was at all surprised by my request, used as she was to the part of me that skewed more melancholic Victorian aristocrat than Southern Californian suburbanite.

"Well, I don't particularly want to send you away, not at the moment anyway, and six is too young for boarding school. And darling, really, we can't afford an American boarding school, let alone a Swiss one."

It was a shame. My vision of Switzerland seemed to be exactly the cure for my fledgling ennui. I imagined an existence more glamorous, whether it was a charming chalet vibrating with the singing of refugee Von Trapp children, or an alternate universe populated by graceful beings of light.

With the boarding school plan nixed, I channeled my hope into the fairies. The appeal of becoming a fairy is that it requires no parental permission: you don't choose fairy magic; it chooses you. You could stumble into the backyard or wander into a musty wardrobe and be snatched and spirited away. To be a fairy—magical, fanciful, and pretty—is one of the commonest childhood fantasies. But the thing about the fairy fantasy is that it bestows power, the possibility of power through liberation, precisely the power a child in the backseat of the car on the night after Christmas lacks.

Like most kids of my generation, I knew about fairies from Disney. I wanted a fairy godmother like Cinderella's, to make me a gown and to enchant birds and mice to help me tie all of its bows and do up all of its buttons. I never really wanted to be a princess, but I imagined that I, like Sleeping Beauty, had been enchanted by fairies when I was born. Maybe I had been.

I was born in Dallas. Mitzi and Tom were young and hip—but never hippies. Dad worked in advertising, seventies-era *Mad Men*. They left for groovier pastures in California about a month after I was born. While in Dallas, we lived in an apartment directly below two older men, whom I'll call Garrett and Bruce. Garrett and Bruce had a fluffy white lapdog whose full name was Evelyn-Jean the Maybelline Queen because she looked like she was wearing eyeliner. Garrett and/or Bruce and probably Evelyn-Jean used to babysit me when my mother briefly ran out for an errand. This is when I think they may have cast their spell. I imagine them incanting, like the fairies in "Sleeping Beauty," but with a little twang: "She shall be blessed in many ways. She shall develop a deep love of false eyelashes. She shall escape having to grow up in Texas . . . but she shall spend her awkward teen years building character in a fly-over suburb, and only after that, shall she find her people. . . . We are your people, little one. Your people are us." The Lilac Faeries.

From Disney cartoons, I graduated to a book my mother had from her childhood, an illustrated hardcover copy of *Grimm's Fairy Tales*. With a majestic teal-and-bronze embossed cover, and calligraphy beginning each story, it held all of the old and more fucked-up versions of the familiar classics. In the Disney version of *Cinderella* the stepsisters are basically drag queens (as they are also in the ballet version, usually played by male dancers *en travestie*—in drag), and their failure to measure up to extreme standards of femininity is played for comedy. When the Disney Prince Charming comes knocking after the ball, the tell for each of the two stepsisters is her man-sized foot that cannot be contained by the dainty glass slipper, both girls "serving biscuit."

In the grim Grimm's version, Cinderella's stepsisters take more drastic measures, knowing full well neither of them has any hope of fitting into that tiny shoe. One of them cuts off her toes, the other her heel, slicing off shrimp and biscuit in a desperate effort to improve their status. It works for a moment, but as each rides away on the back of the prince's horse with the shoe on her mutilated foot, the blood flows and gives her away.

The prince looks back at the blood dripping from the girl on his horse and knows that she is not The One. Grimm's "Cinderella" ends not with an "and they lived happily ever after" for Cinderella and her prince, but with gruesome punishment for the stepsisters. As the stepsisters, one toeless, one heel-less, enter the church for the wedding there commences an intricately macabre choreography: a dove sitting on Cinderella's left shoulder pecks out the right eye of one stepsister and the dove on her right shoulder pecks out the left eye of the other. Leaving the church, the stepsisters get their remaining eyes plucked out. The Grimm's tale ends: "And so for their wickedness and falseness they were punished with blindness for the rest of their days." More blind girls. Cinderella's gown is festooned with violent birds (instead of assembled by helpful ones like in the cartoon), and the sisters meet an Oedipal fate.

As understandable as the punishment is for the "wickedness," it is less so for the "falseness." This version posits not a problematic "happily ever after" as a reward for being beautiful and good, but serves suffering as a punishment for trying desperately and failing to measure up to beauty standards. I do remember thinking *Poor stepsisters, why do they put themselves through all of that?* I had an inkling then how caught up the stepsisters were in an impossible system of oppression. I may have tucked that information away for later.

As inappropriate as the Grimm's "Cinderella" was for me at that age, its ridiculousness somehow blunted its potential to traumatize. The notion that women would cut off parts of their feet in order to fool a man, and then sit through a wedding with one eye plucked out, was as unbelievable as the resurrection of Jesus or the superhuman endurance of the saints that my mom cherished in her childhood. The gospel of "happily ever after" was more insidious.

V. Faerie Fantasia

In the dress-up suitcase among the nightgowns was a diaphanous yellow polyester peignoir set in lemon chiffon, not Mitzi's shade of yellow, which is probably why she edited it out of her wardrobe. With its embroidered neckline, puffy sleeves, long cuffs, and regal amounts of yardage it was great for playing Fairy Godmother, but my favorite item was a simple ivory-colored shift made of real silk. A little nothing I slipped into one warm spring day when I was seven or eight before heading out to play in a thicket of evergreen trees in the backyard. The thicket of my childhood memory was probably a cluster of three trees at most, but provided shade and shelter enough to make the tiny yard seem like an enchanted wood.

After putting on the nightgown I had taken off my underwear because the panty line was unsightly and unfit for a fairy and for the feeling of the silk on my body, a texture palpably, but inexplicably, different from my cotton underwear and the polyester slips and robes in the dress-up suitcase. I loved how the prickliness of the pine needles brushed against my silk-covered legs, the thin fabric on my cold butt cheeks and the breeze blowing up the skirt. I loved the dappled warmth and coolness on my exposed and lightly covered skin. I loved that I had to walk with fairy lightness or else the evergreen needles would stick my bare feet. I crept. I felt free and wild. I didn't yet know who Isadora Duncan was, didn't know that the lyric "Isadora was the first bra-burner," from the TV show *Maude* was talking about her, but I was living an unfettered Isadora dream.

"How you doin'?" My mom had come out to check on me, knocking me out of my reverie. She gave me a little hug, and noticed my nakedness underneath her discarded silk nightie. "Oh ... let's go put on some underwear."

My parents called me "our little heathen," which I mistakenly remembered as "our little Pagan" until one of them corrected me. I think perhaps through the faerie fantasy I began to understand metaphor and weirdness. *Was I a Pagan? A faerie?* If I harbored Cinderella fantasies, they were less about a prince carrying me off on his horse than about that fairy godmother enchanting animals and animating inanimate objects into a squad of helpers. I didn't so much want to be a princess wearing brocade and silk, as a faerie who could wear flowers for clothes. In wanting to be a fairy or a faerie I began to identify that I felt somehow "other" but also that I desired that otherness. I began to construct femininity around the faerie powers of glamour and enchantment.

While I was running wild in my suburban California backyard, fantasizing my petunia dress and my retreat to the garden, the Radical Faeries were living the dream, only they were worshipping the Goddess and fucking in the dirt. The Faeries picked up where drag freaks, the Cockettes, had left off and took their velvet brocade and glitter-covered beards back to the land. By taking on the label "fairy," one in a litany of anti-gay epithets (fruit, flamer, faggot, fairy), those gay anti-assimilationists of the

1970s were the first reclaimers. They were reclaimers in another way too, as practitioners of witchcraft in a tradition that called itself "Reclaiming." By returning the pejorative "fairy" back into *faerie*, its Old English spelling, they reclaimed fae gravitas, fae edge, the fae potential to fuck shit up. Along with it they reclaimed the slur "faggot."

One Radical Faerie artist I know now proudly brandishes the image of the faggot, from its original definition as a bundle of sticks, as a magical talisman. The Radical Faeries' commitment to liberation started in the carnal, sexual rituals of the Pagans and expanded into queer activism. They were also making costumes and putting on talent shows, but calling them "No Talent Shows," which connected them more to what I was doing as a kid playing in the yard than fancy gays going to the Symphony (although I now know lots of Faeries who go to the Symphony). They were cooking and healing, queering the "old religion" and raising a feminist collective consciousness. I would grow up to know many of these Faeries. Sometimes I entertain the fancy that I unknowingly "called them in" as they themselves say, with my childhood rituals. They would become my mentors and my audience, my sisters and my godmothers.

ENGLISH BOYS
IN EYELINER

I couldn't wait to play Barbie again. When I saw my cousin Suzie for the first time after she and her family returned from two years living in the UK, I was more than ready. I had brought the vinyl case containing all of Barbie's outfits and shoes—tiny plastic pumps, mules, and knee-high boots. I had also packed Malibu Barbie and her prettier friend, Hispanic Barbie, as she was called in the early eighties. The term "Latina" was not in the common vernacular, and certainly not the doll-branding one, the term "Latinx" not even yet a linguistic glimmer.

I even lugged the purple Star-vette. That was Barbie's car, an obvious play on Corvette, but which also sounds to me perversely like a girl pop group with a collective eating disorder: "Please welcome to the stage, The Starvettes!"

I had even shoved my Donny and Marie dolls into Barbie's car at the last minute, which had been prudent, because Suzie, unbelievably, arrived bearing no dolls or paraphernalia whatsoever. *Crisis averted, I brought enough for everyone.* When she arrived, I was in the process of moving the coffee table in Nana's living room so that we could draw the floor plan of a sprawling Barbie ranch house compound into the thick pile of the ivory carpet like we always did. Little did I know this would be the last reluctant doll drama, my cousin managing to be a good sport, rallying on my behalf despite her diminished interest in the games of little girls.

Suzie had returned from the UK a changed person, not only because she was now twelve, but because she had witnessed a cultural revolution: the post-punk music explosion. The soundtrack to our seventies Barbie dramas had been our grandfather Papa Tom's surprisingly hip collection of soul and R&B drifting from the family room, but today, instead of dolls, Suzie brought records.

Music was suddenly all she talked or cared about, and so my cousin put Papa Tom's Earth, Wind & Fire record back in its sleeve and commenced to school me in all things punk and new wave. Not only the clangy, bangy synth and drum machine-driven music, but also the inventive hair, clothes, and makeup that marked the movement. I joined her in a new holiday ritual, taking turns sitting in the beanbag chair under Nana and Papa Tom's stereo headphones with her record albums splayed out in our laps, studying the faces and reading the words of the people who would replace Barbie as our imaginary playmates.

I'd felt the rumblings of this new wave even before then. Our coolest and most favorite uncle, Bill, had brought the first album by The Police into the house the Christmas before. Their reggae-tinged staccato and snappy rasp appealed to me then just as much it would to the rest of the world a few years later. I had also seen Debbie Harry perform "One Way or Another" with a bunch of monsters on *The Muppet Show* and gone crazy for her. And I had managed to see The Buggles' "Video Killed the Radio Star" at my best friend's house when it aired for the first time on HBO before MTV even existed.

I had been too much of a little girl for any of that to change me overtly, but my brain filed all of it away for when it might become relevant. I was six years old in 1977 when punk hit, and I remember seeing a gang of outrageous kids on a daytime talk show. Lots of them had mohawks, and one of them even had a safety pin through his cheek. This disturbed me so profoundly I burst into tears and hid under my bed. I couldn't explain my terror. Was it his willingness to self-harm or the fact that the boy with the safety pin in his cheek just seemed so blasé about it? His lack of interest in his own spectacle of pain seemed to have been exactly concocted to scare wimpy little girls like me and old ladies like my Nana. Or maybe his pain was so tremendous that he had to numb it with more pain? His gesture could be read as part of an undeniable cultural movement: an anti-establishment, anti-Thatcher, working-class revolutionary force. But for me at age six it was a total shock. I think what I saw in those kids, what I didn't have a word for then but now recognize, was nihilism. Nihilism still makes me cry.

When I was a tween, the faces on the covers of Suzie's records had the opposite effect: they drew me in immediately. The Human League's *Dare* and Culture Club's *Kissing to Be Clever* were the selections she brought to Nana's house. Both album covers showed their front men in makeup, and I fell in love with them before Suzie even dropped the needle into the groove. *They were men, right?* I didn't really know and I didn't really care. Or I should say I cared, I cared deeply, about the faces and what they had to say, but not whether they were performing their assigned genders to the satisfaction of the dominant culture. I was so intrigued, so smitten with these masculine-feminine-masculine faces that I probably would have loved whatever music came out of them.

I'd seen men performing heavy rock in makeup before; everyone knew about Kiss and Alice Cooper. The painted faces of Human League front man Phil Oakey and Culture Club's Boy George, however, were simultaneously both more subtle and more extreme in their subversiveness, their androgyny riskier than the obvious pomp and costumery of the rockers that came before. "Androgyny" is the word we used then, but now we might call them gender nonconforming or gender fluid or gender-ambivalent. Any way we would describe them, the lead singers of post-punk and new wave didn't scare me the way that the punk kids did. In these singers and the kids who followed them I could imagine finding someone to play dress-up and dance with.

"Take a cruise to China, or a plane to Spain," sang the deep humanoid voice coming out of the Human League record. "Meet a girl on a boat, meet a boy on a plane . . ."

I wanted to meet a boy on a plane. A boy wearing eyeliner.

After I listened to my cousin's copy of *Dare* about ten times in the space of three days around Christmas, it would be the first album I would buy with my own allowance money. Even today, if you threw me on a stage and randomly skipped to any spot on that record, I could lip-synch for my life and slay.

In the following years I would pine for many of those men in makeup as potential boyfriends, but like I said the one I wanted to be best friends with or really, just be, was Boy George, a pale white Brit who sang like he had spent a girlhood in the Black church choir and who painted his face like a queen from drag heaven. The amalgam of his being, none of it belonging where he seemed to have come from, suggested that he had totally created himself and this made him totally queer. He may have been the first out queer person I ever encountered. When Boy George started putting on a lot of weight in the public eye, he owned it with style, giving the impression of a Renaissance angel in full bloom, draped in layered blouses, festooned with rag-tassel braids, serving flawless, flawless face. Later he would succumb hard to drugs, and being the hyper-visible person he was, would have a hyper-visible fall. Boy George's descent into drug-addled infamy broke my heart and offended my delicate sensibilities. I was angry at him for squandering that talent, threatening to ravage that beauty, but later I understood. It must have been exhausting to be Boy George. One would need to blow off some steam, and then one might need a little help getting some rest.

When I went to Suzie's house the next year, she had cut her long, thick, wavy hair into a mushroom cloud like Robert Smith from The Cure and lopped all the extra letters off of her name. She had been making this transition in the notes she wrote to me throughout the year, on what was left of her little girl pink stationery, signing them Suz then Sue then Sioux, in imitation of her punk heroine, Siouxsie Sioux of Siouxsie and the Banshees, then finally to something that was hers alone, a name more streamlined, but with a double meaning. Su: "yours." Super chic, a true signature. When her pink stationery ran out, she started using black paper and a silver pen.

At Su's house, I studied her Pee-Chee folder and all of the band names she had written on it. Siouxsie and the Banshees, Adam and the Ants, Kid Creole and the Coconuts, Bananarama, Blancmange, Orange Juice, Yellow Magic Orchestra, Yello, DEVO, Madness, Killing Joke, Talking Heads, Altered Images, Public Image Ltd., Visage, Bauhaus, Culture Club, The Human League, The English Beat, The Psychedelic Furs, The Go-Go's, The Specials, The Buggles, The Waitresses, The Clash, The Jam, The Cure, The The, A Flock of Seagulls, Tears for Fears, Gene Loves Jezebel, Romeo Void, Cocteau Twins, Eurythmics, Ultravox, Nina Hagen, Lene Lovitch, Xmal Deutschland, Japan, Blondie, Haircut 100, UB40, Heaven 17, ABC, Funboy 3, Gang of Four, Fine Young Cannibals, Men at Work, Midnight Oil, Orchestral Maneuvers in the Dark, Einstürzende Neubauten, Yaz, Duran Duran, Kajagoogoo, Haysi Fantayzee, Scritti Politti . . . There wasn't enough room on a folder for all of them. The one name everyone made space for, regardless of style allegiance, was Prince.

Through these bands we traced history backward and discovered the ones who came before: Kraftwerk, The Sex Pistols, Roxy Music, David Bowie. And a couple of years later would come The Smiths, Sade, and Everything But the Girl. This act of historical reconstruction depended, in those pre-internet days, on mentors like Su and my friend Susan's older brother Doug. Doug would introduce us to The Velvet Underground, whom we took to like mother's milk. But when he tried to do the same for R.E.M. we just giggled, rolled our eyes and asked, "Why are you listening to *country*?"

My parents had a respectable record collection when I was growing up. A smattering of what I like to call "Brown Corduroy Dad Rock" belonging to Tom (Bread, Harry Chapin, Jim Croce), although mine was less a brown corduroy dad than an oxford and khaki one. He also had some Doobie Brothers, some Linda Ronstadt (perennially brown-corduroy-adjacent), and his favorite, Elton John.

Mitzi, by contrast, did not generally like music by white people. In this respect she followed in her own father's footsteps. I would find out later that the reason my Papa Tom listened to Lou Rawls and The Spinners when most white men his age listened to Frank Sinatra was that the woman who raised him, Mary Swagerty, took him to the Black church every Sunday. Soul music reminded him of her love.

My mother made space for a few exceptions. She loved Steely Dan, Carole King, and Carol Bayer Sager. She could deal with Barbra Streisand only in tandem with Donna Summer or Barry Gibb. She could groove with Carly Simon, but I had to learn about Joni Mitchell decades later from gay men.

In Mitzi's car and living room, soul, funk, and disco ruled (Ohio Players, Al Green, Barry White, Dr. Buzzard's Savannah Band, Aretha Franklin, Millie Jackson, Minnie Riperton, Stephanie Mills, Natalie Cole, Dionne Warwick, Ashford & Simpson, Al Jarreau). My mom would get really into one song and play it over and over for a couple of weeks. "Upside Down" by Diana Ross, "Déjà Vu" by Dionne Warwick, "Forget Me Nots" by Patrice Rushen, and "Superfreak" by Rick James all spun round and round as did "Down Deep Inside" from the soundtrack to the movie *The Deep* (on exotic aquatic blue vinyl sung by what sounds to me now like a partied-out Donna Summer). A decade later when my mother pulled up to the airport pickup curb on one of my visits home from college, her jam was Ice-T's "New Jack Hustler," booming from her Jeep Wrangler. *Yo, Mitzi! Oh, Mitzi.*

The first album I borrowed from my mom and never returned was Donna Summer's *On the Radio*. Because she brought me up with so much great soul and disco during my childhood, I always kept roots there, but after Su introduced me to the British bands, I had a genre to claim as my own. Although most of my records were made by pasty English boys, this era seemed to herald the beginning of greater integration in music, different from the either/or division between white folk/rock and Black soul evidenced in my parents' collection.

Post-punk practiced plenty of appropriation, but there appeared to be a growing sense of acknowledgment and awareness among white artists about the origins of their music. A mixing of sounds, cultures and styles linked the disparate artists of the post-punk moment. There were people of color making amazing post-punk and new wave—Poly Styrene of X-Ray Spex, Grace Jones, Romeo Void—that bore little or no connection to soul, R&B or funk. There was also a heavy soul influence in the voices of white artists Alison Moyet, Boy George, and Annie Lennox, all of whom my mom ended up loving because of it, but their soulful singing was juxtaposed with cold synthesizers and offset by confrontational queerness.

♕ ♕ ♕

Su and I made up a game called "spot the punk" which came in handy as a way to pass the time during a family road trip in the summer of 1982. We already had an inkling that simply saying "punk" oversimplified the intricate taxonomy of subcultures we were learning about, but it worked as shorthand to identify anyone who appeared over the top and away from the mainstream. "Punk!" Any hairstyle resembling a mohawk or with the spiky volume of Siouxsie Sioux earned bonus points. "Real punk!" In suburban Colorado where I had just moved, and even in comparatively cosmopolitan San Diego where Su lived, our options were so limited that our criteria had to expand. The game turned into "spot the people with remotely interesting hair," but we still said "punk!" This would become a valuable practice, clocking the signifiers: the hair, the makeup, the shoes, the shape of a jacket, the length of trousers, and the drop of a crotch that might let us know that someone was a possible ally, or at least presented some glimpse of style to which we could aspire. A total look was a bonanza. "Totally real punk!"

Too bad we hadn't yet started playing the game on our trip to Disneyland a couple of years before. Every year over the holidays from the time I was four until I was eight, when we lived in San Pedro, my parents took lucky me and a lucky friend out of school on a weekday to Disneyland. It was always just us and the Japanese tourists, no long lines for rides, no obnoxious amateurs. The first time I went to Disneyland on a summer weekend, I thought, *Who are all these people!?!* Anticipating my future VIP nightlife, I didn't wait in a *line*.

On the last of these trips, as I skipped past the topiary animals straight up to the midcentury whimsical façade of It's a Small World, I saw six gorgeous people, young and Japanese— three men, three women, dressed to the nines—a candy-colored, fifties-inspired, Fiorucci editorial extravaganza. Pompadours, ducktails or perfectly slicked-back hair, ties, and shiny shoes for the guys; polka-dot circle skirts, pedal pusher capri pants, pointy flats, Audrey Hepburn updos or Betty Page bangs on the girls; the most stylish sunglasses of various shapes from perfectly round to sliver-skinny on everyone; and of course flawless socks. No one does socks like the Japanese.

These kids were divine. They were having a full pop-art Americana experience, meeting Disneyland on their terms and owning it. Forget Minnie Mouse and Cinderella; I wanted to have my picture taken with them. The only people I had ever seen who were this stylish and sublime were the people on *Soul Train*, which my mom and I watched religiously. If you have ever wondered where any seventies or eighties fashion inspiration started, look no further than *Soul Train*. Shiny stretch pants before Olivia Newton John in *Grease*, leopard-spotted tube tops before Blondie-era Debbie Harry, shoulder pads before Alexis Carrington, drop crotch trousers before anyone. The fashion of *Soul Train* was *the* avant-garde. Even though "punk" was our suburban teen shorthand for the kind of cool to which we aspired, my style longings carried a torch for punk's glossier antecedents, peers, and descendants.

Though not devoid of political content, post-punk was more aspirational than anarchic, more utopian than dystopian, infused with genetic material from pop and disco and pop art. When the diehard punk and rock devotees threw around the slogan "disco sucks," I knew theirs wasn't my team. Disco was the music of my mother, my soul. If punk was about smashing everything in sight, post-punk, new wave, or its subgenre, new romantic, was about getting out and building something, whether it was Adam and the Ants' ship full of foppy pirates, Culture Club's multi-culti queer Zion, or Ultravox's ballroom in an imagined Vienna. Some dismiss these artists and their labors of finery as all style and no substance. For me, the style and the substance were of a piece, informing and fortifying each other. In conjuring fantastical worlds, worlds constructed around the act of dancing in nightclubs, the new wavers, new romantics, and post-punks embarked on a project of celebratory self-creation. They staged a reaction against punk's rockist musical strictures, masculinist gender construction, and nihilism. If back-to-basics, strip-it-down class warriors were into punk, new wave was for fantasists and creative queers.

Growing up in Mitzi's house, I had access to nearly every fashion magazine that existed, with a stack of them in every room and an archive in her closet. *Vogue* and *Harper's Bazaar* were telescopes to the most fashionable parts of the cutting edge, but it all reached a new level when I discovered the British music, fashion, and culture magazine *The Face*. I still have my copy of *The Face* with Haysi Fantayzee in it. The lead singer Kate Garner—with her dreadlocks piled on her head, graffiti-sprayed outfit of tiny denim skirt and bra, giant unlaced boots, and skinny body—displayed a kind of feminine cool I had never seen. (A little bit toxic too. I would keep this photo as "thinspo" before there was a word for it.)

The three or four imported copies of *The Face* I was allowed to buy during my teen years sustained me. "Five dollars for a magazine?" cried Mitzi. Overpriced back then, priceless now, *The Face* gave me fuel, lending hints for what to read, watch, listen to; how to have a conversation and how to live, its pictures adorning the inside of my locker door.

In those first months after we moved to the little town of Broomfield, Colorado from California, my burgeoning artistic sensibility also found solace in the form of a cable access show, which as soon as I discovered it sent Saturday morning cartoons to join Barbie in a land of banishment. *FM-TV* packed two hours with music videos before the genre had a formal designation and appeared on Broomfield's local cable access station KBDI, a full six months before MTV came along and served a cease-and-desist letter forcing its name-change to *Teletunes*. *Teletunes* picked up where my cousin Su's coaching had left off. The medium of music video was a purpose-built vehicle for the visually compelling, anti-rock artists of post-punk. Not content simply to present footage of themselves strumming guitars onstage, these performers created stand-alone works of art. The Buggles'"Video Killed the Radio Star" aired weekly on *Teletunes* as if to remind us that it was the mothership, along with mind-bending experiments by Snakefinger and The Residents and all of the efforts, earnest and flamboyant, from my beloved boys in eyeliner. I willed myself into the imaginary nightclub of Visage's "The Damned Don't Cry," bopped and flailed to Soft Cell's "Tainted Love," and of course swooned to Duran Duran's "Planet Earth." And then one Saturday a new enchantment arrived.

The camera focuses on a set of gold-painted eyelids under a mane of vibrant auburn hair, as a red mouth enunciates breathy, plaintive words. The camera dollies back to reveal a nymph folded into the fetal position, fists trembling, swathed in what looks like plastic wrap. As the camera reveals more of the picture, we see that she is inside a vinyl bubble. Her insistent brown eyes bore into me from inside the bubble, from inside the TV, as her pouty mouth incants wails that climb to the peaks of her multi-octave range. Another video: she is clad in a white dress, standing in a sea of fog, backlit by changing colors, her slender body swirling and attacking with the skills of a real modern dancer, her long-nailed fingers pushing rhythmically at an imaginary windowpane.

I was eleven years old when I first witnessed the wonder of Kate Bush, the same age she was when she started writing music. Though she wrote "The Man with the Child in His Eyes" when she was thirteen (!), Bush's uniqueness captivated me more than her youth. She wasn't a rocker, though she found a champion in rock god David Gilmour, and rock queen Pat Benatar would cover her unlikely hit "Wuthering Heights." Nor was she a folk singer, though unmistakable strains of Joni Mitchell undergird her earliest work. She didn't have the cool edge of new wave, and though her entire catalogue is suffused with romanticism in the literary sense, she was not a new romantic. Kate Bush articulated the obsessions of bookish kids like me, writing about lovers lost at sea, young boys wrecked by war, taking on the voice of a literary ghost or fetus in utero during a nuclear holocaust. Kate Bush's resolute resistance to the prevailing categories available to women, or really anyone, in music at the time revealed her as her own artist. Not a boy to crush on, but evidence of what a girl could accomplish if she kept her focus and, to quote her, "let the weirdness in."

I added another lesson to my Saturday schedule of extracurricular art education. As *Teletunes* rolled its credits, I switched over to CNN where a soundtrack of French horns began a royal-sounding march. A posh lady welcomed us for an hour of "news from the design worlds of fashion, beauty and decorating." *Decorating!*— the shameless eighties saw no reason to invoke even the legitimacy of the word "design." This was *Style with Elsa Klensch*. I glutted my eyeballs on runway shows: Claude Montana's giant-shouldered glamazons, Vivienne Westwood's haute hobo buffalo gals, and Rei Kawakubo for Comme des Garçons, with her black and indigo collection of oversize shirts and sweaters full of holes, which she framed as a recontextualization of lace.

Westwood had all but created punk fashion, but Kawakubo had taken the elements of the look and elevated them to sculpture. Seeing Kawakubo's collection later that season in *Vogue*, its revolutionary importance resonated. I wanted to participate. My mom, goddess love her, took one look at that editorial, thought *I can do that*, and drove me to the men's department of Kmart, which we scoured for the extra-largest T-shirts we could find. One in black and one in white. When we got home, we cut the sleeves off the black shirt and cut holes in it to approximate the sack dresses that had walked the runway for Comme des Garçons. I layered the black shirt over the white one on top of some black leggings and wore the cutoff sleeve remnant as a headband around a teased-up nest of hair. I added black eyeliner on my lips as well as around my eyes to complete the styling, copied assiduously from the *Vogue* editorial. The kids at school had a field day with my look ("Um, like, there's a HOLE in your shirt! And, ugh, I think you have gum in your hair. Or maybe it's cum! Heh heh."), but I had a higher calling. I was living a fashion-historical moment.

With my newfound appreciation of fashion as an intellectual pursuit, I was ready to set aside childish things, and so, after a major Duran Duran phase propelled by teenybopper lust ("I get John, you get Roger!" "No *I* get John, *you* get Nick!" etc.) I moved to the more rarefied aisles of the record store. This is when Su introduced me to my new favorite band whose name and aesthetic encompassed those new wave rockabillies at Disneyland and Rei Kawakubo's design provenance. A group of just-post-teenage, mostly English boys had named their band after that most singularly stylish country: Japan.

The lead singer of the sophisticated art pop quartet, David Sylvian, was once described in the music press as "the most beautiful man in pop." I certainly thought he was. I knew Japan was my new favorite band just by looking at the image of him on the cover of their album *Tin Drum*. Winsome and delicate in sepia tones, horn-rim glasses, and lipstick under messy bangs, he sits at a table with a lacquer bowl in one hand and chopsticks in the other, under a single light bulb and a picture of Mao Tse-tung. Yes, *problematic*. Also intriguing.

My teen worship of the band Japan offers me questions, in hindsight, about their relationship to colonialism. Where Duran Duran's colonialism gleefully refuses to examine itself, celebrating the seduction of exotic beauties and the conquering of exotic locales, Japan troubles theirs. Though unabashed in their use of Asian instruments and tuning, it wasn't all appropriation, as they collaborated consistently with Japanese artists Ryuichi Sakamoto, Masami Tsuchiya and Yuka Fujii, who was romantically linked to Sylvian. These artistic and personal collaborations in no way preclude racism in art or life, but do deepen their project beyond mere name.

Sylvian enraptured me completely not just with his face, but with his voice, a tremolo that telegraphed melancholic isolation, a feeling I felt regularly. His voice was described, perhaps by the same journalist who praised his beauty, as "glass breaking in velvet." It was.

The cringeworthy pastiche of imagery on Japan's album cover nonetheless signaled what I needed to know about its subject: in his glasses, eyeliner and lipstick, he was smart, pretty and unafraid to appear aware of either. Japan was glamour from another world, the vinyl of their record emitting sounds to bewitch me out of the banalities of my suburban teen life.

The place I spent my teen-hood was an endless prairie of what we would now call "toxic masculinity." In Colorado at the time, it seemed like the only models for masculinity were cowboys or football players, the limited variations of which surrounded me on all sides in that landlocked state. I could see in David Sylvian's made-up face a different kind of man. His makeup may or may not have signified queerness, but either way it signaled a man unconcerned with middle-American convention. These men in makeup, whom I found nonthreatening and beguiling, were totally threatening to the status quo of masculinity.

They were also threatening perhaps to some unexamined idea of authenticity, an authenticity fabricated out of the pretensions of masculine performance. Femininity, no matter who performs it, is often suspect, assumed by the masculinist culture to be false and manipulative. Conversely, the culture often grants masculinity and its adherents the mantle of "real." At the time, nonconformity to gender norms was just as, or more, threatening than artists who played at physical and political violence. 1980s post-punk gender play started to pull these ideas apart.

It never occurred to me that Japan's makeup could have been the brainchild of a stylist instead of an authentically personal challenge to the mores of masculinity. After all, they had been a glam rock band in the style of The New York Dolls before settling down into their lush, multi-rhythmic anti-pop. But as far as my teen self was concerned, the gesture was engineered to draw me in specifically. I was fully crushed out.

For a moment. Then I changed my fickle mind. Japan had supplanted Duran Duran. Bauhaus supplanted Japan. Bauhaus wore their makeup not to express well-traveled, world-weary sensitivity so much as obsessive theatricality. For the expression of their particular brand of anguish, they embodied the trappings and gestures of silent horror film. Instead of naming themselves after a foreign country with great design, they had gone further and named themselves after a design movement.

There was something else too, coded into my fandom. Except for David Sylvian, I was not usually into the front man. The one behind the piano, the one in glasses, the one who loved Brian Eno and wrote all the band's weirder stuff. He was the one for me.

I arrived at both bands too late, their ensembles fragmenting and imploding just as I was discovering their transformative genius. What I realize now is that those bands were made up of boys at most only ten years older than I was at the time, teenagers when they first formed their groups. My imagination froze them in the moments their albums came out, so I could imagine these art pop stars and me meeting and living together in the bliss of some cultured Euro happily ever after. I did not imagine the junkie squalor in which some of them must have lived, or that others were, like me, using music and style as an escape from their own versions of Broomfield, Colorado, outside of Sheffield or Birmingham or Manchester under the Iron Lady thumb of Margaret Thatcher.

♔ ♔ ♔

Lots of 1980s parents were deeply threatened by the forceful cultural and political phenomena of fashion and music, some even calling their kids' music satanic, but not my parents. They never said "Turn that noise down!" or "You are not leaving the house in that!" Mitzi and Tom never even busted me for anything explicit or risqué music-wise, leaving me alone in my room to listen to Peter Murphy's unhinged wailing about "screaming whores," Lou Reed pining for a dominatrix in "shiny, shiny, shiny boots of leather" and Siouxsie Sioux's command to "fuck the mothers, kill the others." My mom had little recourse in the parental advisory department since she was the one who had listened to Rick James's "Superfreak" on repeat when I was seven.

"Mom, what's a kinky girl?"

"Oh, um . . . a weird girl, darling. A weird girl."

Mitzi exacted a small price for her permissiveness by tormenting me at the breakfast table with imitations of my mopey white boy heroes and their doleful baritones. I still shrink from the memory of her interpretation of "Love Me to Death" by The Mission. *God, Mom!* She knew she had dodged a bullet, though, when other girls who were into Van Halen and Def Leppard started cultivating looks that she found "cheap and tawdry." My 1980s teen fashion choices led me to avant-librarian or Hasidic Laura Ingalls or Japanese peasant but never jailbait slut. And yes, believe it or not kids, "jailbait slut" was a phrase in circulation during my high school years. Over the next decade, my generation would explode the assumptions it made. We would "take back the night," and insist that no matter what a woman wears, she deserves respect. That project is still in process. Regardless, you're welcome.

Though true *self*-respect would be a lifelong cultivation, there may have been something about my choices in fashion and in boys that germinated it. I was never into bad boys, thank my lucky stars. And even though I looked mature beyond my years and could have gotten into a lot of trouble, the fact that I was kind of an uptight prude saved me a lot of anguish.

While I mooned over men in makeup, I swore not to trifle with boys and their worst shenanigans. I would get out and build my own world. If I found someone to share it, that someone would be a fellow arty dreamer who respected me.

Style, Teletunes, The Face, and my record collection were windows. They showed me the freaks making things happen in a world beyond the tract houses and prairie-dog towns where I lived. When my mom made that T-shirt combo in imitation of Comme des Garçons, she made one for Su too, and we wore those looks one summer on vacation on a lake in the wilds of whitest Idaho. Some guy in a boat yelled at us, "Ha ha! What are you, the moth sisters?" It's too bad my fandom didn't lead me to want to make music of my own, because The Moth Sisters is a great name for a band.

ART
DAMAGED

I. Read My Lips

As much as I love the art of drag, I am always a little bit embarrassed by lip-synch. My friend the drag queen Precious Moments once said, "Yeah, when people ask me what I do, sometimes I just say," and he continued in the halting upspeak of an eleven-year-old girl, "Um, well, I . . . um, dress up like a *lady*? And, um, I pretend to sing a *song*? But, um, I'm not really singing it? And well, I'm not a *lady*?" That sums it up. We are a bunch of grown-ups (so we say) dressed in ridiculous costumes pretending to sing songs. As *LADIES*.

Later in my career, when I fulfilled my teen anglophile dream of traveling to London, I learned some queens there looked down on lip-synch. I understand their bias. Singing comes from the body—the heart and the guts, and even unskilled singing produces something authentic. Lip-synch plays lower stakes, pilfering the talents or notoriety of a singer in order to carry the drag performer. Lazy lip-synchers are legion and bad lip-synch can downgrade drag pathos to bathos. Bad lip-synch is just really, really bad.

If I were writing a lip-synch bible, the first commandment

would be "Thou shalt not lip-synch with a naked face." The plain face, whether made so through lack of drama or lack of makeup, does not serve the "you know it when you see it" camp requirements of lip-synch. Charming exceptions crop up in the landscape of entertainment. The rendition of Aimee Mann's song "Wise Up" in the now classic film *Magnolia*, in which the lip-synching cast enacts the montage trope as a music video, served to move both the plot forward and the audience to tears. Social media sensations serve hilarity with everyday faces, and the Funny or Die series *Drunk History* never fails to kill. But unwatchable cringe-fests abound, and I stand by my rule. Lip-synching is best left to the drag performers.

To move beyond banal pantomime, lip-synch begs for exaggeration. Exaggeration on multiple levels. Makeup is, well, the *foundation*. Movement begins to communicate. But the necessary drag flourish usually arrives in the form of a diva voice—whether that voice belongs to Diana Ross, Maria Callas, Barbra Streisand or Freddie Mercury—emerging from a body to which it does not belong. And while divadom is by no means a requirement, the more different the synching body is from the singing body, the better. This is why the exceptions to my "no un-made-up faces" rule are usually children. A pretty queen mouthing Marilyn Monroe's "Happy Birthday Mister President," is lovely, but we vivify the picture through a lens of difference. In order to render drag as art, lip-synch must push beyond its position as the primary technique in the archaic form of gender-binary "impersonation."

The classic elements of the drag face—giant eyelashes, arched brows, overdrawn lips, plus a studied over-annunciation of every utterance through mouth and jaw—whether on a queen, a nonbinary beauty, or a creature from another universe, help to send lip-synch into the realm of drag art. Oh, and hands! "Thou shalt beguile with hand gestures" would be my second commandment. And I don't mean miming the lyrics. A drag queen miming song lyrics is like a standup comic talking about airplane food: a hack move in all but the deftest, most self-referential hands. I want to see deep, informed, weighty gestures. Give me art-historical hands, please.

A great drag king makes up for a lack of lip-enhancing lady makeup and gesture-enhancing long fingernails with extraordinary character and exaggeration. With less glamour to hide behind, he must work harder, like Ginger Rogers backwards in high heels. Retrograde.

For the dancing queen, lip-synch is as indispensable a tool as the high heel itself. It expands the possibility of the production number, allowing physical feats that only the most seasoned vaudevillian could enact while actually singing, and we all know they don't make 'em like that anymore. Hollywood has known the creative value of lip-synch for decades (even Julie Andrews and Barbra Streisand were lip-synching to their own voices in *The Sound of Music* and *Funny Girl*), and Bollywood leads the charge with a shameless transparency of voice replacement, valuing long, lavish numbers that involve multiple edits, locales, and costume changes, and on-camera actors who can really dance over those who sing.

When a lip-synch fully clicks in, it is its own kind of dance. The best lip-synchers understand what they are doing as a rigorous choreography, a kind of dialectic companion to the improvisation of singing. Lip-synch begins to transcend its state of simply "pretending to sing" if the performer also manages to coordinate their breath with that of the original singer, to make the words seem to come out of their body. As a drag performer I learned quickly that if I could actually sing the song I was trying to synch, if I learned where to breathe in order to make the sound the singer was making, I could deepen its physicality into dance.

But to truly sell the weird face dance that is the lip-synch, and alchemize it into an art form, the drag performer, no matter their gender, must engage in some kind of energetic transformation. This is one of the reasons I almost always synch to male vocalists. If on the surface it appears that my existence as a cisgender female precludes my having to work to achieve the Studied femininity of the drag queen, then the art form requires me to push the concept of transformation. If the voice coming out of my body is legibly male, it complicates my presence. The work starts to approach that mysterious state of *werq*.

II. Drag Nerds

The clubs that spawned Trannyshack (Club Uranus, Klubstitute) and the ones the 'shack spawned (Midnight Mass, Some Thing, The Monster Show, The Broni Mitchell Show, Stereo Argento, Media Meltdown) were and are the projects of total nerds, people who overthink for fun. There are two words that best sum up our type of drag, and the first time I heard them, they came out of Heklina's mouth: "art damaged." The phrase served cleverly both to embrace and undermine the concept of drag as art. "Art damaged" alluded to performance that was a product of art school, and thus beholden to arcane references. Smart. But the word "damaged" immediately undercut the smartness, insinuating that there was something off-kilter, just not right, about our drag, or any drag that might have the audacity to consider itself art. We were never the ones who valued the pretty or the popular, not in high school and not in the club. My Yoko Ono "Cut Piece" number for Phatima's going-away party was textbook art damage, and after having done it, I was liberated to create a catalog of other work in the context of the 'shack that pushed both "art" and "damage" to their edges.

The quintessence of art damage was another night Phatima hosted in 2002, specifically skewering avant garde performance. Her invitation came at a time in my life when I needed to shake art loose from seriousness, and inspired a performance too silly and self-referential to live in the context of contemporary dance, but custom-built for the framework Phatima had created at the Stud. There was power in recognizing that we performance artists often have our heads up our asses. I had been waiting years for my chance to celebrate this fact. My chance to be a clown.

For my number I had devised a kind of mime drag with the addition of a set of panniers, those eighteenth-century accoutrements that sit under a gown to take the hips to extraordinary widths, compelling a lady to have to sidle sideways through a door. I wore the panniers over a black-and-white-striped turtleneck and black tights, topping it off with a fuzzy white clown wig. The panniers conveniently doubled as giant pockets, and into them I placed a collection of props: a banana, three tomatoes, and a giant ring made out of tin foil. My song was a short piece by Meredith Monk called "The Tale" which consists of her laughing in a specifically composed way: "Ha-ha-ha-ha-ha-huh-HA" from the diaphragm. At least I think it is specifically composed.

My friend, the choreographer and singer Miguel Gutierrez, tells a story of performing Monk's "Gotham Lullaby" for a special event, laboring over every detail, every "wa-lalala," to get it exactly right, only to meet her afterward and find out that she actually did it differently every time. But I was lip-synching this art diva's recording, so I would need to embody every breath and idiosyncrasy of her vocal/physical exploration. Between her bouts of laughter and nasal hums, Monk recites a list, "I still have my hands . . . I still have my telephone . . . I still have my allergies." The result is a sort of twisted take on "I Got Life" from the musical *Hair* rendered by one of our most inventive contemporary composers.

I balance for as long as I can on one leg and then the other during the vocal parts of the song. During the staccato piano notes, I exaggerate precise hops and weight shifts. Merce Cunningham as

*buffoon. It is one of the dumbest and most fun things I've ever created.
On the line about the telephone of course I fish the banana out of the
pannier pocket, hold it to my ear and lip-synch Monk's "Hello? Hell-
ohhh?" into it. I take a bite and hand it to the most scared-looking
spectator. Near the end of the song, during which Monk introduces the
sound of falling and breaking bottles into her composition, I throw
the tomatoes at the audience. The tomatoes aren't rotten, but still it is
a clownish offensive tactic to beat them to it, a winking admission
that my performance is kind of "rotten." And in topsy-turvy queer
clubland to call something "rotten" means you are in love with it.
My tomatoes also signal that I know our audience is up for anything,
eager to see the tables of the power dynamic flipped.*

Those panniers are the best! Their designer gave them to
me as a gift after a photo shoot for which he made them by
hand, and they ended up functioning as a kind of good luck
talisman, prying open a little door to the kind of deep absurdity
that would serve to generate, and then liberate, my performance
work. In a turn of events, the type which happens a lot in our
small, queer, intersecting art world, I found out the designer of
the panniers, Gregory, was best friends with Jim, who became
my close friend much later. In the earliest days of the 'shack,
before my time, Gregory and Jim performed as a duo called
Shindig. Shindig were ur-art-damage wonder twins, performing
in anti-drag, punk drag, and of course clown drag. A precursor
to and inspiration for antics I would devise later with my bestie
Kevin. In 2009, Jim painted a giant blue portrait of my snarling
drag face (I am sitting under it right now), which sparked our
friendship. The portrait is from a photo taken backstage during
"Berlin" night at the 'shack, when I served more art damage,
aping German choreographer Pina Bausch to three songs from
David Bowie's "Berlin album" *Low*. Art-damaged drag nerd
lineage.

For a cult movie-themed night in 2005 hosted by an art
queen who had christened herself simply Kiddie, I grabbed the

opportunity to exorcise a demon (you'll meet her later). The demon was by this time nearly squashed, but in retrospect I can't discount the value of the ensuing maintenance-based banishing ritual. I paid tribute to *Superstar: the Karen Carpenter Story* by Todd Haynes. Exiled to an underground network of art-school bootleg VHS tapes after Karen's brother Richard filed and won a lawsuit against its gay future superstar director, the film uses Barbie dolls as actors to tell the story of Karen's struggle with and death from anorexia and bulimia. It is as campy as it gets. Abject pathos from a director who would, in subsequent decades, train his adoring lens on Julianne Moore and Cate Blanchett.

As he tells it, Mr. David, aka the drag queen Glamamore, had, during his life in 1980s New York, designed costumes and makeup for the Barbie dolls in the film. He had been the one to alter the doll playing Karen Carpenter to emphasize her anorexic wasting, even applying contour to her cheeks for maximum gauntness. The appearance in the film of wan, gray-faced Barbie/Karen, and the gesture itself, whittling away the plastic of Barbie's already skinny limbs, make a harrowing but hilarious analysis of the culture's abusive beauty standards.

I use the song "Tunic (Song for Karen)" by Sonic Youth, the ultimate art school band. In a long, prim polyester gown and a limp brown wig held away from my face with a ribbon, I pose like Barbie, fingers stuck together, arms bent at the elbow, mouth fixed in a big toothy smile. Mr. David himself is on hand to alter my appearance, so that with each round of Kim Gordon's deadpan refrain of "You aren't never goin' anywhere" he steps onstage and brushes contour makeup onto my cheeks, collarbones and arms to make me look like I am gradually wasting away, just as he had the Barbie in the film two decades before. The degree of anorexia realness that the makeup produces is less important than the ritual act of its application. In this moment Mr. David is my shaman/ priestess, having struggled with body dysmorphia as a teen like I had. This shared information is a deeper code that thrums under the campy in-joke of the drag performance.

This was Art Damage at its best, a bunch of smarty-pants queers sorting through the jumble of our anguished youths, the things that had inflicted damage and the things that had helped get us through to this moment. Laying it all out onstage as art.

I also once concocted a number that featured me as Ophelia from *Hamlet* drowning myself in a rising tide of blue silk to the tune of Massive Attack's "Teardrop."

Two black-clad death maidens wave the silk around my knees and up to my waist, and on the music's final crescendo, billow the blue over my head and stretch it behind me. As I stand in front of the fabric I appear to be floating on its surface. To enhance the effect of floating on the blue silk "water," the attendants each grasp a tendril of my wig hair which I have woven with fake flowers and fishing line so that it spreads out as if on the surface of water as in all of the classic images of Ophelia. A hair marionette. A hair-ionette!

On that tiny stage at the Stud, we often discovered the surprising power of the simplest stage magic.

When I had performed enough at the 'shack for Heklina to offer me the opportunity to co-hostess, she asked me if I had any themes to offer.

"Feminism 101," I said, at this chance to reveal my dream theme.

"No."

"My Literary Heroines."

"Honey, I am a *business*woman."

"So . . . no?"

"Hahahahahahahahahah. HA! NO. Absolutely not. Never."

Years and years later, I would unveil a new drag identity, "Fauxnique," and Glamamore would become my faerie-drag-mother. She included me in the club she started with the next generation of art nerd queens, called Some Thing.

"Faux-ne-quay!" said Glamamore, one drag name never being enough for her who, like a true parent, coins at least two nicknames for all of her familiars. "Let's get you up on that stage to co-host one of our nights. Whaddya wanna do?"

Some Thing theme nights always had the phrase "something" in their titles, so, remembering my old fantasy of My Literary Heroines my choice was easy.

"Something to Read. A night of Literary Heroines . . . and a little bit of shade."

"Gorgeous!"

"Really?"

"Why not?"

Glamamore and her coproducers VivvyAnne Forevermore and DJ Down-E were businesswomen of a different stripe. If Heklina was Martha Stewart, these queens were Amy Sedaris.

My literary heroines number had been planned in my head for nearly a decade before this opportunity to do it finally came along. The soundtrack is "One of These Things First," the tender, devastating folksong by the most delicate seventies hippie flower, Nick Drake.

I am Virginia Woolf, writing at a table with a pen. A friend playing Vita Sackville-West comes in to check on me and I give her a little kiss. I put rocks in my pockets. As two stagehands raise that same blue silk to drown me, I hide behind it to make my first change. I use a double wig maneuver, and under my Virginia Woolf 'do is a demure blonde one with bangs. Under my canvas car coat in the pockets of which I've placed the stones is a twinset-and-pearls look. Voíla! When the blue silk drops, I am Sylvia Plath. I sit down at my desk and type on a typewriter. "Ted Hughes" comes in and I give him a little kiss, repeating the earlier choreography exactly. I stick my head in a cartoonish cardboard oven, made for me by Some Thing's resident prop master Nathan, who doubles as stagehand. While my head is hidden by the oven, he switches my wig from the blonde to a teased black one, reminiscent of Elizabeth Taylor in Who's Afraid of Virginia Woolf. *He sticks a fake cigarette in my mouth. Meanwhile, I swiftly unbutton my cardigan, under which is a silver and black sixties tunic top. As I stand, I peel down my skirt to reveal slim cropped pants. Suddenly I am Anne Sexton. Two people in the audience get the literary reference, but the quick change inspires many people to yell "Woo!" and "Yas! and "Work!" I sit down at the table, type, and drink whiskey. No one comes to check on me or give me a little kiss. Nathan has stealthily replaced the oven with a car: hood, windshield, dashboard and steering wheel all rendered in cardboard. I sit behind the wheel, turn on the ignition, and gas myself. The end.*

Suicidal poetesses to the tune of a suicidal poet. I really tried to figure out a way to end as Joan Didion and make it a redemptive story of resilience, but there just wasn't enough time. Maybe when I make an entire one-woman drag show about my literary heroines there will be.

III. Poses

You can always tell when you are in the home of a drag queen if you know what to look for. The signs tend to spill out of boudoirs and dressing areas into the flow of the more public spaces of the drag house: spangle-crammed rolling racks in the living room, Styrofoam wig heads piled high with shellacked curls on top of the fridge, and of course, the entropic law of glitter lending most surfaces a crusty shimmer.

But not in my apartment, nor that of Juanita More! The first time I visited Juanita's stylish, cozy studio in 2002, just after she had opened up the castle gate of drag for me and welcomed me in by taking me on as one of her backup dancers, I caught a rare glimpse of her out of drag. Grand and baroque as Juanita is in drag, out of drag Juanita is trim, tidy and serene, with a home to match. I noticed right away what I didn't notice: there was no drag mess anywhere. *A fellow neatnik-Nancy*, I thought. *I knew I liked her.* Then I wondered the same thing most people do when they come over to my place: *so where the hell does she keep all of it?* The answer lived behind a heavy velvet curtain next to the bed, a Wunderkammer of Juanita's daily effects. Among the drag accessories, organized with every imaginable space-saving gadget, was a little desk at which she sat herself every weekday morning no later than seven thirty for phone calls and emails, and most evenings in front of her lighted makeup mirror to bring Juanita's face to life—the business of San Francisco's hardest-working queen.

I would later find out that a chunk of Juanita's daily work was the upkeep of an ever-expanding archive of cherished pieces, which occupied a storage unit. Even still, her apartment was a feat of editing and discipline. What visible wall space there was in Juanita's closet treasure cave was papered with magazine pages, a heady collage of images culled from high fashion and gay porn in conversation with each other, a confluence that inspired Juanita's drag persona, a high-class lady who is not afraid to get her hands dirty, I for my part, had harbored a long-term love/critique relationship with glossy fashion magazines. The fashionista in me lived for that dreamworld of impossible outfits, but the feminist in me knew firsthand that images of perfection could reach toxic doses. Juanita's juxtaposition of images, my beloved fashion models with scenes of blatant gay sex, and her shameless delight in it all placed it in another context that heightened the camp value of both.

In 2003, after a battle with cancer, Juanita was well again and raring to take a victory lap through the club scene. She planned a show at the 'shack, calling it "Guts and Glamour" to celebrate her birthday and her triumph over illness, a night to highlight beautiful resistance and drag sisterly alliance. I was one of the lucky ones she invited to participate. Juanita is more than an opinionated queen with a point of view; she was a true curator in a world that is too free with that title. She made her vision clear. Juanita harbors old-fashioned values and practices, sending handwritten cards and care packages to her loved ones. After we agreed to perform, each of us received an envelope in the mail. This fashion care package contained two sets of huge false eyelashes, a pair of oversize eyebrows and a beauty mark cut out of black pvc, a tiny packet of sequins and a photo from a recent runway show with makeup by the peerless Pat McGrath.

McGrath, herself a former club kid who had gallivanted around with Boy George in the eighties, upheld drag tradition in taking her makeup design inspiration for the Galliano show that year ('02/'03) from camp icon Joan Crawford and from the Cockettes, the San Francisco hippie drag collective whose legendary acid-soaked shows had formed our own queer consciousness: full-circle inspiration. We were to use the tools Juanita provided to render the models' exact runway look, appearing at the club as a united squadron whose mission was to deliver outsized femme glamour. Some of the queens were nonplussed to receive such specific instructions and took it as an insinuation that Juanita didn't trust their drag skills. I, however, a perpetual student who loves an assignment, was more than happy to get schooled. With images of Juanita's closet plus my love and my gladness at her endurance dancing in my head, I began my home-werq. Soon I knew what I had to do: I would make a costume out of collaged magazine pages. As a magazine addict, I had piles of images ready to be scissored to bits, which the tidy housekeeper in me was just about to toss into the recycling bin.

As I cut and pasted images onto sheets of brown butcher paper, the costume began to take shape. Then came the performance. As I carefully cut around the models' faces and bodies, I started pondering their inner lives. What triumphs and heartbreaks had they endured? What was it like to do their job day to full-calendar day? Were they happy women living their best lives in the big city, or were they sad teenagers tortured by self-doubt as I had been? A drag number began to materialize. It would take me through a session as a model—one who represents a world of breezy glamour, but who bears the weight of it on her bony shoulders, a wistful wisp who must "model through it," as Tyra Banks commanded on TV. She would model through it all: summer, fall, winter and spring. I needed seasons. I needed costume changes.

The piece starts in summer, for which I fashion a sun hat, fifties-style bathing suit and beach ball out of the collaged glossy paper. Fall features a wrap in russet red tones, and winter poses a little fashion joke—a bikini with a hat and muff. The piece ends in hopeful spring with a gown and boa of flowers made from images tinged with bright yellow. To evoke the seasons, I would use the ultimate drag tool: not the false eyelash, not the wig, but the electric fan. Blow an electric fan at any person or thing and behold instant kinetic glamour. Think of the fashion photography of the 1970s, or almost any context in which you've seen Beyoncé. A fan at the foot of the stage activates each season by blowing its signifier into the proscenium frame: leaves in fall, snow in winter and pink blossoms in spring for a hopeful finale.

The costume changes required a dresser, a stylist—and of course I immediately called upon my collaborator, Kevin. I wanted his role to resonate as a character in a theatrical space, not just as a prop boy. We both already knew a few versions of the character he was to play: the trusted, trend-making gay assistant, the exacting creative director, the man behind the diva. Kevin's job as The Stylist, his "motivation" as theater people say, would be to stay absorbed in the work of assembling and dismantling my various paper costumes and to remain unmoved by the emotion of the music or by any empathy for my character, treating me almost as a mannequin ("mannequin," indeed being the archaic term for fashion model). Kevin would evoke no malice or frustration toward my character, but simply present a thinking person doing his work. This difference in objective between us, my ennui and his task-oriented precision, created subtle but palpable dramatic tension. As we figured out the choreography, we found unsurprisingly that the stylist character ended up doing all of the labor. "Oh, don't worry, Mary; you just stand there and look pretty. I'll take care of your number," Kevin joked.

This was one of the few times I chose to do what I criticize so many queens for doing: I basically stood still and moved my lips to the song. I gave myself a handful of key gestures, but all of the responsibility, the cues and potential mistakes belonged to my trusty stylist.

The act of posing, the model as poser, the authentic feelings that might lurk in the mind of the *poseur*, all started to creep into the thematic landscape, and of course I thought of the title song from the album I had been listening to on repeat for the entire previous year, *Poses* by Rufus Wainwright. The song "Poses" had exactly the right weight for what I wanted to convey. The lyrics pondered the surfaces, crevices, and depths of identity. "I did go from wanting to be someone/Now I'm drunk and wearing flip-flops on Fifth Avenue." Rufus puts his showy range to plaintive use in order to convey disappointment. The song is perfection from its gentle piano intro to its swelling strings to its ending full of key changes and scales that sound like late fall blowing the leaves off the trees and down the street as the days get shorter.

Time marches on over our sadness, dread and busted dreams, but we keep standing and trying in our tired ways to create beauty. We "model through it," however we do it. I was inspired by Juanita's collaged closet-office but also how she may have felt dragging herself out of bed to her desk through the days of her illness, treatment and recovery, to keep propping up the business of her life and all of its sparkling details.

I was a little afraid of the song. At five minutes, "Poses" runs too long for a drag number, which usually thrives when it clocks in at a crisp three. To choose a long, slow song that may also be unfamiliar to the audience is asking for trouble in a crowded bar full of drunk chatty-Cathies, but the "Poses" number hit the crowd right somehow that night. It also worked on Juanita and Heklina, cementing their opinion that I ought to compete in the

Miss Trannyshack pageant, which was happening two months later. "You could just go onstage at the pageant and do that," Juanita said. I was relieved that the number had played well to the audience, but elated that I had done Juanita proud.

♔ ♔ ♔

Live performance, theater, dance and drag, consist of hundreds of little moments, choices, reveals, gestures that their creators hope will punctuate the audience's experience with delight or surprise, recognition or horror. I love this aspect of performance-making. I am a *detail queen*. As such, my reliance on those details being correct can veer into pathological, and once they are in place I nurture a superstitious belief in their power.

One of the details in my "Poses" number that I love and curse, besides my decision to place the choreography in the hands of someone besides me, is the big papier mâché beach ball I use to symbolize summer. In a literal throwaway moment, I pose with it, then crush it in one second and toss it into the audience. This insouciant instant of magic starts with a balloon. I breathe as much air as I can into a balloon and tie it off. Then I soak bits of paper in a bowl of glue and water and apply them overlapping each other until images cover every bit of the strained rubber surface. I sit, on edge as I wait for it to dry, praying that it doesn't pop or deflate and collapse the whole thing in on itself. I have learned over the years to leave a hand-sized opening at the top in case this does happen so that I can reach in and knock it back into place.

Drag spectators always comment on the costumes in this number and never fail to cheer at the stuff flying around in the fan. If a fan blowing a wig around prompts shouts of "*Yas queen*," some confetti, snow, and flowers thrown in make the drag crowd go batshit bonkers. However, after years of my performing "Poses" no one has ever commented on that ball. Yet I insist on constructing a new one and transporting it to and through the crowded nightclub every time I am booked to perform the number. I give myself unnecessary stress with the precarious task of keeping my prop pristine until I crush it. Though I have taken "Poses" across the country and the Atlantic, I cannot carry that situation on a plane. I even shipped it ahead of my arrival once, but it came out of its box like a sad soufflé. Every time I perform the poses, I must construct a fresh ball, which is fine if I am at home, but always a pain if I am traveling, often necessitating a hotel-room crafting session when I would rather be going out for a drink.

The first time I performed "Poses" in New York, at the legendary Stonewall Inn in 2008, I was staying with my friend Aaron, who worked in prop and set design for television, a real-life version of my stylist character. Aaron made my crafting dreams come true when he invited me to his workplace to make my silly drag prop. This was not just any workplace, but *Martha Stewart Living!* The show was on break, and Aaron opened the door to the workshop of every crafter's dreams. And yes, from what I could see that day, Martha's empire was run by an army of brilliant, dedicated, and detail-oriented gay men, plus a few astute and fastidious women.

I can be fairly certain it was the nation's expert on papier mâché who coached me through my project that day. I sat on a stool at a workstation in *crafting heaven*, fresh brown butcher paper to catch the glue runoff, strips of newsprint precut and ready for my first layer, a selection of high-end magazines for my second, and a dish of water mixed with just the right proportion of Mod Podge for soaking my paper. I sat among and marveled at rows of gleaming metro-shelving stocked with an abundance of plastic bins labeled with their contents, whatever bit, bob, or notion anyone might need in order to realize their wildest, most festive décor dreams. "It's a good thing," I heard Martha's voice saying, as I said yes to a tour of the set, giving my hollow paper globe ample time to dry. When I returned to the work table, I beheld the most magnificent, glossy beach ball anyone in clubland would ever see, not that they would notice. But I was in love with it.

Later that evening on the Stonewall's tiny stage, as I hold my creation aloft in a pinup girl pose, panic flashes through my mind as I realize this thing is indestructible; *my crafting coach was too good. When the time comes to crush my beach ball on cue as a moment of punctuation, it won't budge. I consider throwing it into the crowd intact, but giving an audience something to throw around is a risk for any performer. I can't afford to upstage myself with my prop. I harness my upper body strength and manage to crush it— the ball and, in the lingo of straight-dude optimization, perhaps the performance as well.*

The messy work of collaging carries me into an alternative mode of artistic production. The practice remains with me as a complement to and complication of performance-making, part not only of Fauxnique's image, but her DNA. For me, the paper "Poses" outfits deepened my analysis of drag, encouraging me to play with image as object: images of fashion as fashion, images of jewelry as jewelry. Fauxnique's collaged costumes, made up of images of women, of models, those embodiments of impossible beauty standards, worn in pleasure and also as critique, are a proclamation of my project of feminism and of drag. The jankiness of my level of paper construction points to the "faux" in Fauxnique.

Fauxnique wants to remind you that she is pretending, wants you to remember she is a drag queen and not hoping to "pass" as anything. She likes to create illusions and then destroy them. My practice of using fashion magazines involves the artificial image in the predicament of my imperfect drag. The surface is a shiny trick to lure you to look deeper into the problems and intricacies. The paper is an impossible material for clothing, always pointing to the fact that nothing we put on our bodies can ever be neutral, that all of our packaging is imperfect and subject to decay. Paper will never be completely wearable, in the same way that gender is always doomed to be an unwieldy and insufficient construct for the expression of the complex and mutable self. Paper breaks down. Gender breaks down. It is all drag.

IV. Weird Sisters

The first time I went out for coffee with Precious Moments, we ventured quickly and deeply into the subject of Kate Bush, which was all I needed to surmise we'd be great friends. By the end of the hour, we had schemed a Kate Bush tribute night, which Presh would host. A surprising first for the 'shack.

When the night came, I arrived, backup dancers in tow, with whom I had prepared a spirited rendition of "Sat in Your Lap" from *The Dreaming*, the bizarre funhouse ride of a concept album Bush self-produced at the age of twenty-four. Normally, drag shows at the 'shack moved along in the cabaret style, Heklina prefacing each number with a few words—salty, sweet, or shady—about each queen. But for Kate Bush night we needed to pull the audience into our fantasyland and submerge them there, retaining the fourth wall for the duration of the show. So that the show could flow as one long mood piece, Precious Moments implemented a narrative structuring device in which she, in the guise of a benevolent witch, would guide a little boy, played by the impish queen Peggy L'eggs, through our drag wonderland.

I walked under a festoonery of tulle around the stage and ducked behind the heavy vinyl curtain to enter the dressing area all aflutter with chiffon, queens adding the final touches to their ethereal looks. Stage manager Bobby Barber readied the fog machine and stood by with his clipboard full of light cues. In addition to my own number, Crickett Bardot had enlisted me to pantomime terror in her rendering of "Under Ice," Bush's song from the point of view of someone trapped beneath the surface of a frozen lake. I prepped my extra wig for the quick change on a narrow shelf designed for pints of beer.

"Oh, Glory!" said Suppositori Spelling, the 2002 reigning Miss Trannyshack, arriving breathless, gorgeous, and late as usual. "Can you help me out with my number? Where are we in the lineup?" she muttered, looking at the set list penned in Bobby's tidy hand with Sharpie and duct-taped to the wall by the stage entrance.

"Oh yeah, three numbers between mine and yours."

"I'm also in Crickett's," I reminded her. She glanced at the list again.

"Plenty of time! Here," she said, pulling a piece of cream chiffon out of her bag and pushing it into my hands to throw on over my leotard for her "Waking the Witch" number.

"What do I do?"

"Just dance in a circle around me during the part with the voices."

"You mean the chorus?"

"Duh. Heehee! Yeah," she said, turning around to attend to other business.

"Wait! How do you want me to dance and what do I do during the other parts?"

"Like a witch dance? And uh, when you're not doing that, just, y'know, duck out of the way. Ohmigod, thanks honey."

Out of the way of what? I wondered. And whatever I was wondering about could be anything with Suppositori Spelling. She was a lightning bolt of charisma known for jumping offstage, swinging from drainpipes, and snatching drinks from the audience, one of the most talented physical improvisers I had ever seen. *Who knew what she was planning? Did she even know?* I prepared to serve whatever it was and otherwise take shelter from the tornado of her presence. Presh and Bobby began the preshow ritual of shooing any remaining nonperformers out of the cramped dressing quarters.

Latest to arrive was Glamamore, whose relationship to time had taught anyone casting a show to always save the last slot for her. She arrived at what would have been referred to in the legit theater as "curtain," just as the Muppet Show theme was ending.

My number succeeded early in the show with spot-on lip-synchs and tight choreography by my backup dancers and me. I reached for the pigtails and coat that would turn me into Crickett's traumatized child skate-mate.

"Gloria!" Glamamore said to me with a flick of her fingers, using them and her current drag nickname, her riff on my drag name at the time, Glory Holesome, to cast a quick spell in my direction. (More later about these hands.)

"Oooh! I'm gonna need you. Where are you in the lineup?" she said, looking at the list.

"Oh, Glama, I don't know if I can. I'm in Crickett's number and in Suppositori's—"

"—what're you wearing for Spaz?" She rolled over my attempt to protest. Spaz was Glamamore's nickname for Suppositori, which fit her so well it stuck forever.

"This," I said, fluttering the chiffon in her direction.

"Oh, that's fine. Just flow right into my number from Spaz's. She's in my number too! So each one of you will just grab a sleeve of my straightjacket, wrap it around me and pull! Okay?" Madwomen with their figurative and literal straitjackets made a lot of appearances on that stage.

"Uh, wait, what's the cue?"

"It'll be obvious. I'll let you know. Right, Spaz?"

"Totally," said Spaz.

I ducked offstage after Crickett's number, threw off the pigtails, threw on the chiffon shift, and put my auburn wig back on, ready to enter on the cue for the witch dance, doing my best to stay out of Spaz's way so she could bust out. Then from the floor, I watched for her cue for me to grab one of Glamamore's sleeves. We stayed on the floor where only the front row might see us until it was time, at the break a few minutes into "Night of the Swallow." The music suggested a folk dance, so we grabbed Glamamore's sleeves and skipped around her in a demented Ring Around the Rosie to bind her madwoman outburst, even adding a little rhythmic tug-of-war. It was total chaos, but we pulled it off. And no one ended up getting trampled.

On a normal night at the 'shack, I would slide out from behind the stage door curtain after my number and find a discreet spot next to the platform to peep at the rest of the show, but this night I was lucky to keep my head on straight, let alone my wig.

"Ohhh, Glory, we did it. You were so good!" said Precious, in the cheek-pinching tone of a proud auntie as I caught my breath and took my drink ticket from Bobby's hand.

"You were ALL RIGHT, Gloria," Glamamore said. "All Right" was what Glamamore said when she was very proud.

"Oh. My. God. Did I just get hazed?" I half joked.

"I think you did," said Presh.

"You didn't *not* get hazed," Glamamore said. Had a bunch of drag nerds tossing Kate Bush and community theater into a witches' brew created a spell to reclaim hazing?

Two weeks later the three weird sisters—Precious Moments, Glamamore and Suppositori Spelling—showed up at my house to watch the recording of Kate Bush night. I put the VHS tape into the player, and we relived the chaos magick.

"We came here with an ulterior motive," said Precious.

"But we were never here," said Glamamore.

"You should succeed me," said Spaz.

"But we were never here," said Glamamore.

"Me? Miss Trannyshack 2003?"

"Totally," replied Spaz.

"Do you really think we need a *woman* Miss Trannyshack?" I wondered, not wanting to step on any toes.

"I think it's high fucking time," Presh said.

"But we were NEVER. HERE," incanted Glamamore. So mote it be.

Kate Bush night and its hazing served to dramatize an unexpected outcome of my drag fandom and involvement in the drag community: suddenly I had a regular art practice. Performing nearly every Tuesday at the 'shack gave me the kind of committed, creative laboratory that had eluded me in the dance world, where performance opportunities were relatively rare and came with a lot of logistics and hand-wringing. Dance rehearsal processes were high-pressure situations in which I often ended up in floods of tears on the floor of a studio for which I paid by the hour. Dance classes had the regularity, but were basically for exercise, and even the kindest ones centered on a teacher telling me what to do. The creative process of drag was, by contrast, easy and loose, non-precious because of its frequency. There was always next Tuesday! When I jumped into that fast-moving current of weekly drag shows and let it pull me along, I learned more about art than I ever thought I would.

PAGEANT I:
PAGEANT QUEENS

The annual Miss Trannyshack pageant was both a subversion of the idea of the pageant, and the thing itself: a shameless spectacle to end all spectacles and a skewering of everything a beauty pageant holds dear. What started as an in-joke grew into a giant forum where the most cutting-edge drag queens in the most cutting-edge drag city pulled out all the stops, sometimes literally out of their butts. We lived for The Pageant.

Like most pageants, this one included swimsuit and talent competitions, but unlike most it skipped the traditional introduction in which the contestant tells her would-be subjects what to expect should she come to rule. At the Miss Trannyshack pageant we put the body forward, the swimsuit competition functioning as introduction, an opportunity for each queen or king or genderfuck masterpiece to make her, his, or their terms and presence known, to establish their lexicon. A grand dame might enter carried by her minions, a drag king on roller skates. An elder might play up matronly modesty to comic effect; one who identified as neither king nor queen, or as both, could use this moment to intentionally misdirect the signals. The trope of the bathing beauty got a lot of play, as did that of the fish, from queens dressed as pretty mermaids to monsters with dead sea-life hanging out of their bikinis.

In the talent competition, performers were not only expected to, as RuPaul would command a decade later, "lip-synch for their lives," but blow everyone's minds. The pageant stayed true to the Tuesday night gender representation, and always included at least one drag king, one faux queen, and one performer who fell outside any category. But no drag king or faux queen had ever been crowned Miss Trannyshack.

"I hear you're doing the pageant," said Juanita.

"Oh? From whom?" Still pondering, I was averse to competition and always had been. And I was terrified.

"A little bird told me."

"Oh really? Which one?" *Damn birds.* "Well . . .I'm not sure I'm really ready. I—"

"Well, I think you should," she playfully cut me off. "I'll add you to the list. You can always drop out."

Ha! Lies! I thought. I wasn't the sign-up-and-drop-out type, and she knew it. Besides, one does not flake on Juanita. She expects . . . *More!*

Juanita did kind of steamroll me, but, like the mother and mentor she is, she also began to shovel the bullshit off my fear and expose it as pointless. What would happen if I competed? There wasn't any reason not to. As Kevin and I always said, it was a *drag show*!

"Ooooh!" Mr. David/Glamamore exclaimed to me after hearing the news, "Let's make you something!" He rubbed his supremely skilled designer hands together and flung all ten fingers in my general direction. There was that spell again.

Now I was in. Mr. David was going to "make me something." An understatement. How could I pass this up?

The phone rang.

"Hi, it's me, Heklina! Juanita told me you're doing the pageant."

"Well, I don't know, I . . ."

"What?!?" she theatrically raised her voice. Even though

we were on the phone I could see her making a stink face and half mockingly, half genuinely shaking a raised fist. This was her tactic: pretend bullying that flirted with the real thing.

"Yeah, Hekles. I guess I'm doing the pageant."

"Good! Hahahahahahaha! You're swimming with the sharks, Fish! Hahahahahahahahaha!"

Oh boy. Ooh Girl . . .

With the blessing of Juanita and those three witches, and cackles of encouragement from Heklina, I was ready to take off down the drag runway and pose on its red carpet, to ease on down its yellow brick road and watch its disco tiles light up under each of my steps. *Well,* I thought, *if this fish has any hope of making a splash, she'd better get to work.*

For our pageant numbers, we contestants had license to do whatever we wanted, as long as it met the most basic of all drag-pageant criteria: be fierce. As a young ballerina, I was trained to be lithe, expressive, and charming; as a college dancer I was trained to be nimble of spine and placidly devoid of affect. Now I would have to be fierce. *Fierce*—a broad and arbitrary term, but like camp and porn, we all know fierce when we see it. Fierce always attacks. Sometimes fierce attacks in that unmistakable choreographic sense, like when one says that a dancer "has attack." This brand of fierce is the physical equivalent of an exclamation mark. Sometimes fierce attacks with stealth, when the performer looks almost bored and then manages to transform the energy in the room and make the smallest change feel monumental. This brand of fierce is audacious, *how-dare-she-oh-no-she-didn't.* The past Miss Trannyshack pageant winners were each singular sensations: some monstrous, some glamorous, some silly, some sexy. And they were all Fierce.

In 2000, Vinsantos had snatched the crown by opening with a fake-out video of her doing the most lame, wan little drag number she could barely muster, after which she is ridiculed, then rescued by a fairy godmother. Vinsantos had brilliantly included her own failure as a meta-narrative. After the failure, she rises from defeat as a cult leader, brandishing her own drag sigil: two black platform heels emblazoned on a hot pink circle, printed on a black flag. Glam, punk, and graphic, the drag flag created an emblem for the outcast queers who were cynical about the rainbow while critiquing the mob-like frenzy of their connection. This was the bullied queer child emerging as badass ruler. Vinsantos plugged her punk/goth/genderfuck image into our need for a glam power-top leader. She would command us to reenact our collective problem with authority. We bowed down.

The next year, 2001, Precious Moments took the crown with a sort of *One Million Years BC* meets *Last Temptation of Christ* number in which she, in sexy Raquel Welch fur bikini (plus tail) gets captured, colonized, and crucified by a cast of drag kings dressed as priests. She overtakes them with her sexual magnetism and seduces all of them to fuck her with a strap-on. When later interrogated about this by the perturbed club owner, who feared for his liquor license, Precious answered, "Well, I'm not really a *woman*, and those weren't really *penises*, so technically it wasn't a *real* sex act."

Though, um, technically *anticlimactic*, this was no defeat, but a triumph, like when Barbarella short-circuits the evil Duran Duran's "excessive machine" with her erotic power. In the end, Precious saunters offstage, jauntily swinging the horsetail butt plug that had been pulled out of her body and dragging her cross to the outro of Mahalia Jackson's version of "Go Tell It on the Mountain."

Redemption, resuscitation, and transformation narratives always work in a drag pageant number. It's all about getting knocked down and rising up from the rockiest bottom. Resilience wins the day. St. Jude, the patron saint of lost causes, loves a drag queen.

"You need to overcome an obstacle, and you need at least three reveals," said my now dear friend Precious Moments.

"That's the recipe for a winning pageant number." She knew. Duly noted. In no way was I "in it to win it," but I have always been a good student who thrives on doing the assignment. This is my biggest strength and weakness combined, the legacy of my ballet training. I really, really want to please the teacher.

And who doesn't love a good reveal? The reveal is the most primary action of practical stagecraft, and if done well it can bring about total transformation. The reveal can take the form of an object or new character appearing, new information coming to light, though in drag the reveal is most often an instantaneous, unanticipated costume change. The reveal is magic, the "ta-da" moment. I had practiced the reveal in many forms on that little stage at the Stud. Now I had to come up with some reveals on a scale befitting The Pageant.

AT THE
BALLET

I. Magic Spells

Lots of little girls want to be ballerinas when they grow up. Most of them don't get to. Many find their young hearts and bodies broken in the process. When ballet casts its love spell over you, it makes no promise, nor any effort to love you back. The effort is all yours, and the spell is both faerie-gossamer fragile and forcefully magnetic. You have to be a little bit gullible, a little bit blinded to fall completely under the ballet love spell.

There is a sweet spot in which to start your child in ballet lessons so that they are mature enough for it to sink in, but young enough to still fall in love with it. Start her too early and it's drudgery—a constant battle with a short attention span. Start her too late and it is tragically clear that she'll never catch up to where she should be for her age group, try as she might with all her heart. Conventional wisdom points to pre-ballet (lots of skipping and waving of arms) for little ones and serious study starting at age eight. I say "she" because ballet is a different story for boys. While girls in ballet are a dime a dozen, boys are rare and precious. If you are male and you hang in there with ballet into adulthood, you'll most likely find a job. Some men can even start their ballet training as late as eighteen. Need I mention that ballet relies heavily on the gender binary? Though rare and cherished exceptions exist, it does.

I wouldn't say "Ballet is Woman," as Balanchine said, but I would say that ballet is a way of performing gender and especially femininity. Ballet is drag. Ballet is an unnatural set of conceits that you put on your body, but also something you spend hours breeding into yourself until it is second nature. Second nature—the uncanny, like but not like, akin to drag but deeper, a constructed way of being in the body.

Ballet came out of the courts of eighteenth-century France, which was really one of the highest points in the history of drag, when men and women alike cavorted in high heels, wigs, and makeup until the guillotine blade came down. The costume of ballet—the pointe shoes, the exaggerated makeup, the layers of tulle netting that evolve outward to form the most gravity-defying and ridiculous of skirts, the tutu—it's all drag. The whole practice is drag, a codified way of embodying ancient gender stereotypes and archetypes. All of this is still with us in the technique, a technique of rarefied femininity, like the practice of the geisha.

I started ballet training at age seven, but I looked like I was nine. I always looked older than I was, which would always work against me. My class was in the gigantic studios of Rosalie & Alva, a married couple, he from Croatia, she from Missouri, who had found success as a Hollywood dance team in the 1940s and then settled in San Pedro, California. In my memory, from when I was fairly child-sized, their studio was an airplane hangar. What remains from those lessons are Alva's charming accent and the enormity of that studio. I got bored and used the ballet barre as a monkey bar, hanging upside down, wasting my parents' money and trying the patience of my teachers, so my mom pulled me out of class. I spent my crucial eighth year not studying ballet, but instead, playing ballet. "Let's just let her be a kid." Being a kid consisted of playing Barbie or aping *Little House on the Prairie* in the practically nonexistent and un-prairie-like backyard of our new house in Modesto. When I wasn't playing Barbie or Little House, I played ballet.

I pulled all the scarves, the camisole, and the crinoline from the yellow dress-up suitcase and twirled around the living room to the only two classical records we had: Beethoven's Third or *Eroica* Symphony, which for years I incredulously misread as "Erotica Symphony," and Ravel's *Boléro*, which was used as its own kind of "erotica symphony" in the movie *10*. That Blake Edwards post-sexual revolution farce made Bo Derek a breakout star with slow-motion beach running, extreme side boob, and white lady cornrows. Her sexy character, while seducing a guy played by Dudley Moore, claims that Ravel's *Boléro* perfectly mimics the rhythms of the sex act from foreplay to orgasm. I really, really don't want to know if my parents purchased the Ravel because of the magic attributed to it in *10*.

I blasted the Beethoven and Ravel and pranced around on the coffee-with-cream-colored carpet of the sunken living room. I was a fairy, a gypsy, a genie, and a general drama queen. The crinoline was a tutu, a flamenco skirt, and also a wig. Shirley Temple made the occasional appearance in my repertoire of characters, as did Cher. I leapt and spun until the needle skipped on the record, until my performance and its flounces had to be contained. That year of reckless scarf-twirling may have imprinted too much liberty onto my best dance-learning moment, skewing me more toward the glamorous abandon of modern dance pioneers Loïe Fuller and Isadora Duncan than the worshipful dedication of contemporary ballet stars Suzanne Farrell and Gelsey Kirkland. By playing, not studying, through my crucial eighth year of life, I likely sealed my destiny as a ballet outsider. After the umpteenth record skip and much begging, my parents sent me back to class at age nine. I could do ballet supervised by a professional, and Mitzi could listen to Donna

Summer in peace.

When I was nine, I looked eleven, and I attended the local garage-turned-studio of the tanned, sweet, and lanky Julene Frowen. Class with Julene was not rigorous. Hers was one step above what the dance cognoscenti condescendingly call a "Dolly Dingle" school—your generic ballet/jazz/tap one-stop shop. Though Julene taught only ballet, her motherly kindness diluted any serious artistry. It was a great place to learn the basics, and the basics bored me nearly to tears. But I refrained from hanging from the barre this time and simply hung in there with the other girls. I learned to fantasize that I was really dancing when I was just doing tendus (pronounced *tawn-doo*, the move in which you stick your leg out and point your toe from a standing position, and then close it again) and pas de bourrées (*paw-duh-boo-ray*, step right foot behind left, open your feet, close, repeat). I infused those basic steps with enough drama and meaning to keep me interested. I made up stories in my head about why I might be sticking out my foot, or doing that triplet step, back, side, front, back side front into infinity. It's a skill that served me well in my future as a dancer in postmodern group works in which I had to keep myself engaged in my role as an agent of pure movement with no character to anchor me, but in those cases I often received the note that I was being too expressive. Julene indulged my excesses of expressivity, and I stayed enthralled enough to start to learn technique. I *played* ballet while I was learning ballet, and its mystifying logic began to sink into my body.

After about a year our school put on a little show in the amphitheater of a local park. I have a friend in my life now, a would-be big brother, who will often refer to my work as "your little show" just to infuriate me. It's how he shows love. But the performance of Julene Frowen's first year nine-year-olds was the definition of a little show, all tendus, piqués, and pas de bourrées. There was barely any dancing, nor, to my shock and disappointment, were actual tutus involved, but there were powder blue leotards with pink tights and chiffon skirts. Good enough.

Right after the little show we moved to Broomfield, Colorado, in 1981, at the height of a late summer grasshopper plague. My mom and I both cried when we arrived, having envisioned the alpine evergreen of John Denver's TV Christmas special, not the hot, dry brown we found. That first week we drove from house to house, trying to find a home, opening the car door to driveway after driveway alive with grasshoppers popping like popcorn, the unlucky ones squished beneath my sandals. Our consolation was the Royal Wedding between Prince Charles and Lady Diana, which we woke up before dawn to watch. In September I did a report on it as the new girl in sixth grade. This did not endear me to any of my classmates, and I remained basically friendless. But everything, as that song from *A Chorus Line* goes, was beautiful at the ballet.

II. Lessons

Rachel Taylor's class at the Arvada Center for the Performing Arts was a sanctuary of adult calm away from the senseless barbarism of the sixth grade. Of all my teachers, I remember Rachel's body most, since it was the first I had occasion to scrutinize. In the dance studio bodies teach other bodies, both teacher and student offering their physicality for deep analysis. I didn't just learn ballet; I learned bodies, my own, my teachers', and those of other students. The dance classroom is one of the only places it is totally appropriate to study bodies, to fully check them out.

Rachel had dark hair, a long neck and sloping shoulders. There was a slight downward turn to her ice blue eyes and the corners of her mouth, which, with the slope of her shoulders, gave the effect of wistfulness, a soft Victorian ideal of femininity.

Her wrap-style leotard lay neatly on the long plane from her collarbone to breastbone, nearly uninterrupted by her small breasts. Her torso was long and her waist small and she was super slim from the side but ever so slightly pear-shaped when viewed from front and back, which I am sure she thought of at the time as an imperfection, but made perfect sense with the general weeping-willow inclination of everything else about her. Her feet were narrow with a nice but not fashionable point, not the extreme arch that has ruled the ballet aesthetic for decades. Her whole physical affect was old-fashioned, suggesting the etchings of nineteenth-century Italian ballerina Marie Taglioni I had seen in my book about ballet history; but when she got a snappy short eighties haircut, asymmetrical, with a bit of a tail in the back, she seemed to come into her own.

Once she taught class in a fabulous outfit: makeup, spangly top, high-heeled shoes, perfume and all, literally ready to run out the door. She looked and smelled like she was going on a date, the haircut, we found out later, having come on the heels of a divorce. I wondered where she had to get to so quickly that she didn't even have time to change her shoes, but I loved that a glamorous woman was giving us the time of day before her date. I wanted to be a woman with someplace to be.

"No white knuckles on the barre" is the first thing I remember Rachel saying. And then, almost immediately after, that the tendu must be "like a cat's tongue licking the floor." These lessons keep on giving. Not white-knuckling your support system, whatever it is, be it the barre or anything else, shows the primary and gracious yogic virtue of "practicing non-attachment." It illustrates the role of the support system as a place from which to evolve and learn to hold oneself, not as a crutch. The tendu as a cat's tongue licking the floor shows commitment, intention, sensuality, and specificity, which are important traits for dancing, and also for living.

So much of the learning of ballet feels awkward, twisted, stiff where it should be fluid and wild where it should be composed. I watched Rachel and her control, the way she knew exactly where everything was—her neck, her right big toe, her little finger, her left cheekbone—and longed for it.

Little by little I started to find it, first in the tendu, then in the feeling of self-support. A lot of people talk about how good ballet's "self-discipline" is for young dancers, but I think it's more complicated than that. The feeling of self-support is far more profound than mere discipline. You start with the teacher supporting you, holding up your back and stabilizing you while she helps you move your limbs in the proper codified way. And then it begins to make sense: the feeling of your arms radiating from your back, the feeling of the movement of the pinky finger starting at the base of the shoulder blade and the connection of the crown of the head to the tailbone. You learn to stand in turnout. Turnout presents the body to the audience and to other dancers. It is a beveled and baroque way of relating to the world. You learn to relate to and from those positions: first, second, fourth, fifth. "What about third position?" you may ask. Third is a kind of default of which no one really speaks because lots of people do it naturally, the heel resting comfortably in against the instep of the other foot. Third is too easy, too natural to mention. Then you learn that toe-ball-heel way of walking from first or fifth, through second and fourth. Strength builds in your inner thighs to make a through line to the floor and a buoy for the torso, from which you step, kick, jump. You learn to walk silently. Then you learn to jump by pressing into the ground from plié. You learn to kick by disengaging your leg from tendu (degagé) then you learn to unfold your leg as gradually as an unfurling fern frond (developpé).

Ballet is totally unnatural, but when it is good, it feels supernatural. You can pretend to do ballet, but the specific illusion of flying and floating really only comes with the mastery of technique. Stephen, two teachers later, would quote one of his mentors saying: "You must be like a swan, gracefully skimming the water and paddling like hell underneath." What he meant was that, in a sense, the work of the legs in ballet is not glamorous, but earthy and gritty and resistant—dealing deftly with gravity so as to give the illusion of levity. The great thing and the not-so-great thing about ballet is that it allows us to, but also demands us to, transcend humanity.

At the end of my first year of study at the Arvada Center I was eleven and looked fourteen. It was time for us to take the stage. Rachel was careful to point out, though, that this would not be called a show, no matter how little, but a "Lecture Demonstration." I was confused about the "lecture" part—wasn't this about *dancing*? I learned that the lecture would be Rachel explaining what we had learned in between rounds of barre and center exercises, basically class onstage. *Bo-ring!* There would be powder blue leotards again, but no chiffon skirts this time. I was a little bit crushed.

Then I started my period for the first time.

Fairy fantasy swiftly shattered, dropped down sloppily to fecund earth.

My biggest concern was what the hell to do about that stupid powder blue leotard! I was still in sixth grade, and had just had the preliminaries of Sex Ed, which was, at that level and in that era, plainly called "Health Class." Health Class was conducted by one of the sixth-grade teachers, a woman who, in her symphony of earth tones and lank dirty blonde hair, gave the effect of a middle-aged and not-at-all-groovy Jan Brady. She had an extreme version of an accent I now recognize as coming from Michigan, and she inexplicably pronounced tampon "tam-poon," or rather, *tampoo-un*, which I took as evidence that she had never encountered one and made me instantly suspicious of everything else she told us.

The Health Class starter kit with which she sent us away consisted of a "Your Body Is Changing" pamphlet featuring a photo of another Jan Brady-looking creature, this one young and standing backlit by afternoon sun in a field of wildflowers, and a paper bag decorated with cartoonish daisies containing a sanitary napkin. The "sanitary napkin" (is there a worse phrase in the English language?) that came with the Health Class starter kit was enormous and attached at either end to a weird elastic belt. "Are these dead stock from the fifties?" my mom marveled, when I brought it home. "I didn't know they still made these. When the time comes, I'll teach you how to use a tampon. This thing is barbaric." I had stashed the Health Class starter kit in the back of my closet for a possible distant future emergency. I had vague plans to dismantle it in the meantime—to attach scarves to the belt for a Salomé vibe and to repurpose the pad as a spare bed for Barbie's Dream House—plans hatched by a child unknowingly careening into the realities of the menstrual info pamphlet.

Despite the kit and the class, no one was prepared. I was defying age category again, just like in kindergarten. And if I hadn't been moved up to first grade back then, I would have been a fifth-grade bleeder. The powder blue leotard had been assigned to a class of little girls, age nine to eleven, not young women prepped for the onset of menses. The girls in the next age category wore black, perhaps accounting for possible menstrual disasters ahead. My mom was prepared in theory, having cavalierly dismissed the outdated sanitary throw-pillow in the back of my closet, but in practice not so much. She was going to have to soldier on with her plan and show me how to use a tampon right then and there. That pad had no business under the powder blue leotard. Everything, every panty line or panty liner, would show through the light-colored, thin stretch polyester. When she showed me the tampon, the cardboard applicator, and how to use it, her voice went up an octave. She both stammered and over-enunciated and chirped "Okay" a lot. Her hand was shaking a little, but she did an excellent job, even reassuring me, like all the commercials did, that there wasn't anything I couldn't do while I was menstruating, that it should never get in the way of any girlish fun or ambition.

I did not bleed through my costume in front of those assembled at the Arvada Center, thank Goddess. But the heat was on. I was no longer a little girl. At eleven, I was aging.

III. Ballet Is Woman

Once upon a time, the ideal ballerina looked like a woman, and audiences could suspend their disbelief in order to place their favorite curvy star in the role of fairy, ghost, or swan. But the ethereal and youthful supplanted the earthly and adult as the choreographer superseded the ballerina in the power structure. The ideal ballet body is now and remains one that is beyond girlish—a stick figure with long, beveled curves for joints.

Legendary game-changing choreographer George Balanchine was the prime mover for the girlish look. Over time his muses, a few of whom he married, grew younger and younger, thinner and thinner. In Balanchine's 1960s heyday, those ballerinas, mainly Suzanne Farrell and Allegra Kent (is there a better name for a ballerina than Allegra Kent?), were like their fashion-world counterparts Twiggy and Jean Shrimpton, revolutionary beauties, gliding onto the scene like a bracing breeze against silk chiffon. Their thinness and girlish athleticism served Balanchine's ultrafast choreography (*Allegra!*) at a time when audiences had reached maximum boredom with ponderous old story ballets. But then these women, representing not characters but qualities, not women but ideas—fleet, fast, spare—became the standard against whom all others were measured. Then they became the norm.

Balanchine famously said "Ballet is Woman," but his woman is an idea, an economical rendering of a woman. Now you have to be a line, a dash. If you are a woman at all in ballet, you are to seem like one birthed from the head of George Balanchine like Athena from the head of Zeus, only not like Athena because you have no real power. But that is what we all wanted to be: that Balanchine muse.

The problem is that to appear supernatural one needs superhuman strength. To a degree, form follows function; dance your ass off and you may well literally dance your ass *off*, but different body types react differently to activity. Some bodies like to build bulk. The ideal condition for the female ballet body, the Balanchine-style body that has ruled for decades, is one that needs the absolute minimum of muscularity to sustain itself, a natural sense of economy. She needs to be as strong as Athena, but we must never see it.

Men in ballet, of course, are allowed a certain amount of bulk. If the bulk results in a truly superhuman jump, as in a Baryshnikov, he is allowed quite a lot. But not the women, never the women. A bulky woman is not allowed in ballet, and it is amazing to see what ballet considers bulky, just what small degree of feminine mass threatens to upset its scale. In eighth grade I was twelve and looked sixteen and was fast approaching my current height of five feet eight inches. I weighed between 112 and 115 pounds. I was considered bulky. My muscularity is what made me capable of what I was attempting. I could move. I could sustain. I was learning to dance and actually getting pretty good at it, but learning to dance is not exactly the same as learning to *be a dancer*.

I wasn't the biggest girl in ballet class—that was Katherine— but I was tied for second-biggest thighs with Tammy. Tammy and Tracy were fraternal twins who looked only vaguely like sisters. At the start of the year, they were equally good at dancing, but Tammy swiftly grew discouraged, while thin, long-legged Tracy became the star, evidence of the kind of spectacular improvement students can achieve when they are favored, undermining ballet's strategy of expecting good results by berating students. Good attention and praise for her little girl thinness spawned confidence in Tracy, which produced better and better dancing. Disdain for her big thighs (I say "big," but they really weren't) slowly crushed Tammy's dancing. Tammy's thighs taught me that the world is not a meritocracy.

Katherine had breasts and hips *and* thighs. There was no hope for her. Even my mom used to mock her behind closed doors after watching her at the end of class through the fishbowl window of the suburban studio. "Ugh, every time she lands it's like 'baboom baboom baboom!' She shouldn't be allowed on pointe." My mom, in her compact, easily athletic body, had little imagination for what it might be like to have big breasts and still want to do ballet. Katherine's curviness would have been favored when my mom was twelve, in the 1950s. In the 1850s, the time of Maria Taglioni, Katherine might well have been a star. Her soft, pretty pink face matched her old-world body, making her look like a Russian doll when she was relaxed and a put-upon matron when she was stressed out. Our teacher, Marcelle, stressed all of us out.

As the tallest person in the room, I was an easy target for the tiny velociraptor that was Marcelle. I have no patience for people who casually toss around the adjective "shrill" to describe women. If you never took ballet with Marcelle, you don't *know* shrill. Marcelle was shrill on a good day, which was rare. Most days she actually shrieked. Younger than she looked, Marcelle almost certainly lived on coffee and cigarettes, which sapped any possibility of kindness or patience along with most of her collagen. Although she verged on anorexic, she had a massive head of long, wavy blonde hair cascading from her head to graze her tiny tight butt. I'm sorry, but it did "cascade"; there is no other word for it. It was a Niagara of hair. It was the only remotely sexy thing about her, an anomaly.

In class, Marcelle would grab the flesh of our thighs and turn it out away from the midline of the body, in the shape of what we were trying to get our muscles to do on their own, and we would try to hold ourselves that way, to make the shape stick as if we were clay girls. Once she grabbed my foot, bent the arch and pulled the heel forward and the toes back and down and yelled "That! That! That's a gorgeous foot! Why am I not seeing that foot? Every time?!? Every tendu, every dégagé, every battement! I wanna SEE THAT FOOT!" That was the closest Marcelle ever came to giving praise.

Right before holiday break, Marcelle lined us all up, and looked us all over. Standing a head taller than the others, I was, as usual, the first one she noticed. "You!" Her eagle eye landed on me and moved down my body and back up to my face. "Don't eat too many cookies." With her command Marcelle squashed not only my innocent enjoyment of Christmas treats, but also my pleasure in finally being able to dance ballet.

After Marcelle came Erin. She taught a strange, bastardized form of Cecchetti technique, which basically negated everything we had learned until then about how to stand, how to extend, and how to jump. She was about twenty-one years old, barely older than us, but she had us in her thrall because she was *going to start a ballet company and train us all to be in it!* Or so she said.

Erin's bobbed hair was always dirty, she never wore makeup, and she let her armpit hair grow, which none of us had ever seen on a woman before, and which scandalized us. She was short and kind of stocky, built more like an ideal gymnast than a ballerina with broad shoulders, well-muscled hips about the same width as her waist and a high, perky butt. All her leotards fit really low on the leg, totally out of fashion for the moment, which was all about high-cut aerobics wear. "I don't understand why all of you want to wear leotards that show the fattest part of the leg," she would say. I took this to mean she thought our legs were fat and tried to eat less and work harder.

Amy didn't have to do much in terms of encouraging my pursuit of thinness, since by then I was already self-policing. She continued to reward skinny Tracy and to call Tammy "lazy girl," because by then, Tammy was phoning it in. She called me "crazy girl" because I cried when I got frustrated. I cried a lot because I cared a lot. I really, really wanted to be perfect. I probably also cried because I was really, really hungry. This is something I have realized years later. No wonder most of my female ballet teachers were short-tempered. They were hungry, too.

What does it mean when a woman who can't enjoy herself or her body or her beauty has regular access to the mutable egos of pubescent girls? There was an entire culture working behind Marcelle and Erin and even Rachel. The ballet culture and the culture as a whole made these women powerless, second-in-command sergeants entrusted with carrying out the orders of the general (the general was ballet), some of them doing it in the most abusive way possible short of actual hitting. So why did I keep going back? It was hard, but it felt great to come as close as I could to mastering the technique. Getting through one of the combinations without being stopped in the middle for an egregious mistake was rare. Doing it well was a miracle and that feeling was addictive.

Along with self-discipline, laypeople also love to glorify how hard dancers work and how much they abuse their bodies. That all exists in ballet for sure, but under the hard work is the mysterious work, the body learning to think, developing an instinct inside the codification. It all starts to come together when you internalize the technique, getting your foot and leg to make these arcane shapes: the point, the turnout, but then at the same time coaxing expression out of them. A good ballet dancer can express and think with the body, not just with technique layered on top of the body. A foot can express, a leg can think.

Just as my body was learning to think in ballet terms, as I was learning to dance and also to *be a dancer*, I simultaneously was developing a deeply antagonistic relationship to that same body. My combination of curviness and muscularity was unruly, too earthy, at once both too womanly and somehow also unfeminine. My body developed into a useful instrument and sometimes a source of aesthetic pleasure, but more often a zone of constant criticism and emotional pain. I continued to work. I wanted to be capable but with no evidence of that capability I learned to hate my body more quickly than I learned any of Marcelle's impossible combinations or Erin's confusing technique. I did not experience puberty primarily as a burgeoning of sexual desire, but of aesthetic desire. I channeled one into the other.

It isn't that I never desired or had a crush, but what I longed for most was to embody that intangible quality that would make my dancing into something magical.

I remember the first time I saw a girl who actually embodied that thing. I was at a statewide audition, where I was already out of my league, and when I saw her standing at the barre I knew. *Oh. That's it.* I didn't know humans could look like this girl. She looked like Charlotte from *Charlotte's Web*, like a beautiful spider. Only skinnier. She looked like her natural state was to float away, like the one thing holding her there was her light touch on the barre. No white knuckles for her. No gravity for her. When her leg started to unfold and kept unfolding through developpé, effortlessly past her ear to the perfect point of her high arch, she transformed the energy in the room. A friend tells a story about once seeing Catherine Deneuve crossing a street in Paris: everyone tried to be cool and French and pretend not to notice, but everything slowed down all around her so the mortals could sneak a peek into another realm. It was like that.

The feminine performance in ballet is the highest femme, a stylized bouquet of expression, faces whose lexicon seems only to include innocent, awestruck, coquettish, and wistful. She is a femme so high she floats, usually not a woman at all but a fairy, a flower, a jewel, a swan, an *idea* of what Stravinsky or Balanchine had in mind. Ballerinas are gender illusionists in the deepest sense, for the heights of ballet femme are enabled by wells of superhuman physical strength and endurance that are, ideally, invisible. All gender performance in ballet carries that feminine aspect—of turned-out leg and pointed toe, of baroque flourish and silk jacquard. It is about gender, and of course about class, a fancy fantasy of refined movement.

I was an eighties teenager, born after the sexual revolution and during the women's movement, but I steeped my burgeoning gender identity in an eighteenth-century caricature of femininity.

I was called names and yelled at and developed body dysmorphia, and still my ballet experience was far better and less abusive than many. My ballet training encouraged a kind of sub/dom relationship with the teacher and also between myself and the art form and between myself and myself. "Why are you so hard on yourself?" "Why are you beating yourself up?" These questions, usually coming from my mother, always confused me. Had anyone actually given me any other choice? How does one engage in the passion play that is ballet and not end up, literally or figuratively, beating oneself up? The fact that there are no winners or losers in ballet makes it seem like there would be some kind of expanded sense of success, something beyond a metric, but it's the opposite. You can't win. When you win at soccer for instance, you win. It is absolute. In sports there is also that practice of celebrating small milestones that sane people say is healthy. Ballet doesn't have that. In fact, ballet tends to decline the celebration of small milestones the way it declines chocolate cake, and tends even to undermine the big achievements. You just end up thinking you're never any good. Be it a standing ovation, a lead role, a sold-out show, no triumph is good enough. Perfection is a myth.

In a college class I visited a few years ago, a young woman asked me: "Which was more feminist, the world of ballet or the world of drag?" I answered, "drag, by a long shot." She was surprised, and I was surprised that she was surprised. She had a vision of the ballet world as a supportive sisterhood, bless her heart.

In ballet, women far outnumber men, but men hold most of the positions of power and superstardom, making it one of the most sexist cultures in the world, not to mention one of the most racist. In my female ballet teachers there was often a guardedness, an adherence to rules, a submission and a cynicism we see in many women who uphold the tenets of patriarchy— mothers who put their daughters on diets or cut their genitals or marry them off or send them to fat camp or pray-the-gay-away camp or even tout the value of "leaning in." They are already damaged from trying and failing to live their lives in a world in which men are constantly, maddeningly more prized.

Tales of misogynistic ballet masters are legion, but the two male teachers I had early on happened to be wonderful, liberated as they were from the baggage of embodying a feminine ideal. Stephen was the first. He never yelled. In fact, he often spoke so quietly we had to focus deeply to hear him. When he stopped us mid-combination, he didn't berate us for doing it wrong, but ran his fingers through his thinning hair, adjusted his wire-rim glasses, and helped us figure out for ourselves what we could improve. He talked about physics and quizzed us on the composers of the pieces the accompanist was playing for barre exercises. He treated us like thinking people and emphasized performance quality.

"Why are you so obsessed with your feet? You're *people*. So's the audience. People look at faces; then they'll notice your arms, then your feet. What are your arms doing? What is your face doing?"

Stephen taught me Kitri's variation from *Don Quixote*, the first time I would perform part of a real ballet onstage. Kitri's dance is a showstopper full of kicks, leaps, and impossible hops en pointe, all while maneuvering a Spanish fan, which one opens and closes as bravura punctuation. Kitri's dance is high drag, a woman playing a woman playing the coquette, not a sylph or a girl, or an idea of what Stravinsky wrote, but a woman. I loved pretending to be a woman.

IV. Spanish Chocolate

After Stephen came Mr. Clouser (Jim to his colleagues, but never to us). He walked into the dance studio as onto a Shakespearean stage, classical, imposing but generous. With his ear-grazing hair, vandyke beard, and barrel chest he looked like he was meant to be wearing a brocade doublet and velvet cape. Instead, he wore the next-best look for him: a uniform of wide-wale cords, button-down shirt, sweater vest, and black jazz shoes, his only piece of dance attire.

If he could have taught ballet in an actual tweed jacket with leather elbow patches and a pipe, he may well have, but there was a real dancer under the professor drag and he filled you with the ballet spirit. In his class, packed to the rafters with better dancers than I had ever encountered, real adult professional dancers, the baseline of formality gave way to little ripples of jubilance. Mr. Clouser made you want to dance, the best gift a ballet teacher can give, and surprisingly rare. After months in his class, months of subtle encouragement and dogged repetition, of watching and learning from all of those good dancers, Mr. Clouser asked me to demonstrate a waltz combination in front of everyone. We had already done the combination a couple of times across the floor in groups of five, and usually this kind of singling out would lead to an analysis of my mistakes: how to make the arms, or the timing, or the angle of the head better. I threw myself into the waltz with all the ballet spirit I had, and Mr. Clouser did not stop me to analyze the technique, but yelled, "Look everyone, look what she has. She has *ardor*!" He used my dancing to remind everyone of the importance of loving what we were doing. I was over the moon.

Then I was cast as the Spanish dancer, or "Spanish

Chocolate," in *The Nutcracker*. My first role in a real ballet! "Spanish" became my wheelhouse. In ballet, when you are tall and muscular, and tend toward the fiery and dramatic, you are often cast as "Spanish," regardless of ethnicity. Back at the Arvada Center for my farewell performance in Stephen's class, my costume for Kitri's variation had been a black leotard and a black chiffon skirt with a rose pinned behind my ear and a spit-curl (my idea). My Spanish costume in David Taylor Dance Theater's *Nutcracker* was an actual dress with a bodice made of black lace over red taffeta and tiers of flouncy ruffles. The best thing I had ever worn, better even than my favorite crinoline from the dress-up box.

This production of *The Nutcracker*, besides taking us on tour to the Aurora Mall and various local senior centers, initiated me into the particular responsibilities of performing in a big theater. The best thing about this was that it would require real theatrical makeup for us to be seen from the balcony. I had long fantasized about "playing to the balcony" and had kept myself occupied by imagining doing so all through barre exercises since age nine. Now was my chance to see how far my fledgling allure could travel. My theatrical makeup included false eyelashes, which I had never worn. "Oh, so you're gonna wear *falsies*, eh?" the little kids' teacher Henrietta said to us, with suggestive sass. My mom helped me practice with the lashes at home since she'd had a little experience with them in the 1960s. When I glued them on and looked in the mirror, I thought, *This. This is what my face is supposed to look like.*

The Nutcracker, every ballet company's holiday cash cow, is the first and often only live ballet most people see. *The Nutcracker* is the story of a little girl who goes on an adventure with a nutcracker-turned-prince; its second act takes place in the "Land of Sweets," where we see dancers—athletes sustained by diet soda and cigarettes—personifying what they fear and desire most: candy. Clara is the protagonist, often played by a little girl in Act I and then swapped for the closest thing in Act II, which in the most widely televised version by American Ballet Theater on PBS in the 1970s was the famously collagen-lipped and coked-up Gelsey Kirkland.

The first time I saw *The Nutcracker* I was in fourth grade in Modesto. The Sacramento Ballet came to my elementary school and performed some excerpts on a three-foot-high carpeted platform. The Sugarplum Fairy had a nipple-slip issue that she didn't seem to be aware of, but most people's experience of *The Nutcracker* doesn't involve that much humanity. Along with sugar and spice, the ingredients of *The Nutcracker* include a lot of what goes into the average four-year-old's princess drag at its factory source: oppressive labor and sexism. Ballet dancers suspend our disbelief with the force of their wills and muscles, but under the sugary icing is a layer of unyielding tension. I read somewhere that the occupation of ballet dancer is up there with firefighter and merchant marine in terms of stress level.

The movie *Black Swan* reads ballet's darker aspects as the ingredients of horror, as subjugation and oppression, rather than glamorizing them as passion and sacrifice. *Black Swan* is, to me, a totally accurate, if psychedelic, portrait of the inner workings of the addled ballerina brain. It hits me in my nervous system. The film hinges on one dancer's desire to take on the most demanding role in the ballet pantheon, Odette/Odile in *Swan Lake*. Natalie Portman, as Nina, deserved the Oscar she won for the fluid grace of her ballerina arms alone, the form and function of which are surprisingly difficult to master, always the tell that an actor lacks classical training. More important, she telegraphs perfectly the character's psychological and emotional suffering. Portman lost something like twenty pounds for the role and I have no idea where she found it on her slight Hollywood frame. You can feel how literally hungry she is.

At the end of *Black Swan*, (spoiler alert) Nina cracks up into bloody, violent megalomania and utters her final line: "It was perfect." Any ballerina knows there is no such thing as perfect and yet they devote themselves to embodying it. There is no black (swan) or white (swan), only the gray of working harder, getting back to the barre the day after the stage triumph and doing it all again. There is always someone there to tell you that your best could be better. And, of course, as *Showgirls'* Cristal Connors says, "There's always someone younger and hungrier coming down the stairs after you."

Most of the girls in my class made the pursuit of thinness into a whole other hobby. One girl, Heather, had gone all the way with this project. She was older than I was, maybe late high school. It was hard to tell though, because she had gotten to where her anorexia made her look even older—hard and sallow. The hardness was enhanced by her eyeliner, which she did rocker-style, lining the inside edge of her eye like Joan Jett. She was sweet and shy, but the eyeliner made her look mean and aloof. She was also the first kid I met who smoked, which added danger to the mix.

As *The Nutcracker* opening night drew near, we watched Heather try to perfect herself, but since perfection can't exist, what we actually watched was her disappearing. She had an awkward body for ballet, skinny but not supple. Her lack of fluidity was tragic because no matter how thin she got, she never appeared weightless, never defied the earthly realm. She had been cast as the Snow Queen, which fit her brittleness. She looked like a death's head in her stage makeup, with her hollow cheeks and eyes, teeth too big in her bony face giving that same skeleton effect that Karen Carpenter's face had toward the end. The night of dress rehearsal, when she removed the cardigan she wore to keep warm backstage just before her Snow Queen entrance, the sharp angles of her bony shoulders and the protrusion of her sternum shocked us all. She went into the hospital the next day, and Marcelle had to step in at the last minute as Snow Queen.

Heather never came back to class. Before dress rehearsal,

none of us had seen how skinny she had become because she always hid under bulky layers for practice, boxy sweatshirts from The Ltd. The Limited. That's what we were, I think. Girls limited and thwarted by the twisted evolution of an eighteenth-century social dance. It would take me a long time to rediscover the joy of dancing. At fifteen I looked twenty-one and ballet had broken my heart.

ST. VITUS
DANCE

"Crickett's Buggin' Out. . . . She Has Ants in Her Pants and She Needs to Dance!" That was the theme night that had me digging in the back of my closet in 2003. Crickett Bardot was hosting a dance-themed show at the 'shack. With the encouragement/warning/assignment from Precious Moments to use every drop of talent I could scrape from the bottom of my creative well, a kinder version of Marcelle's command to "SEE THAT FOOT," I knew what I had to do: break out the old ballet skills or else. I still owned pointe shoes, which I hadn't worn in years, save for every so often during a deep closet clean-out just to see if I could still stand in them. I found the old hard-toed satin slippers and pulled them out. *Wow*, I had forgotten how tenuous pointe work was, how inflexible those damn shoes were and just how much they smooshed my toes. I had forgotten the special effort it took to appear effortless. I rented rehearsal space and started thinking about how I might incorporate these ancient torture tools into a drag number.

I knew and loved the Ballets Trockadero de Monte Carlo, the all-male drag ballet company who, under all their fluff and camp, could really *dance* in their pointe shoes. At this point in my life I was thirty-one, and felt like ballet would look as camp on me as it did on the Trocks. Comedy would open the door for my return to the ballet studio, even if it was the back door. In drag, as such, if I were to portray a ballerina, being good at ballet was secondary to embodying the character. I didn't have to be pretty or ultra-feminine or even make it look easy. Really, my main task was to make it known to the crowd at the Stud, most of whom could not actually see my feet, that I was dancing en pointe. Of all the ballerina tools I had allowed to rust over the decades, the exception was my flexy hamstrings, which I'd kept well-oiled. I could yank my pointe-shoe-clad foot up past my ear, that much I knew.

I combed through my music collection for any song that mentioned dancing and could conceivably evoke some notion of ballet and landed on "St. Vitus Dance" by Bauhaus, goth idols of my youth. In fact, I had gotten deeply into Bauhaus and ballet around the same time, the band's dark drama dovetailing with teen angst cranked up by the tribulations of ballet.

"St. Vitus Dance" sits in the punk section of Bauhaus's oeuvre, fast and twangy with a fucked-up, pared-down guitar intro that veers into surf-rock. But Bauhaus don't surf. The intricate, wordy lyrics refer to an invention, an electric light show triggered by dancing. It evoked a different take on the fairies I used to fantasize about as a child, the singer Peter Murphy perfectly cast as a malevolent manic pixie.

The concept for the number fell into place instantaneously: the Black Swan. This was many years before the film and its psychological horror. Odile, the black swan in the ballet *Swan Lake*, was already sort of a punk figure to me, a party-crashing witch who beguiles a prince with near-impossible feats of virtuosity—thirty-two fouetté turns—that is to say, thirty-two consecutive turns on one leg that entail hopping up to and down from pointe again and again. Odile is a badass. I would portray badass Odile as if she were a real swan, and real swans, in case you've never encountered one, are, to put it plainly, total cunts.

I enter the stage on the rapid-fire descending bass line of the song's intro with my back to the audience, performing bourrées en pointe, *tiny little steps that, if performed correctly, make a ballerina look like she's floating. Here though, I take advantage of the punk context to introduce the quality of jaggedness. I face upstage performing wing-like arm movements borrowed from Swan Lake, which I push along the jerky-to-smooth continuum. When I turn downstage to face the audience and deliver my lip-synch, I am all spitting fury, like the swans I've read about, liable to attack hapless brides and small children. Drag's comedic permissiveness allows me to indulge in literalism without guilt, so when the song's vocals exclaim "what flexibility," I show off my high leg extension, a gesture that also performs the essential duty of proving to the folks farther back in the club that I am legitimately wearing pointe shoes.*

In the recording of the song, vocalist Peter Murphy sputters and gasps between verses that stumble into the vacant lot between punk and rap. He finishes the song with a long string of utterances that veer from "Ohhh" to "Oooh" to "Ow!" to "Aghhh!" perfect for telegraphing my actual pain as I raised and lowered myself on and off of my mean old pink satin pointe shoes. This show of pain, verboten in "real" ballet was welcome, even essential in its drag version, and did a lot to soothe my trepidation about shining a spotlight on my rusty balletic abilities. In fact, I would find that as a drag ballerina no one would really care if I was sardonic, or silly, if my thighs were too big or I didn't move softly enough. No one would care if my technique was subpar, as long as I was fierce. And with the help of my goth superheroes, I was.

My Black Swan number folded my ballet history back into my burgeoning drag practice and stayed in my repertoire for years, making "ballerina" the bedrock of my drag identity. It turns out that the suspension of disbelief it takes for us to be moved by a big queen pretending to be Judy Garland is the same suspension of disbelief it takes to hoist a grown woman back up en pointe.

SHE'S
A MANIAC

My first apartment was in a basement. I furnished it with family castoffs—vases, my grandma's old chair, a rag rug, a wobbly floor lamp, and a giant brass Moroccan plate as a coffee table. It was my own version of an urban loft—cement floor, dubious light, sweltering in summer and freezing in winter—just the right amount of hardship to make me feel like I was struggling on my own. I was thirteen and the basement was in our house. Down there in my fake apartment I created space to dance and found peace and quiet to read, my two favorite things.

I was one of those kids who got busted for being awake way past bedtime with a book and a flashlight. I read whenever, wherever I could. Never a particularly fast reader, I always loved weekend nights on which I could stay up as late as I wanted and stay in bed reading through the next morning, plowing through a whole book.

Having graduated in short order from the Little House books to an autobiography of Helen Keller, my early teens sent me on a nonfiction rampage: a biography of Audrey Hepburn and then straight to *Mommie Dearest.* In a box in my basement sanctuary, I found my mom's discarded copy of *Lauren Bacall: By Myself* and tore through the first quarter of it sitting there on the cement floor, the rest of it over the course of the weekend in the old chintz chair by the light of the brass lamp. Ms. Bacall's authorship pun and her state of being were all I wanted: to create my life and to be alone; "by myself" sounded good to me. I could read anywhere, but in my fake basement apartment I felt like I actually lived on my own. Except for when my mom came down to do the laundry. It grated on me when the clothes she had sorted began to migrate into my meticulous space.

My mom didn't teach me to do my own laundry until I was about to leave for college, but she never had to tell me to clean up my room. I was a neat freak from day one, veering into the obsessive. Even my dollhouse was impeccable. Once, when I was eight, I "cleaned" my mom's desk so well she couldn't find the bills she was in the middle of paying. Shortly after that, as I knelt down to play with my dollhouse, I sensed something was amiss. I found the tiny toilet inexplicably in the living room. The miniature tabby cat and roast turkey, which were the same size and color, had been switched, the cat on the platter in the dining room, and the turkey on the rug in front of the fireplace. "Mom! Have you been playing with my dollhouse?!?" Perhaps, either as retaliation for the desk incident or an irresistible test of my fussiness she pranked me.

The first time Heklina came to my apartment she sensed the same possibility. "Oh my GOD. Your apartment is so tidy!" she said as she took one of the Hershey's kisses from the bowl I had set out for the group of us who had gathered for rehearsal. I left the room and when I returned, noticed one of the little signature pieces of paper from the chocolate in the middle of my living room floor. I immediately picked it up, and Heklina lost her shit. "HahahahHaHA! I knew you would do that!" And I thought, *Of course I did. What am I? A monster?* We all need ways to feel in control of our lives. Some are healthy and sustainable, some not so much.

Two books shone as beacons in the midst of my teen celebrity nonfiction immersion and I imprinted on them like a cygnet. Or a kidnapping victim. One was *DV*, the autobiography of style-editrix extraordinaire Diana Vreeland. The other was *Edie: An American Biography*, which my mom had borrowed from a friend and tossed aside. I picked it up and walked with my nose lodged in it, straight down the stairs to my basement lair. *Edie* went with me everywhere for the next ten days. I literally could not put it down. What had my mom not seen in this book? While my parents were in and out of stores on a Sunday—the hardware store, Radio Shack—I stayed in the parked car, slightly nauseated by the vinyl interior off-gassing in the summer heat, and read all about Edie.

That book, later retitled *Edie: American Girl*, focuses on the life and white-hot image of 1960s icon Edie Sedgwick—one of the first of a parade of figures Andy Warhol called his "superstars." The format of the 450-page saga is an oral history, a series of interviews by Jean Stein that create a map where all roads lead to Edie, the major thoroughfare running through Andy Warhol's "Factory," where he and his team made his paintings and films. Warhol never had qualms about admitting that his works were products made by a team, sometimes not even touched by his hands. In this sense, the Factory was a *factory*, and of course it was also a scene, and a queering of the Hollywood studio system that Warhol adored. It was also a cult and, like most cults, left a trail of ruined celebrants. In keeping with this, it seems eerily notable that Jean Stein ended her own life by jumping out a window at the age of eighty-three.

Interspersed with the stories in the big book about the enigmatic superstar were images: riveting, entrancing, and necessary. Edie—like Marilyn Monroe, like Lauren Bacall and Audrey Hepburn—was a creature of visual magic. One had to see her. I had been mad for Marilyn since age ten, but I dropped her when I picked up the Edie book.

One of my favorite images from *Edie: An American Biography* was of the fledgling art goddess getting her hair cut on the fire escape of the Factory. A fire escape was foreign to me, a suburban ranch-style-raised kid. The concepts of "fire" and "escape" being part of the architecture of one's home was so exciting! *How cool*, I thought, to designate this as the space where one did things like smoke and drink cocktails and cut hair. I could pretend my Broomfield basement was an urban apartment all I wanted, but would I ever be hip enough to have a fire escape? Would I ever be muse to a gay bestie who would photograph me getting my hair cut to match his so we could cavort and confuse people and make a scene?

The Edie book was my first introduction to the concept of a scene and what it meant to be part of one. And the scene at the Factory—lawless, and senseless, fraught and fabulous—ignited my imagination. The fact that many of its denizens ended up the dead or near-dead drug casualties of their generation's legendary tumult didn't really register at all, the gloss of time making it seem unreal enough not to frighten me. I would, however, remain an obedient product of the Nancy Reagan "just say no to drugs" brainwashing well into the Clinton years.

The mess of Edie Sedgwick was not lost on me, but I longed for her brand of gritty glamour. I loved the haircut image, but the picture of Edie I most wanted to embody, the one that dug a deep groove into me, was of Edie dancing at the Factory. With her long, thin thighs in black tights and a dress that wasn't really a dress at all but a spangly tank top over a leotard, and her arms, skinny but with the slightest tone to the biceps and deltoids (ballerina arms) she looked like an urbanized version of one of the mischievous sprites in my *Faeries* book. Her slightly closed eyes under layers of lashes and dark kohl, her pale lipstick and pixie haircut, were perfect simplicity with the dangling earrings, so modern, despite the image being twenty years old at the time. I wanted to embody that. The energy. The zing!

"The girl has . . . zing!" was something I could hear Diana

Vreeland saying out loud before deciding to feature Edie in *Vogue* and coining the term "youthquake" in reference to her. Vreeland's *DV* was the book I dove into next, flinging myself like unformed clay into it as if it were a mold to shape me. In the *Vogue* editorial, Edie's hip bones and ribs jut out like hangers for the sculptural, futuristic Rudi Gernreich creation she wears. These images seared into my young mind before I realized how dangerous it was for me, an impressionable girl, to go worshipping someone like that. My obsession deepened and darkened.

👑 👑 👑

Fashion, in its twenty-year cycles, steeped the early 1980s in the looks of the early 1960s. I wanted to look perfect in the opaque tights, minidresses, and flat shoes that were the rage at that moment—the sixties youthquake that had an aftershock in my own youth—but hardly anyone who isn't Edie or Twiggy looks good in the styles they made popular. I spent the years of my lowest self-esteem grappling with clothes that were the least flattering to my long-waisted, muscular-legged, athletic body type. Instead of making me look like a cute little fashion-illustration version of the sign on the ladies' room door, the tunic dresses hid my small waist and hit me right at the biggest part of my thigh, the flat shoes dragging it all down. When the seventies came back around in the nineties, I discovered my fashion sweet spot. A-line skirts, skinny T-shirts, and knee-high, stacked-heel boots were a godsend. (And I challenge you to find anyone who doesn't look good in a wrap dress. So does Diane Von Furstenberg—all the way to the bank). The seventies return dug into my earliest fashion memories, of watching my mom get ready to go out, Barbie of course, and also the kids' toy Fashion Plates, clearly inspired by Faye Dunaway's clothes in *The Eyes of Laura Mars*.

⚜ ⚜ ⚜

Ballet had already led me to idealize impossible bodies and had begun to misshape my perception of my own. It was back when I was studying ballet with Erin that I figured out what I had to do to begin to cross the threshold into ballerina thinness. I started to "cut back" as my mom called it. "Cutting back" was innocent enough at first. My mom and I did it as a team, counting calories together, supporting each other in what seemed like healthy eating. Then I cut back more and more.

Edie lured me deeper into skinny girl idolatry. Edie became my anorexia totem, *my* muse. Lucky for me I didn't know how to get the drugs that took away her appetite and kept her so thin. I was always hungry. All I thought about was food, how to burn it and how to avoid it. I would have loved a drug to take away that hunger.

My basement crash pad fantasies expanded. I began to project myself beyond the grit and glamour of Edie's New York into a warehouse belonging to another urban style-maker. *Oh, to sleep next to an exposed brick wall with the city lights bleeding into my window all night and then roll out of bed in the morning, into a cut-up sweatshirt and some legwarmers, tape my feet, and then hit the floor like a maniac to dance it out. Because I live in the dance studio!* This warehouse loft belonged to Alex, the welder by day/dancer by night of the ultimate eighties movie *Flashdance*. I wanted Alex's relentless drive and I wanted her apartment. Little did I know that actual live-work space for urban artists would be practically extinct by the time I moved to my own place in a real city.

I also coveted Alex's body. The role of Alex made Jennifer Beals famous, but Alex's body belongs to her dance double, Marine Jahan. The French actress and dancer goes uncredited in the film, and in fact it took the labor of a total of three dancers to embody Alex in her tour-de-force audition scene at the end of the movie. The video for the song "Maniac" renders *Flashdance* the movie superfluous. It opens on a masked welder, sparks flying. She removes her mask to reveal lovely young Jennifer Beals/Alex underneath. She wipes the sweat from her brow and daydreams for a split second. We witness Alex perform a succession of tasks, each sweatier than the next. At the Studio, a.k.a. *her home* (I'm still jealous), she wraps tape around her hardworking feet and then pulls on legwarmers and that sweatshirt with the collar cut off, the look that would dominate the rest of the decade. To warm up, she does tiny little runs in place. Soon the sweat pours off of her as she swirls her hips, her curly hair spraying sweat around the Studio. In her exertion she looks beatific. As she runs her tiny steps, she also runs her hands up her thigh to her waist and lets us experience the feeling of tightness, the efficiency of existing in that slim, sweaty body. The camera moves down and you see that she is wearing not a leotard, but high-cut briefs that show her perfect abs and butt. Or rather, the dance double's perfect abs and butt.

This butt was a revelation. Even without tights, it barely jiggled and had a hint of that indentation that boys' butts had. I had never really seen a body that was both sexy and athletic in this particular way. The ballet bodies I had seen until then were little girl bodies and ballet teacher bodies, allowed to be only remotely sensual, no accessible or visible flesh, always held in by tights, every measure taken to avoid the possibility of jiggle. Marine Jahan's butt instantly became my new standard.

In reality I didn't have any weight to lose, but I tried to lose as much as I could. I sustained a constant state of exercise-induced euphoria or exhaustion in pursuit of those bodies: the *Flashdance* body double, Edie, Suzanne Farrell, a fairy. . . My body was, in the grandest of scopes, not dissimilar to a ballerina or a fashion model, or Marine Jahan, but to anyone whose business it was to pay attention, myself included, I looked like a different creature altogether, a hopelessly imperfect one. I had muscular curves in proportion to my height, so I always looked "healthy," a word I hated. A couple of years later it would be Madonna (with her own set of problematics) who would give me permission to express myself, as it were, and take pride in my muscles, my relentless heartiness, to exploit the natural tendency of my limbs toward the "cut." But when I was thirteen, I had no image of strong quadriceps as a form of beauty. I wanted to be delicate. I longed for concavity.

In search of it, I began setting an alarm for 5:30 a.m. so I could work out before heading to school. Every day I headed down to the basement for barre exercises and petit allegro jumps or moved the wicker coffee table in the living room and dropped to my hands and knees to "feel the burn" with Jane Fonda in her purple-and-red-striped leotard on a VHS tape ("Are you ready to do the workout?"). Little did we know that the impossibly lithe forty-something Jane was still bulimic at that point. Then I ate half a grapefruit and a single piece of dry toast, or an egg or a carefully measured portion of cereal: a quarter-cup if it was granola, or a half-cup if it was Special K. At school, starving by lunch, I would allow myself an apple, a child-size carton of skim milk, and half a PB&J, which I would edit out if I was feeling especially fat, trying to avert my dazed stare from my classmates' various sandwiches and savor the apple bite by bite.

The ad for Special K cereal asked "Can you pinch more than an inch?" and if you could you were apparently too fat, so I always added a pinch to the end of my workout like the lady in the commercial. Sometimes I couldn't resist pinching myself while I was sitting at my desk at school. There always seemed to be an inch (was it an inch?) I could never get rid of. My mom pointed out "That's skin!" and that it needed to be able to go slack when you sat or "you wouldn't be able to sit!" I would sit and make the inch, or whatever it was, appear and pinch it, then stand and look at myself from the side to make sure my stomach was concave, which it often was, and then suck it in more. Then I would look at myself from the front standing with my feet together and see if there was light between my thighs (which we now have a horrible term for, *thigh gap*, more language for aspirations toward female thinness. #thighgap #thinspo). If there wasn't any light shining between my thighs, I grabbed the "fat" of my thirteen-year-old thighs from behind and pulled it back so that there was more of a thigh gap. Making that gap appear without pulling became my new goal.

On weekends, I let myself cheat after being "good" all week. On Saturdays I tried and failed not to eat an entire can of Betty Crocker ready-to-spread frosting or a bag of chocolate chips, starting with a spoonful, or a chip, which would lead to several more, then end with a spatula to scrape the bottom of the can, or with shaking the tiny specks of chocolate in the bottom of the yellow bag into my mouth. Then I greeted Monday with a new campaign of self-hatred.

Once there was a birthday party for someone in orchestra at school, where my friend Susan and I both played cello. Someone brought homemade cake—that "pudding-in-the-mix" kind that is so moist and delicious—still in a cake pan with that ready-to-spread frosting on it covered in flat, confetti-shaped sprinkles. I tried to resist, but I was so hungry! I took a piece and then offered the cake to Susan, who declined. I don't think she was avoiding it for any reason other than that she just didn't want any: a healthy lack of want. This foreign concept did not sit well with me. I needed her to have the cake too, needed her to be my partner in crime. Because I saw eating cake as a crime. I flew into a sugar-low-to-sugar-high teen girl rage and practically tried to force the cake into Susan's mouth. Still, she refused, so I grunt-sighed in disbelief, rolled my eyes, licked my fingers, and stomped out of the practice room. I cannot remember if I ever apologized to Susan. Sorry, Susan. Body dysmorphia made me a shitty friend.

That scene in *Black Swan*, in which Nina refuses birthday cake and then her mom throws it in the garbage really hit me where I live. I too have thrown cake in the garbage to avoid temptation. I too have fished it back out and eaten it. Miranda does the same thing on an episode of *Sex in the City*. Garbage cake. It's a thing. #garbagecake.

On "cheat days" my workout, aside from Saturday afternoon ballet class, was a dance party in the living room, usually for one, or two if I had a friend sleep over, to MTV, *Night Flight* or *Friday Night Videos*. I really did still love to dance around the living room like I did when I was little to Ravel's *Boléro*, but now I had calories to burn. Now I had goals.

People started to notice me getting thinner, and when I say "people" I mean laypeople, people outside of ballet—my friends, my mother—but I didn't believe them because their uninformed opinions didn't count. None of my ballet teachers remarked on my weight loss. I wonder if they just didn't notice or refrained from commenting for fear of instilling in me some sense of accomplishment and thus turning me lazy.

My mom saw the signs of a burgeoning eating disorder and tried to reverse it. She went to my ballet teacher at the time, twenty-one-year-old Erin, ill-equipped as she was—as they both were really—to discuss what was fast becoming my "issue." Mitzi didn't tell Erin that I starved myself and then succumbed to chocolate binges. She just blurted out that all I was eating was "shit." Erin suggested a seventies hippie book called *Back to Eden*, which I heard as "Back to Eating," which made me hopeful, because I actually really wanted to get back to eating but could not figure out how. The reality was I got angry at my mom for baking chocolate chip cookies, tried to resist them, and then ate them or the dough or the chips in secret. The reality was that I panicked at dinnertime and she had to bargain with me to eat.

"Sit down and eat some dinner."

"I don't have time."

"Yes you do. When's the last time you ate?"

"I had an apple at school."

"You had an apple. An *apple*? If you don't eat, your brain's going to stop working. I'll make you a tuna melt. Fish is brain food."

"No thanks."

"Okay then. You don't go to ballet."

". . .!?!"

This was a brilliant move on her part really—recognizing, along with my obvious FOMO (Fear of Missing Out), the urgent issue of FOUC (Fear of Unburned Calories). Mitzi, in a few moments of clarity, attempted to correct my course away from anorexic oblivion, but every time she did, I tried to yank the wheel back. If I crashed into a telephone pole, I would get out and run like hell off the road into the wilderness toward my goal. My mirage. That body.

Mostly, though, I ran in place. Maybe if I did that little *Flashdance* run in place over and over and over until sweat sprayed off me, form would follow function and I could look like that dance double. I ran those little runs in place in my fake live-work space. I sweated. I ran. I ran my hand up my thigh. But I still felt the fat. Or I thought I did. *Did I?* The terrain from knee to waist wasn't tight enough. The butt-muscle divot wasn't deep enough. I wanted to run it off, run away from it. As I ran in place as fast as I could, like a maniac, I silently repeated the mantra *Why are you so fat? Why are you so fat? Why are you so fat?* I couldn't stand to feel the fat or what I thought was the fat, so instead of running my hand sensuously up my body like Alex/Jennifer/Marine, I started to hit myself instead. I would hit my thighs and punch my stomach, hoping to beat the phantom fat away from my fourteen-year-old body. I had read in the Edie book that she had subjected herself to a kind of pounding massage treatment that helped create her slender-but-toned look (it couldn't possibly have been that she gobbled and snorted all the speed she could get her hands on). So maybe hitting fat did help? Maybe I could melt the fat away with the sheer power of hate and fear.

My private ritual of hitting my fat started to creep out of the basement studio. I hit myself sometimes when I was out if I caught my reflection in a mirror. Especially if I was wearing my favorite 1950s pencil skirt, which was a heavy wool bouclé in bright fuchsia that fit snug in the waist. Unforgiving. I needed to remind my stomach not to stick out. I needed to remind my thighs not to go slack and rub against each other. Mitzi caught me a few times. "Did you just *punch yourself in the stomach*? Jesus Christ. *Why*? Stop."

Other kids would become cutters, but that never occurred to me. I do think they're related manifestations of (mostly) white (mostly) girl pain. I've met one other hitter. A gay man who hit himself for entirely other reasons, who used to stand in front of the mirror and slap himself in the face and call himself a sissy loser.

After my mom caught me, I sent the hitting underground, below the surface of my skin, to the muscular level. I replaced the hitting with even more exercise. The hitting morphed into ninety leg lifts and three hundred crunches before bed. I couldn't go to bed unless I did them. This was fine in the privacy of my room, but traveling with my parents, it became kind of an embarrassing problem. When we visited family in San Diego and I stayed overnight with Su, I was full of anxiety because I needed to do those crunches but didn't want to do them in front of her. I knew she wouldn't ridicule me out loud, but I was sure she'd think I was crazy, the way my ballet teacher Erin referred to me as "crazy girl." I *was* a crazy girl. I was a maniac.

THE HOUSE
OF MORE!

S eeing drag queens backstage in their stuffed bras, pantyhose, and foam hip pads warms my heart like nothing else. Even when mockery peeps in, it has always been a celebration, these queens embodying the parts of myself that I have been told to be most ashamed of. Some drag queens, of course, are all about skinniness-as-perfection—about the tiny waist, the perfectly proportioned hips, and tight, high booty. But even on skinny queens, hips are usually a priority.

"I am in LOVE with your *hips!*" Mr. David exclaimed the first time he put me in one of his dresses. Sure, he was objectifying me, but if someone—my tiny, mean ballet teacher, for instance—had said that when I was thirteen instead of telegraphing a general terror of hips, I might have felt differently about my body. His exclamation functioned as inoculation against the creeping self-loathing of my past.

Mr. David/Glamamore is the grand matriarch of the House of More!, "Granny" to a select few, and drag mother to Juanita. When I dove into the world of drag, I was lucky to land on this sturdy and supportive branch of its family tree. I've told you about Juanita's closet. Well, here's a little more about the house, the people who live there, and the bodies who wear and create the items in that closet.

The dress that highlighted my hips was one of two outfits Mr. David custom-made for me to be a backup dancer for Juanita. Being a backup dancer in one of her numbers in 2002 would launch me fully into a habit of performing at the club on an almost weekly basis. It would also show me the heights to which one could elevate the art of drag. Custom-made couture for backup dancers: that is how the House of More! lives life. The theme of the show for which Juanita had enlisted me as dancer in that Mr. David dress was San Francisco in the 1950s, a time when fashion was body-conscious and adult, when hips were all the rage. The dress was a navy taffeta mermaid concoction with a smocked organza bust and form-fitting bodice that hugged the waist, hips and thighs, blooming into frothy white ruffles at the knee, and begging for a cha-cha. We built a deep friendship and lots of collaborations on that first cha-cha dress, Mr. David and I.

The second outfit was a smart suit out of a scrumptious iridescent Thai silk that gave the impression of a Cara Cara orange, the kind that are pink inside. That suit is the most well-made thing in my closet. The skirt has a nipped-in waist that reaches just below the bustline and a generous square pleat that makes walking easy despite the appearance of pencil-cut severity. The jacket is a mysterious masterpiece of engineering that sits roundly on the curve of the shoulder and stands perfectly away from the body despite or because of the fact that it bears a single tie closure at the neck and consists of a single seam. Ponder that for a moment. A *jacket* with one seam. I have worn it to imitate Connie Marble, Mink Stole's snobby/filthy character from *Pink Flamingos* ("I guess there are just two kinds of people Miss Sandstone: my kind of people and assholes."), and I have worn it to a dear friend's wedding at the Metropolitan Museum of Art, and it was perfect on both occasions. Fully lined in tangerine cotton, it is so splendidly finished that I could wear it inside out.

I would soon learn about Mr. David/Glamamore's history

as an actual bona fide living legend in a world in which that term is tossed off like a tired old bra. One of the original Boy Bar Beauties, Glamamore wowed crowds at Boy Bar in New York in the late eighties. Mr. David, designer to the drag stars, dreamed up Lady Miss Kier's iconic 1990 "Groove Is in the Heart" harlequin catsuit and constructs costumes as masterfully as anything from the Paris haute couture houses. Glamamore the drag queen still wows 'em. In a perfect world, she will only stop performing when her lifeless body is dragged offstage.

I've mentioned the hands. One of the most striking things about both Glamamore and Mr. David are the hands. They are eloquent, elegant, and ageless with long demonstrative fingers. You would think Mr. David-the-designer's hands might be rough from years of running them through sewing machines, but when he touches you, they are surprisingly soft, as if they've taken on the qualities of the fabrics he uses: chamois, velvet, silk.

Glamamore-the-drag queen's hands can transform in an instant from those of a 1950s fashion model into those of a sixteenth-century witch. When she gestures at you, you receive magic energy, that spell I have mentioned: "The Hand of Glamamore!"

These hands, and the mind that commands them, have created almost everything that adorns Juanita. Juanita, in turn, created the empire.

Juanita is classy. She gossips just enough not to seem snobbish and is always effusively but sincerely gracious, thank-you texts landing with her collaborators during post-event cab rides, and I've mentioned the handwritten notes and packages. Her famous Pride parties always serve as fundraisers to benefit those in need. This practice of civic altruism has, over the decades, yielded a kind of queer urban garden of good works.

Juanita is mother to a select few drag daughters, but the ones who help keep the house in order are the More! Boys: the worker bees to her queen. They help promote parties, design flyers, and cook gourmet feasts. They create her custom jewelry and blend her custom perfume. They choreograph and dance backup in her production numbers. All of them at some point modeled in next-to-nothing for her photo project, suggestively titled "Booty Call," the fictional premise of which was that these were Juanita's conquests, photographic notches in her bedpost.

Side note: I was one of the few lucky women photographed for the project. Naturally, the adorable More! Boy Isaac styled the shot of me sitting, in a thong and wig cap, before Juanita's famous makeup mirror in her famous closet. Now that everyone has high-quality camera phones full of nude selfies, the following piece of advice is probably unnecessary, but I will offer it anyway: if you are in the prime of physical life and a drag queen offers to photograph you in your undies, say yes. Even if you do not feel young or cute, say yes. Decades later, you will not believe how young, cute, and cool you were.

The first time I saw Juanita More! onstage, she was sporting a psychedelic caftan ensemble that looked like it sauntered right off of the pages of late sixties Vreeland-era *Vogue*. This has always been my own favorite fashion moment, and I knew I had found a kindred spirit beyond the valley of the avant-divine.

Juanita always ups the ante of outsize beauty in any woman she portrays, envisioning her as queen of her world. As a Spanish dancer trussed up in fifty yards of polka-dot tulle or a tough greaser girl balancing a cigarette on her lower lip to barely pout out the refrain from "I'm Blue (The Gong-Gong Song)." Passing a gigantic spliff through the crowd as a sassy chola (Juanita is Mexican-American), or as Erykah Badu, head-wrapped, caftan-clad, admonishing her man to "call Tyrone." As a glamorous transport worker in an official SFMUNI uniform with the voice of Mavis Staples, assuring the audience "I'll Take You There."

Juanita's women can stand, or kneel, with the filthiest of them too. In one of her legendary performances, she appeared as Snow White in a picture-perfect rendition of the Disney costume complete with a little bird on her finger, to whom she directed her lip-synch, the preamble to "Put It in My Mouth" by Akinyele and Kia Jeffries. As the song gets to the part where she hooks up with the best friend of her man, he appears in the form of one of the seven dwarves, played by the adorable drag king Rusty Hips, literally dwarfed by Juanita as she steps up onto a platform. Rusty (as Happy, Sleepy, Grumpy, Horny?) deftly removes Snow White's dress in one gesture, to reveal her voluptuous naked woman's body, rendered in foam padding and caramel-colored spandex with a bountiful bush, with which he is eye level and where he buries his white-bearded dwarf face.

Juanita has a couple of bodies: this naked lady body—often revealed in all of its glory or partially concealed under filmy, see-thru negligees—and another more practical one, which she wears under everything else. The creator of these bodies, in an act of supreme and literal drag mothering, is naturally—and artistically—Mr. David.

As genius as Mr. David's sartorial creations are, so too are the drag performances of his alter-ego Glamamore. Sometimes a gestural dance of punctuated precision, sometimes a dervish of unhinged emotion, Glamamore embodies the fullest potential of drag, pushes its limits and blurs its lines. She has brought me to cathartic tears during many a club night: in classic Judy Garland mode, as a sad clown, as a madwoman smearing her lipstick and opening her mouth bigger and wider than I have ever seen a human do. Kevin likes to joke that Glamamore can disengage her jaw like a snake. She also, on more than one occasion, has sat perfectly still and enthralled a bar full of rowdy drunk queers without lip-synching at all, looking nonetheless as if the words to the song were coming out of her eyes. One time this culminated in a perfect tear rolling down her face, another with rose petals falling out of her mouth. The great opera diva Maria Callas once said "never move your hand unless you follow it with your eyes and with your soul," advice Glamamore may as well have invented. Glamamore's body knows what it is doing, transforming at will but giving the impression of being acted upon by an outside force, shapeshifting from show to show, moment to moment. Glamamore is a method actress of drag.

One of my favorite moments involving Glamamore's body was for a Björk tribute night at the 'shack. Juanita had rendered Björk's famous swan dress and joked that she had to do research before choosing a song because this was "music for white people." Words that could have come from my own mother. Glamamore chose the song "Pagan Poetry," a plaintive proclamation of visceral, sexual love. Glamamore entered the scene with white fabric draped seductively across her nude, un-padded body, Venus arising from her lover's bed. She let the sheet fall to reveal not the man's body we knew she walked around in by day as Mr. David, but something else. With her chest un-enhanced and waist nipped in with an ivory satin corset, she drew our attention down to a surprise, a juicy pubic mound, what looked like actual but outsized labia majora. With a twist on the usual drag queen tuck, Glamamore had pulled her penis between her testicles and pushed them forward to make her lady parts. (I would learn later that she had tied a nylon stocking to the penis head and then secured it to another nylon stocking around her middle under the corset). In this state Glamamore brandished an x-acto knife and a roll of tape and with these she fashioned the draped white fabric into a goddess gown right on her body.

It was astonishingly vulnerable, at once grotesque and exquisite. By making a pussy out of her cock and balls, instead of tucking them all away and under multiple pairs of tights to form a Barbie crotch like most drag queens did with their tucks, Glamamore expressed the complexity and acknowledged the presence of female anatomy, like a live interpretation of French feminist theorist Luce Irigaray's essay "This Sex Which Is Not One." At this point I already knew David/Glamamore respected women and their bodies, but his willingness to put his own sensitive male parts on display in such an extreme way, to literally weave them together in the service of creating female ones was a revelation. This gesture came from a place of commonality and of love, which I would see from Glamamore/ Mr. David for years to come. This was solidarity.

Mr. David has always railed against drag misogyny in his various gentle ways. A favorite tactic of his is to make gowns for drag queens that open in a pink ruffled front slit and then say cryptically, "I don't *think* I made a big pussy dress for her. But maybe I did?" Or deadpan, "I would *never* intentionally make a drag queen look like a big vagina!"

Glamamore would eventually become my faerie-goddess-drag mother and Mr. David would make me many more outfits, some of which transformed my own body in various ways, making me into another shape or creature, or integrating me into the architecture of a room. Some garments he constructed by draping them right on my body and, once finished, they felt like nothing, as light as the faerie dresses made from flowers I fantasized about as a child. Mr. David's design practice is also one of radical inclusion, a favorite part of which is to adore and adorn the bodies that the rest of the world tends to marginalize, the giant ladies, the large lovelies, the modern-day Willendorf Venuses who reign on the stages of cabaret, burlesque, and drag.

The House of More! and its politics and practice of inclusion presents a template for what drag can be. Rigorous attention to detail and adherence to the traditions of drag coexist with a liberatory practice of expression. Performing at drag clubs emboldened me to get naked for the first time onstage. I was comfortable being vulnerable in that environment because I felt powerful, valued, and ultimately, safe. One night backstage at the 'shack, I looked over at Suppositori Spelling as she was intently studying my breasts and then looking in the mirror and highlighting her own chest in imitation of them. Instead of making me feel picked apart like I had as a young ballet student, her gesture made me feel strangely valued. That environment gave me the perspective to step back from constant scrutiny and enjoy creating performance, and ultimately to learn to love myself and my body. I never expected that it would be drag queens who would undo the last stitches binding me into my narrow concept of self, but it was. Being among drag queens who value and celebrate women of all shapes and sizes also made me love women more. Seeing queens celebrate and emulate their real and imagined sisters, mothers, friends, and goddesses deepened my own sense of sisterhood. This is the drag that formed me. These are the people who helped me to heal the old hurts of a child who hated her body and to bloom her into whatever kind of lady I wanted her to be.

WILDE IS
ON MINE

"Fag!" Lots of boys got called "fag" at my high school. My friend, and later my boyfriend, Andy, who wore a bolo tie and an army jacket festooned with a cluster of his grandma's old rhinestone brooches along with his anarchy and Clash buttons, was called "fag." Everyone in marching band was a "band fag," everyone in drama club a "theater fag." Even the trio of senior student council boys with new wave style were called fags by someone. Anyone whose hair veered even a little bit from 1950s-short or rocker-long was taunted as a fag, or more seldom and more harshly "faggot." And not just boys—me, Michelle, Missy, we all got called fags. Michelle and Missy met the scorn by skipping down the hall arm in arm chirping "Gay gay gay!"

Michelle and I became close friends, sitting together at lunch teasing out the details of our emotional lives the same way we teased our hair: obsessively, with fine-toothed combs. Michelle introduced me to Frank.

Frank was what people used to call "flaming." He never even bothered to deny. It was obvious. What was crazy was that his lack of denial never seemed scandalous, never seemed to endanger him, though he must have caught relentless bullying from kindergarten on. The obvious fact that he was smarter than everyone else might have shielded him a little, but in that time and place, 1985 in the brand-new suburbs, basically still the Wild West, it was dangerous to be Frank.

Frank was skinny and pale with dark hair and eyes. He looked like he had fallen asleep on a steam train in a Merchant Ivory film and missed his stop, somehow ending up in our eighties suburban high school. In his oversized Benetton sweater, baggy tweed trousers, and floppy hair he could have been the singer for the band Haircut 100. If someone were turned into a vampire at age seventeen, he might look like a Cullen from *Twilight*, but he would be wry and world-weary like Frank, Addison DeWitt from *All About Eve* trapped in the body of a teenager. He was into everything that was cool and simultaneously over it. He was over all of it before it even had a chance to get started. By the time I met Frank he was basically done with school and on to better things, already moving into the bracing currents of adult life. He never really seemed like a kid, and at a time when youth culture was climbing to its ever-rising zenith (a zenith I don't think it will ever reach because I don't see any sign of its decline, do you?) he made its trappings seem like dead weight.

Frank always had faint dark circles under his eyes, not the kind from heredity, but from low-grade exhaustion. The exhaustion of the queer kid, of being over it, but also of never being understood, of being the smartest one in the room and knowing you'll be stuck in that room with those assholes for a while. The exhaustion too, of being an only child: that is something we had in common. We knew people would always think we were spoiled; they didn't know the half of it. The half of it they didn't know was that we had to bear the weight of all of it, all of our parents' hopes and expectations and missteps too. And for us that was a lot on top of a lot already. As soon as we met, we were fast friends. And then I met Elisa.

The one person smarter than Frank was Elisa. It was from Frank and Elisa that I learned what a "fag hag" was—maybe a new name for myself. She used the term as shorthand for the complicated love she and Frank had for each other, aware of its insufficiency. Elisa was no hag, no hapless hanger-on.

Frank and Elisa, seniors, never would have paid me, a lowly sophomore, any attention at all unless my clothes and hair had broadcast a shared set of values. Likewise, when I first spotted them, something told me that these were the first kids who had read the same things I had. I knew I had to belong to their club, that I already belonged, in fact. I just had to help them recognize it. Within the space of a lunch period I made sure to strategically but casually mention *The Picture of Dorian Gray*. And so I became their sophomore pet.

In addition to Wilde, Elisa was obsessed with Shakespeare, quoting Juliet as she proclaimed her various heroes and heroines "the gods of my idolatry." She especially loved the sonnets and had a lot of them memorized. In college I would meet a girl named Jill who had actually memorized all of the sonnets. Thin and intense in her chin-length bob and jodhpurs, she was a winsome figure out of F. Scott Fitzgerald. Legend had it that the only time Jill had tried pot, she got so paranoid that she started muttering "I'm losing the sonnets. I'm losing the sonnets," and had to repeat all of them right then and there. "From fairest creatures we desire increase/That thereby beauty's rose might never die/But as the riper should by time decease . . ." Jill was also the only girl favorite of the legendary gay Classics teacher who mostly favored only boys. Frank and Elisa would have thrown me over for her in a hot second.

Elisa and Frank obviously liked me because I was smart and because I wanted their mentorship, but they were also the first people who weren't my mother to openly and shamelessly tell me I was pretty. However, their admiration, unlike my mother's, came with no expectation. (Or so I thought. I would learn later that this wasn't the case. I would learn that there were intricacies.)

Elisa and Frank were aesthetes. They liked books and art

and pretty things and people who dressed well. I was one of the things on that list for them. But I didn't mind being a thing on their list. Being objectified by a true aesthete is actually kind of a deep experience, an experience of being valued for something that, though you may have been recognized for it in the past, is seen by most people as valueless, unearned, seen by most people through a lens of spite. Frank and Elisa didn't see beauty this way. They were lovers of beauty and introduced me to the act of taking shameless pleasure in it. If I were to meet us today, of course I would find us pretentious. But I would also love us. We were *anti-establishment* aesthetes. We were for rejecting what *They* told you to do and creating ourselves. Pretentiousness is often a bridge to deeper self-creation.

In terms of self-creation, Elisa was on her way to total mastery. She was short and super curvy and always immaculately put together, better dressed than any of the schlubby teachers at Northglenn High. With a stylist's eye for the thrift score, she crafted a sophisticated wardrobe that accentuated her assets and suited her stature, a capsule collection of crisp shirts and blouses, pencil skirts, pointy-toe shoes, and wool coats with fur collars from the early 1960s. Polished and put together, as my mom would say.

Elisa's dark hair, which she dyed an even deeper blue-black, was cut into an earlobe-grazing bob, and then later in the school year even shorter, into a kind of Robert Smith from The Cure look like my cousin had: short on the sides and back and long in the front, her teased and sprayed curls hovering perfectly over one or the other of her intense, dark eyes. The hair was her only nod in the direction of the goth or new wave, both of which she transcended. I never saw her fiddle or fidget the way other kids did. Her eyeliner was flawless, as was her lipstick, always classic red or deep wine. Frosty, shimmery lips were for cheerleaders, and Elisa's lipstick proclaimed the opposite: she wasn't there to cheer, she was there to judge.

Within a week of meeting Elisa I followed suit and wore a bright matte red always, which meant filling in my entire lip with a cheap, hard, dry lip liner, as the cosmetics industry hadn't caught up to the cool girls. We didn't have access to a good matte lipstick in 1985 and wouldn't until MAC saved our lives in the early nineties. Elisa had a charming crooked front tooth that only a few of us ever saw because she only smiled fully when Frank said something "evil."

Frank and Elisa were irreverent in their humor, surfing a sea of flip puns and filthy language, pushing the edge and upping the ante in fake insult wars that got more and more disgusting. Elisa won when she called Frank "vaginal blood fart." No one could top that one.

Frank worked at the Häagen-Dazs ice cream shop, and seeing him behind the counter in that apron surrounded by all that sticky mess was just wrong, vulgar. Another type of gay boy would have looked adorable in his little ice cream scooper outfit, like a chorus boy in a technicolor musical, but not Frank. Here are the things Frank should have been selling: perfume, ladies' gloves, rare books, watches, antique clocks, art. Not ice cream, and preferably nothing at all. Selling was too gauche, Frank too urbane. He always called his workplace "Nina Hagen-Häagen-Dazs," which at least brought it closer to his milieu, made it seem more like a nightclub than a food court fixture. Nina Häagen-Dazs could have been our version of the Fiorucci boutique in New York, where Joey Arias worked and Klaus Nomi hung out. When our relationship progressed to the exchange of extravagantly folded notes in the hallway, Frank would sign his *God Und Sects Und UFOs*, quoting our bug-eyed, Teutonic intergalactic goddess. Even though he spelled "Sex" *Sects* to approximate Nina's German accent, I found it thrilling that he would refer even vaguely to sex in our exchanges, and I thought him clever for disguising the word lest a teacher intercept one of our notes, which none ever did. Frank also sometimes signed his notes *Phranque*, to make them extra fancy. No girl I knew folded notes with the same origami flair as he did, ingenious folds that I could never get back to their original perfection.

Despite my best intentions, I did fall in love a little bit with Frank. But rather than sulk and pine for him, I grabbed his hand so he could drag me up as if in a balloon powered by the hot air of our gabfests, beyond the embarrassing awkwardness that weighs down teen romance into the swift and sophisticated levity of cocktail conversation, the higher ground of intellectual discourse, unencumbered by the craziness of desire, beyond sex or "Sects."

Despite all the notes and hours on the phone, Frank hardly ever talked to me about boys. There was one he mentioned, someone older, whom he was going to meet at Paris on the Platte, Denver's only real café. There must have been crushes, but any mention of his actual sexuality was guarded, chaste compared to my girlfriends' and my incessant zany musings about Duran Duran years before. As far as I was concerned, Frank was as out as he could be, but he drew a line at talking about actual sex. I wasn't a blabbermouth, but I guess he couldn't be too careful.

My friendship with Frank was a validating stroke of luck. He was the most cosmopolitan person I had ever met outside of a book. He introduced me to Anarchy; Opera; Nina Hagen; John Waters; The Smiths, whose singer sang the words "Keats and Yates are on your side, while Wilde is on mine." Frank was obsessed with George Orwell and *1984*, drawing connections between its dystopian world and the suburban hell we endured. I couldn't wait to read it the next year in CP English. He taught me to hate sellouts, fakes, phonies. Poseurs. Frank used to have this test: he would make up names for bands that didn't exist and casually drop them in conversation with other kids at school: "Hey, do you like The Blue Babies on Toast?" and they'd be like, "Yeah," and he'd be all, "They don't exist, poseur!" He managed to stone-cold them with their desire for his acceptance, when they didn't even like him to begin with.

Despite our snobbery about sellouts, we loved Madonna! This was before she was world famous, when some people who'd only heard but never seen her actually thought she was Black. We played the 45 of "Burning Up" at 33 1/3. She sounded exactly like Pete Burns from Dead or Alive. It was like our gender-bending version of listening to Led Zeppelin backwards, or *Dark Side of the Moon* with *The Wizard of Oz*. We kind of liked her better that way.

Our Madonna listening party was the first time I ever visited Frank's house, and I remember being surprised at how unglamorous his parents were, especially his father. They were as fat as Frank was thin, but not in a fabulous, opulent way like the opera divas Frank loved. His mother was pleasant but harried and distracted, and his dad especially seemed completely out of it, almost absent even though he was sitting right there. I remember Frank saying that things had been strange and tense in their household since his dad "had been abducted." I had never heard the word "abducted" used in a sentence before then, and I somehow thought it meant laid off from work. When I told my mom, in the same casual way that Frank had told me, that his dad had been "abducted," she repeated the word with shock in her voice and I learned then that it meant kidnapped! So we figured they must have had a lot of money, or Frank's dad must have been important. I thought about how strange that would be, to have your father kidnapped, but I never asked Frank about it. This was at a time when people were starting to claim to have been abducted by aliens, and now I wonder if Frank's father was one of those people.

All I knew about Elisa's home life was that her family was strict Jehovah's Witness, and that she seemed to be embroiled in a battle with them. I always wondered if that was why I never saw her wear pants and all of her skirts fell below the knee as if she were goth Tippi Hedren or Latina Liz Taylor. Maybe her mid-century wardrobe was a stylish interpretation of the dowdy skirt and cardigan combo that was de rigueur at her family's church. I wondered if her skirts were a trade-off for her hair, which by strict Jehovah's Witness guidelines should have been kept long. But I don't think it worked that way. I don't think there were any negotiations to be had at the Kingdom Hall. Elisa's battles with her family and the church stemmed from the general "worldliness" that Jehovah's Witnesses railed and warned against (higher education, women's rights, that sort of thing). A worldliness that was so attractive to her, that she embodied, with her Shakespeare and her lipstick, even more than other kids who had actually been places.

Elisa always did love Jesus, though; she always did believe in God, and seemed to be in the process of reconciling her own subtle intelligence with the literal-mindedness of the Christians in her family. Once I made the mistake of thinking she was an iconoclast because of her filthy sense of humor. My family wasn't religious, having walked away from church the way some of the smart young women I knew walked away from ballet. Having never baptized me because their experience of Catholicism had been so painful and so empty, my parents' party line was that I should be allowed to "choose my own faith." I hadn't realized the rarity of their irreverence nor the luxury of it until I met Elisa. I never did choose a faith, going from agnostic to open and affirming atheist, then and now horrified at what people with power and limited imagination do in the name of their sky gods.

I remember finding out, fierce femme that she was, that Elisa thought abortion was wrong. She said that if meat was murder, as Morrissey claimed, so was abortion. Of all the arguments around "the abortion issue," of which there were many, hot topic that it was then (and astonishingly now), hers was at least consistent and logical. She was careful to avoid the piercing tone that marked most high school religious zealots. But still, I didn't believe her. I thought she was playing a philosophical game, devil's advocate. She said all kinds of crazy shit with a poker face, toying with my gullibility. So I thought I was being clever when I replied to Elisa's assertion that every conception was sacred with "Oh come on, Eli-hovah." I knew as soon as the words left my mouth that I was out of my depth and I regretted it instantly. I had gone low, and then she smacked me down to the ground. Elisa didn't yell or anything; she just glared at me and quietly said, "Don't say that." That is the only time I saw on her face a flicker of the tough girl like the ones who threatened to kick my ass just for looking at them in sixth grade. She kicked my ass with a look and a quiet command.

Because of how I'd been brought up, I didn't know how grave it was to denigrate someone's religion, to speak in vain the name of a God that this would-be radical woman worshipped even though He was making her authentic life impossible. Nina Hagen was a goddess and yet we denigrated her by equating her with ice cream and Frank's shitty job. Elisa taught young, stupid me how to retain respect in the face of disagreement. I still found her anti-abortion stance bonkers and sad, but it wouldn't kill me to keep it to myself.

Elisa and I had only a handful of one-on-one conversations. In the last, through streaming tears and a veil of coded language, she came out to me as a lesbian. She hinted, never revealing the whole story. One of the hardest things, the reason she told me at all, was that she had to cut off her friendship with Frank. Flaming Frank was a bad influence. I don't know if her family knew she was queer, but they must have thought Frank's gayness was contagious. As the school year progressed, we saw Elisa less and less. Elisa's absence created space for me to get closer to Frank. Sad as I was, I was honored to sidle in. I wonder if it had been Elisa's plan all along to groom me to be Frank's new hag, to pass the flaming torch along to me, even though I wasn't ready for the relationship of equals they shared.

In February, Frank invited me to go and see Leontyne Price

in concert. My mom seemed weirdly scandalized. Even though it was the most natural thing in the world, and in so many ways she had made me who I am, it was just starting to sink in for her that I was a fag hag. "You know that's *opera*, don't you? Why does a teenage boy want to go see an *opera singer*?" Why indeed. I couldn't go. I had rehearsal. But the vision in my mind's eye of Frank seeing Leontyne Price and his gushing about her divinity in an origami-folded note the next day introduced me to the concept of the opera queens who remain some of my favorite people.

In mid-March, Frank. Asked me. To prom! He wore a white dinner jacket and looked like a matinee idol, and we almost missed the dance because we were talking and talking and talking. I had never spent three hours talking over dinner before and I thought, *this is exactly what I want my life to look like.*

The last I heard of Elisa, from Frank, right before he dumped me as a friend, was that she had gone back into the Jehovah's Witness fold of her family. Maybe she had had a relationship with a girl and they had found out and that was the last straw. They were laying down the law and threatening to disown her, which, in that church, is serious shit.

I couldn't stand the thought of her wicked intellect wasted, the thought of her trapped in a doomsday cult or a marriage to some controlling religious man, with a bunch of kids she may not have wanted. I have a desperate desire for her to have become a scholar, a fashion arbiter, a lipstick lesbian living her life. I hope she's okay wherever she is. Even if she is a God-fearing wife and mother, I hope Jesus loves her back.

👑 👑 👑

My relationship with Frank was a little bit fag/hag, sure, but it was more mentor/mentee. He talked and I listened and took notes. I knew it was not a relationship of equals, and that was fine. I knew somehow there would be plenty of equality in my future. I also sensed that there might always be a hierarchy inherent in my relationships with boys like Frank, that I would be following behind and happy to do so, really. But maybe I could also be an Elisa to them. Or maybe even a Leontyne Price.

I regret not seeing Leontyne Price in concert when I had the chance. My friend Miguel, the choreographer/singer, sent me a text message a few years ago, our current version of the fancy folded notes that Frank and I used to pass back and forth, with a link to footage of Leontyne Price's farewell concert at the Met. I *lived*! Lived! She finished her aria, "O Patria Mia" and then held that space and that applause for TEN MINUTES! She stood there without making a movement. She took it all in. She taught us all about what it is to hold space. She taught me again the lessons I need to learn about stillness. (I always need to learn lessons about stillness.) Miguel has taught me a lot about movement. And stillness. And art. And talking. And talking about art. I think my relationship with Miguel is one of equals, but maybe sometimes not quite. I will always have to put a hop in my step to catch up with him. And that's okay. Relationships that inspire us to aspire are good for us.

When Elisa stopped being friends with Frank, it broke his heart and his worldview. I met up with Frank at Perkins diner the summer before my own senior year. I had just had my nose "fixed," and Frank was one of the few people who noticed immediately and freely commented. "Why? *Why?*" he kept repeating. He couldn't focus on all the good things I had to tell him, like I was in love and had a lead in the school play, and had discovered modern dance. He couldn't get past the nose and what it represented. "Why? *Why?*" I didn't have a good reason, certainly not a reason good enough for him. I had been ambivalent about it anyway. I could have made up a story about how my parents made me do it, which might have been attractive to him, might have given me some tragedy cred. But

I didn't. Because they hadn't. Well, not exactly. In that precise moment I had a lot invested in it being the right decision. We proceeded with an intense debate about plastic surgery: him against, me for. Me for creative, self-aware self-invention, him for authenticity and the rejection of conventional notions of beauty.

"I think the fact that you have done this to your face means I can't be friends with you."

I felt our connection dissolve like the sugar in our bad coffee.

Wait, wasn't it part of our ethos to be decadent and beautiful and glamorous? Wasn't it part of our philosophy to invent ourselves? And if my parents wanted to help me do that, was it wrong for me to take them up on it?

Keats said, "Beauty is truth and truth beauty and that is all ye know on earth and all ye need to know." Yeats said something about loving the "pilgrim soul in you" and the "sorrows of your changing face." Wilde said, "Art, very fortunately, has never once told the truth." I guess, after all, to paraphrase the Smiths, Keats and Yeats were on his side while Wilde was on mine.

And maybe what was in the back of my mind was in the front of his: that I had caved, that my desire to do away with the bump on my nose showed a weakness of character. That my unwillingness to live with it as it was, to agree to squander my parents' good money on "improving" my face was a little bit heartbreaking, and would deprive me of the opportunity to strengthen that weak character of mine. Had I broken a promise to him that I would stay authentic, or was he looking for a kind of authenticity I couldn't prove? We didn't have a term for "basic bitches" back then, but that's what I felt like: a sad, basic bitch with a nice, straight nose. Maybe Yeats was also on my side because Frank couldn't love the sorrows of *my* changing face. Orwell said, "By age fifty a man has the face he deserves." No one was injecting botulism toxin to paralyze their faces when he wrote that. Now it seems like plenty of people have faces they don't deserve, and no one loves the sorrows of a changing face.

Maybe after the agony of Elisa sliding back in with her religious family, Frank just couldn't withstand another disappointment. Maybe he was on his way to being a militant queer, refining that art of refusal and sharpening that sword of political discernment that would become so familiar, and so dear to me, in my early twenties in San Francisco. If you refused the status quo, if you always turned to the alternative, maybe you could build an alternate universe, a place where we could be safe and happy, free and queer. I got it. But why'd he have to dump me?

When I was in college, I did receive one olive branch from Frank, a postcard saying that he had lived in San Francisco for a while, that he went around on rollerblades, skating up and down all the hills, which now that I know how steep they are seems impossible. Then I heard another legend. The legend was that Frank carried a gun, and with it, had stopped a gay bashing. That he held the bashers in place until the police came, a gay vigilante superhero. I would love to believe this story, but I can't. I can't believe it any more than I can believe that Frank's father was abducted by aliens. I think it might be more likely that the tall tales, of taking San Francisco hills on rollerblades and of Wild West fag justice, were some kind of delusional, speed-addled fantasy.

This is the part where I stop writing and try to find Frank on social media. I always fail and fear he may have died, maybe during the AIDS crisis, maybe in the drug-crazy PTSD of post-AIDS clubland. But maybe he is happily settled somewhere with a nice home and a cushy job and a wonderful husband. And the face he deserves.

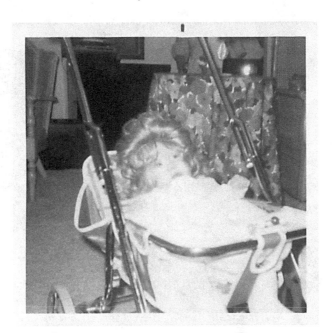

Me, 1971 (Tom Jenkinson)

Me, Mitzi & Tom, San Pedro, 1976 (Tom Jenkinson)

With Superstar Barbie, 1978 (Tom Jenkinson)

As Boy George, Northglenn, Colorado 1983 (Mitzi Jenkinson)

Class photo, 1984

With Marc, Evanston, Illinois, 1987 (Marc Kate)

With Kevin at Trannyshack, 1998 (Marc Kate)

Fauxnique & Falsetta Knockers, "Tired," Trannyshack, 2003
(Reverend Michel)

With Juanita More! at the 'shack, 2005 (Eric Stein/Shutterslut)

With Kevin, "Poses," Stonewall, NYC, 2008 (Mark Kate)

Reprise of my pageant number, Trannyshack Kiss Off, 2008
(Courtesy Heklina/Trannyshack Archive)
Pictured: Joseph Copley, Jennifer Chien, Fauxnique,
Carlos Venturo, Nicole Dessoye

Fauxnique & Marc, promo for "Lipstique" by Silencefiction
(Juanita More!)

Fauxnique as Madonna in Faux Real, Climate Theater, 2010
(Robert Takahashi Crouch)
Pictured: Joseph Copley, unknown, Neil Stewart, Fauxnique,
Damian Stewart, Bobby Barber, Mica Sigourney

With Mr. David & one of his creations, City Hall, San Francisco, 2011
(Arturo Cosenza)

At Some Thing, the Stud, San Francisco, 2015 (Kegan Marling)

The F Word, Oasis, San Francisco, 2016 (Gareth Gooch)

C*NT, ODC Theater, San Francisco 2017 (Arturo Cosenza)

QUEENT, CounterPulse, San Francisco, 2019 (Robbie Sweeny)

Fauxnique 2008 (Fontaine Weyman)

OUR
LITTLE LIBBER

My Feminist consciousness switched on the first time I heard the soft pop hit, "I've Never Been to Me" by Charlene on the AM radio. "Sometimes I've been to cryin' for unborn children that might have made me complete." I was nine years old and knew even then that song was deeply fucked up. Look it up and listen to it. Why did the narrator, this woman who seemed to have so much fun, have so many regrets? Why did she spend a whole four-minute ballad slut-shaming herself? I mean, aside from seeming to be unaware that there is more than one "Isle of Greece," she seemed to have it all. Why did she feel incomplete? That song was a backlash anthem, as if it were written to directly undermine Helen Reddy's insistent pluck or to insinuate that Joni Mitchell should have kept the baby she gave up and settled down instead of living her big, colorful life in ripped stockings and jukebox dives.

Over the next decade the epiphanies would pile up, big and small, weird and obvious, building to critical mass during my first year of college, as they do for so many young Feministas. For a while, though, it was as if the lightbulb of feminist consciousness just hung there, bare and switched on in a room I rarely had to enter.

Despite the struggles with body dysmorphia, which mostly played out in my girls' world of ballet, for most of high school I felt capable and smart and didn't think much about sexism. *Free to Be You and Me* had been filed away in the back of my childhood consciousness and my vehement pro-choice stance was my only feminist issue. I formed my politics around wanting to be creative and not wanting to conform to harmful, mindless social norms, but feminism as such was not a part of this. "Conformity" and being "nonconformist" were big buzzwords among kids in the 1980s. Articulating one's resistance to conformity was also a roundabout way of articulating queerness. I was aware of queerness before I was aware of feminism.

👑 👑 👑

My next feminist epiphany was subtle and sneaky, disguised as an offer of comfort from a dear friend when I was seventeen. I was in AP English class, and after a string of successes, wasn't so sure about the Emily Dickinson paper I had just handed in and feared I had written myself into a hole. Granted, I usually went around with the constant feeling that my work was subpar (all the perfectionist ballerina striving), often pleasantly surprised by the outcome of my efforts because I had no gauge for self-confidence, no way to know what I was made of or what I had to offer. I am still a little like that: Imposter Syndrome.

The day Ms. Sanko returned our papers I entered the classroom with a wan hope for a pleasant surprise. D'ann Sanko was the kind of teacher who made you want to write, to really impress her. She had a calm grace, dry humor, good shoes, and a bumper sticker that read "I'd Rather Be Reading Jane Austen." She also had the capacity to not seem nerdy despite it. She was patient and fair as a teacher, but sometimes I suspected that she really would rather have been reading Jane Austen. She was the teacher who diplomatically questioned my interest in *The*

Fountainhead when I entered the essay-writing contest that Ayn Rand's cult followers put on every year, ensnaring kids with the possibility of actual scholarship money. The next year my no-nonsense brilliant college professor Maura Spiegel would flatly denounce *The Fountainhead* as "garbage" and get me to consider the cruelty of Rand's right-wing position and also, um, that scene where *the protagonist rapes someone.* I listened to what these women said and I wanted what they had.

I retrieved my paper from Ms. Sanko's desk and there it was. B. Minus? Had I misread? No. That was not an accidental mark. It was a minus. I was devastated. Being devastated by a B minus seems ridiculous to me now that I know people who have come out the other end of high-stakes problems like homelessness, imprisonment, widowhood, and meth addiction, but in high school, English class was my domain. I had already written off math and had received the only C in my academic career in College Prep Chemistry, which I worked so hard to earn. I was headed to Bennington in the fall, and that same CP chem teacher, a weird old man with an egg-head, suspenders, bolo tie, and requisite safety glasses strap had said about my choice of college, "it's for people with a lot here" (theatrically pulling his wallet out of his pocket) "but not a lot up here" (tapping the wallet to his head). I didn't really value his opinion, so neither his shady comment nor the C had upset me terribly, instead just driving me to edit out math and science from the long list of things I felt I had to be good at and to put more of my eggs into the liberal arts basket.

The truth was I had received more financial aid from Bennington than anywhere else, so his wallet gesture was moot. What's more, I was finally going to be free from the oppressive conformity of letter grades! I was headed to a school that would encourage me to think for myself. I was always ready to defend the arts and humanities against charges like those of my science teacher against Bennington: that they were for inferior minds, that their subjectivity made them less rigorous. I had begun to read this as a boy/girl thing (few girls occupied the upper echelons of math and science), but I didn't yet have the language to call it a feminist issue. I would take what I was good at and not try to prove myself where I was not wanted or needed, but this feeling started creeping in (was it just a feeling? I was so sensitive!) that maybe what I was good at really wasn't as valuable or as important as things that men and boys were good at. I wanted to resist, even reject, the whole game of metric evaluation. But in the meantime there were still grades to be earned, and I was staring at a B minus in English.

I started to cry in the middle of class. Of course I did. There came that familiar, humiliating feeling of the heat, the tingling, the unstoppable change in my breathing, the snot and the redness, impossible to conceal. I was seventeen, but I felt like such a baby.

The only person who could relate was Larry, who had the previous fall become one of my best friends. Even more than Frank, he was up for processing and dissecting everything, and unlike Frank he actually listened. I could admit only to him, an overachiever like me, how terrible the B minus felt. He knew I was upset because of my attempts to hide my red face and snotty tears behind my long sheet of shiny blond hair. His response was: "If it's any consolation, you look beautiful today."

I shriveled. This well-meaning comment from my sweet friend just ground my shame in deeper. The idea that looking beautiful could make up for intellectual mediocrity was empty; that my friend would offer it as a solution depressed me further. I don't think he knew how high the stakes were for me, but in that moment, I thought he should have.

We had begun a deep friendship—gay boy/girl bestie— although he would not come out to me until sophomore year of college on National Coming Out Day, after which he started using the name Lawrence. We spent long evenings driving around in his powder-blue Volkswagen Rabbit talking about everything, and if he knew anything he should have known this: that it was *not* any consolation. But maybe he didn't. Maybe that was before I really had the words to talk to anyone, even him, about how deeply I needed to be taken seriously.

I had begun to scrutinize and question my worshipful relationship with ballerinas and fashion models and their unattainable bodies. This started to coax me out of the other end of the eating disorder. I was learning that not only did obsessive adherence to beauty standards waste precious time, time that could be spent thinking, but it could actually kill you. Another feminist epiphany. If Frank or Elisa had intimated when I was fifteen that I could find consolation in beauty I would have taken it as a compliment, a poetic quotable, but now it submerged me in sadness. And Frank had dumped me as a friend for the nose job, for conforming to a beauty standard, so even he had rethought all that stuff about beauty being truth and truth being beauty.

What complicated things was that at that point I *was* trying to look "beautiful." I had become disenchanted with punk/new wave/goth, finding, like the kids in *The Breakfast Club*, that the adherents to the alternative culture could be just as conformist, just as snobby and exclusive, as the cheerleaders and jocks. I had decided I had nothing to prove with the height and pointiness of my hair, so I abandoned Siouxsie Sioux as my beauty role model and took up Sade, with her sleek ponytail and proper buttoned-up shirts (still with a red lip, though). I even bought a long, thick fake braid in imitation of hers and wore it for my class picture. Baby's first fall.

Also complicated was the fact that I had chosen fields of study that valued beauty: art, music, literature, and especially dance. I was in the process of setting my life up so that I would always have to consider the problem of beauty. Further, what I had chosen and what I was good at were the fields that the world took less seriously, the things it told us weren't necessary.

When Larry offered me consolation through my efforts at looking beautiful, it turned up that glowing lightbulb of feminist awareness. He never would have said that to a boy, not even (or especially) one he thought was beautiful. We must have processed his comment later as we did so many things, in his car, him turning off the engine so we could sit for an hour in the parking lot of Perkins or my parents' driveway. I even wrote a poem about it, which I searched for and can't find, thank Goddess. I know my poem tried to reckon with expectations and value. What was beauty? If it was in the eye of the beholder, why did people also act like it was a fact? Why did the fashion magazines my mom and I gorged on in the summer as we lay in the backyard and baked in the sun have so many rules and standards about what was and was not beautiful? Who was beautiful enough and why and for what? And why had I received so many conflicting notions? My mom always told me I was beautiful, but also sometimes blamed me for it, like it was something I had done. And obviously I wasn't beautiful enough because the nose issue had to be fixed. Was I beautiful enough after? Beauty standards make such a mess of everything.

♔ ♔ ♔

The feminist epiphany that cinched it, the third one, hit me hard when I was home for winter break after my first semester of college, that pivotal moment of awakening.

I had to go with my dad to his office at the Western Dairyfarmers' Promotion Association ("Dairyfarmer" had only recently been changed from "Dairymen"). I would wait while he conducted a quick meeting before taking me to an awkward lunch at a local Chinese restaurant.

When I was ten, right after we moved to Colorado, I had loved visiting his office, where I would go directly to the kitchen and get a cup of cold chocolate milk from this weird machine with a giant metal lever. Chocolate milk on tap—employees' children must have been the only ones who ever drank it. With my cup I would sit in the conference room enveloped in one of the big spinning chairs at the glossy table with a pile of letterhead on which I would doodle with a ballpoint pen, figuring out creative ways to work around the red swirl logo at the top that said "Real." The "Real Seal" as it was called was one of my dad's team's design contributions to the promotion of the dairy industry. In my childish drawings the logo might become part of a blazing sun, or a fish, or a lady's hairdo, Dairy Industrial Executive *Real*-ness.

The women who worked for my dad, "the gals," as they were known, lightly doted on me whenever I came to visit. My dad's entire team was made up of women, a fact that the men in the industry made a big deal out of, teasing him that he was being walked all over, that there must be endless catfights, "Rowrrr!" But my dad never played into their attempts at low gossip and always respected the competent women who worked for him. Of the gals, my favorites were Faye (quippy, quick, urban and Asian), Ruth (dry, wry, older and East Coast formal), and Roxy (my dad's secretary, who was kind and soft with huge downturned aqua eyes that made her look sad when she wasn't). Faye looked like a Faye, Ruth definitely looked like a Ruth, but Roxy did not look like a Roxy even though she remains the only Roxy I've ever met, so what do I know?

I had been dreading this trip to my dad's office, even though I knew I would probably see the gals. It would be my first visit since my parents' split, a rough laceration really, like the time my dad had accidentally cut his palm with a serrated knife. Not a clean cut at all and still fresh. They weren't even fully divorced yet, that is how fresh it was, and my dad and I had both left home in the space of a few weeks; that is how sudden and life-altering it was for my mother.

It was only the previous July that I had been on my way out the door to meet Larry before he was Lawrence and ride around in the powder blue Rabbit. Our unspoken plan was to do what we always did, talk and talk as he drove south, and then get out of the car in Cherry Hills to sneak a peek into rich people's windows. That was the official pastime of summer 1988: talk therapy and aspirational trespassing. I was on my way out the door when a man called the house.

"Mom, it's for you!" I yelled upstairs.

"Got it, baby! Have a good time! Take a wrap. It might get cool."

"No it won't! Love ya!"

I left. That was the night Larry and I got a little bit too close to the gate of an over-the-top French chateau kind of situation and a Doberman lunged out of the dark at us. It was thrilling.

It turns out the man had called our house to tell my mother that their spouses were having an affair. I came home to find my mom in more or less the same position I had left her, sitting up in bed, but now with the TV off, in shock.

The moment a kid leaves for college is supposed to be a bittersweet milestone, but the revelation of the affair had scraped the sweetness out of that moment for all of us. My mom's experience was suddenly, openly all bitter and I was one of her few confidantes. I suddenly had divorced parents, a "broken home" as they used to call it.

My dad borrowed my mom's habit of listening to a song on repeat, and his heartbreaking choice was the theme from *Heartburn*, "Coming Around Again," by Carly Simon. Two years later, my mom, still deep in process, spun "Fairy Tales" by Anita Baker.

My dad's strategy was just to keep moving forward as if everything was normal, to live his life, which we all need to do eventually. I didn't quite grasp this at my age then. I wanted to parse and process everything that had gone wrong. At the same time, I did not want to deal with any of it.

Back at the office, my dad's meeting was with a man whom he was in the process of hiring and he planned to introduce me to him. I would have preferred to sit at the conference table with a pile of Real Seal letterhead and scrawl. However, I had long ceased to be that kid, and even when I was a kid I was the one with social graces, the one who's good with adults, a buffer and a charmer. I guess this is why my dad decided to introduce me to this new hire. Or maybe he was using his new hire as a buffer against me.

"This is Molly," my dad said as he patted me on the head, using the nickname I had shed, "my little girl."

His expression of fondness rankled me fiercely. Everything my dad said or did rankled me at this point of course, and I was in the process of cataloging each word and deed so I could judge it. During my first semester of college, still a seventeen-year-old girl, I had learned that to allow anyone to *call* me a girl, even to refer to myself as a girl, was obviously demeaning. It had become absolutely crucial to me to be identified as a "WOMAN."

"Dad, please don't call me 'your little girl,'" I said, in front of this stranger. "I am not a girl."

At college I had learned that the personal was political and figured the articulation of my feminist stance had to start at home, with my parents or, if need be, right here in my dad's office as he was welcoming a new hire. It was he who had brought me there after all.

"Well then, what do you want me to call you, sweetie?"

Sweetie. I fumed.

"How about Monique? And I'm a woman, not a girl."

"Aw, well . . . that's our little libber!" he said, patting me on the back a little too hard, as he always did when he was amped up, as if I were choking on a bite of something and he was trying to dislodge it. Then he laughed a little and winked at the new guy.

Our. Little. Libber. Those words landed hard and knocked me down my first time in the ring outside of the training grounds of liberal arts college. I had gone from feeling like a righteous, serious woman to feeling ten years old again. My demand for my father's respect had taken him by surprise, but his reaction made it seem like my request was a silly routine born of a cockamamie idea, the crazy notion that almost-eighteen-year-old girls are women and that women are people. As far as many men like my father were concerned, the women's liberation movement was a crazy idea.

I was under no illusions that my father was a feminist, but the way he said "libber" made him sound like one of those other men, the sexist ones. The ones who said "Rowr!" when they talked about the gals. The whole sentence really needed to be unpacked. "Our," the possessive, like I belonged to him. "Little," the demeaning diminutive. "Libber," to trivialize the word "liberation," a derogatory term for the brave people fighting for women's freedom from oppression. My dad *knew* women were people. Weren't Ruth and Faye "libbers" too? They had to be. But the people who said "libber" the way my dad did believed that those women were man-haters, bra-burners, and castrators. I wasn't any of those things. I was a feminist! I was a woman! I was not anyone's little libber. Or maybe I was. Fine!

When my dad called me "our little libber," of course I think he also meant it with love. He had met my intensity, my righteous indignation, my awkward petulance and refusal to make him and the new guy comfortable, with relatively good humor. He could have been out and out derisive, he could have been flustered, he could have punished me. With the perspective of distance, I can hear a kind of sweet exasperation in my dad's "our little libber" comment. Like it was his way of saying "you do you!" Still, it hurt. It felt like everything I had learned in school would be made fun of in the real world, that men would never wake up and see the strengths of women. If this was how it was, maybe I would never be taken seriously; maybe I could never fully exist with men around. I started to understand separatism then, too.

"Women's Lib," or the Women's Liberation Movement, was the seventies iteration of feminism, the version of feminism that the backlash of the Reaganite eighties thought it had vanquished. But it hadn't. Women's lib was just getting started. In fact, the backlash just helped it to mutate. The daughters of the libbers were rising with the torch in hand. "The third wave," if you believe in those distinctions, was me and my generation. Though some of us were raised by women who claimed feminism explicitly, many of us struggled with the insufficient tools we were given. I was told I could do anything I wanted, but I was shown something different.

My mother was not a libber. I don't think she was against the women's movement, but maybe it was just that she was, as she often said, "not a joiner." She had, however, checked out *Free to Be You and Me* for me from the library, so there was that. My mom effectively demonstrated strength and self-sufficiency for me. She had self-righteousness, but self-confidence was more elusive. I struggle still with how to parse self-righteousness with self-confidence. A lot of us bluster through to cover up that vulnerability, the open spaces that make us feel unfinished, weak, and wrong.

If it's any consolation, you look beautiful today.

I know lots of girls would find consolation in looking beautiful. We all have our experiences. The narrative that went along with mine was this: you have it easy; therefore, the story you have to tell is of no consequence. No one wants to hear the story of a lucky, happy white girl who had it easy. No, not unless a tragedy befalls her. And even then her story is not hers to tell, but that of the omniscient narrator. "Once upon a time there was a beautiful princess . . ." The hero's journey is one of non-belonging, of bad luck befalling, of temptation, of close calls, and then of overcoming, of living to tell the tale. "If it's any consolation you look beautiful today" got me where I hurt because I had come to the conclusion that my hurt was not valid. I had been checking my privilege since I was nine. I still walk around a lot of my days wracked and burdened with the discomfort of it, as well perhaps I should. Although I don't know if I serve the world best in that state: the state in which I spent the better (or at least the prettier) portion of my adult life.

This subtle message I also received from my mother: I looked beautiful so how could I possibly be upset? I have to admit that I think this sometimes now when I see a beautiful young person going through a hard time. It's not that I don't respect them or their pain, but with the perspective of time, and not without hypocrisy, I just think, *Oh sweet angel, with that skin and that body how could anything be that bad?*

I really discovered feminism deeper into college, first through my friend Jessica, and then from my roommates and teachers, and then from those cool, confident women a couple of years older, who grew their armpit hair and got tattoos, who talked openly about their periods without shame and made weird performance art dances and weren't about impressing anyone. Then there were the riot grrrls, in rock bands and at school, with combat boots and lipstick and hairy legs and baby barrettes and slips and eyeliner.

The shadow side to discovering feminism means discovering the extent to which sexism and misogyny exist in the world. Because feminism entered my life at a time when I was just starting to come into myself, it shook my still-setting foundation. The more I learned about oppression, the more oppressed I felt. I couldn't believe there were structures with a real interest in keeping women down, in keeping *me* down. I wanted to believe in meritocracy. I didn't want to need feminism. I just wanted liberation from everything I had tried to shed: ballet, the eating disorder, trying to fit myself perfectly into a world obsessed with surfaces. I wanted the benefits of feminism without having to be weighed down by the awareness. I sometimes thought that if I didn't know, if I had never known, my life would be lighter, easier; but there was no going back. I started to notice all of the structural ways in which women and girls are held back and had been held back for so long, especially those for whom race and class compound the struggle. It was real and so complicated. My eyes were open and I couldn't un-see or un-know.

One day a few years ago, during Feldenkrais class, a subtle somatic technique that attracts mostly injured dancers and creates momentous sensation through subtle movement, my teacher said, in her sassy deadpan, "Awareness ruined my life." *Preach, lady,* I thought as I burst into tears.

⚜ ⚜ ⚜

When I was a junior in college, I made a dance installation that drew a correlation between pointe shoes and corsets. I had read some history about corsetry and had been shocked to find that in some extreme cases of tight lacing, women allegedly suffered prolapsed uteruses. I was lucky to find a corset to wear in my performance, which I had bought from a girl selling her stuff on the college commons lawn. It was not the sexy kind of corset, but more orthopedic, and too big for me so, though it worked, it didn't do any extreme tightening. (I wouldn't have the real corset experience for another ten years.) I performed in a window in the dance studio with the audience standing outside. I attached the corset strings to eye hooks in the walls on either side of me, so that I looked like a marionette being pulled to and fro en pointe by the corset strings, or rather, by *The Patriarchy*! I had written a poem that I displayed in the window about being an outsider on the inside with insides being pushed out. I remember that Tom Sachs and DD Dorvillier, who both are now big art stars but were then college seniors about to graduate, liked the piece and said something about passing some kind of torch to me, which made me feel like I was one of the cool kids and like I might have a future. The performance was as earnest and terrible as everyone's work is in that time of life (well, except for DD's or Tom's), but in the scheme of collegiate performances, exactly what it needed to be. If there had been grades, I definitely would have gotten higher than a B minus.

I needed to reckon with the pointe shoes, but in order to do that, I had to put them on again. I had to contend with them in order to figure out what they represented to me: a fetish, a tool, a form of compulsory femininity, and finally, a curiosity. Someone said once, good art takes a thing, changes it, and changes it again. My college dance program, more than any place I could think of, rejected the pointe shoe. It was a little bit perverse of me to bring that despised object into that zone, to make that historic place the location of my reckoning with ballet. But reckoning was what I needed to do.

I have held that piece in my mind and body. Even though it was the clunky work of a nineteen-year-old, it delved into costume history, drag, feminine performance and feminism, and began to touch on what I would be doing for the rest of my life.

A few years later the riot grrrl bands sang my feelings, about "not waiting till I grow up to be a woman" and snarled sarcastically through a megaphone, "Go out on the lawn! Put your swimsuit on!" as if to my high school self, the tan, blonde good girl I didn't want to be anymore. All of those women taught me what a feminist looked like, which is, as we know now, any way she damn well wants.

THE
FIERCINGTONS

Picture one of those dogs that is really good with children, who lets them pull its ears and tail and never snarls. That's my husband Marc in the club with all the drag queens. For the short time I was Glory Holesome, queens called Marc "Mr. Holesome," but Mr. David, master of nicknames, chose one for him that stuck: "Husband." If anyone says "husband" in our drag world, you know whose they mean: mine.

Our inflection for the word "husband" is the same one writer Dan Savage uses: "*huhhh*sband." I had adopted this campy inflection long before I started hanging out with drag queens, even before I heard Savage say it. It came from my friend Rick, who had also uncovered the camp joy in "waitress." "*Huhhh*sband" peeled the dark wood veneer of heteronormativity off of the word, and the role it signifies, making it way more fun to say than "partner."

"How's my *huhhh*sband?" Mr. David always asks. The possessive "my" is telling. Marc is a community resource. But his position in the drag family goes beyond tolerant golden retriever. He isn't just along for the ride with me in the queer nightlife; it's his home, too. He worked the door Fridays and Saturdays at the Stud in the early 2000s before I became a regular on its stage. He has edited sound for several queens, collaborated on musical projects with them, and even ran the lights at the 'shack for a stint. When Marc started his own club night, spinning old-school house with DJ Derek, formerly of the 'shack, the dj moniker Marc chose was "Husband." My friend Gregory, himself husband to drag performer Vinsantos, pinpoints one of Marc's less tangible, but no less valuable, skills. "He's a fag whisperer," Gregory says. "He talks sense. And girl, the fact that he's so easy on the eyes doesn't hurt."

Heklina puts it differently. I was once standing around the Stud with her when Marc walked up. I squeezed his face and pushed it toward Hekles for her to admire, the way she always does with boys she thinks are cute, and said what she always says.

"Look! Look at this sweet angel. Isn't he an *Angel* from *Heaven*?!?"

"Meh," she replied. "Too nelly."

👑 👑 👑

I arrive at the National High School Institute at Northwestern University the summer before my senior year. I am like a creature released from a net and thrown back into the sea. Studying theater and dance all day: this is what I want to do, who I want to be around, who I am.

There are 120 of us and soon we are a bustling utopian village. I have already made about ten new best friends. Then I notice him. He's hard to miss with his teased-up Daniel Ash-from-Bauhaus hair on top of his six-foot-two height. Drapey jacket over a Frankie Goes to Hollywood T-shirt, clamdigger pants, slip-on Vans. He is unbelievably handsome. Square jaw, intense brow, smoldery eyes, dimples when he smiles, Prince Charming handsome. He is Marc with a *c*. He listens intently, like an adult, and speaks with unshowy ease, and only brief flashes of the nerdy bravado endemic to teenage boys who are into theater. I learn that he lives in California, and that he is Canadian, which makes perfect sense. That he is an atheist, which makes even more sense. And that he likes Bronski Beat and *Wuthering Heights* and is a vegetarian because of Morrissey. I imagine he will be my new gay bestie. *Yay!* Then I find out he's into girls. *Uh-oh,* I think. *I came here to fall in love with* theater, *not with a* boy.

We flirt a little and then a little more. He offers to massage my hands. My *hands.* The offer is almost pervy in its restraint, but sends the message that he is not the kind of boy who'll suggest a shoulder massage and then try to touch my boobs. With this, he places in my hands the power to steer this thing between us, whatever it might be.

Our entire group goes to Chicago to see a play, *Road* by Jim Cartwright. The playwright is young, his characters despondent, living in a Thatcher-torn England, yearning for purpose. At the end of the play two couples dance to Otis Redding's "Try a Little Tenderness" and then chant "Somehow, a somehow, a somehow, might escape." Most of us are kids whose parents paid for us to spend six weeks bellowing and swaying in Voice and Movement class, analyzing Brecht, and perfecting monologues, but we identify with these struggling youths, especially those of us who have added the red flag of punk music fandom to our identities as "theater fags." We are all "somehows" in some way, trying to escape. I am wrecked by this play. It has busted down my fourth wall. It has altered my life.

I look across the crowded lobby and my eyes meet his. We've had the same experience. I find him and fall into his arms. Yes, I do. And he is not freaked out by my tears. I fall. I fall in love with theater and with the boy.

We talk all night about the play, about life, about everything. We kiss. It's perfect. We fit together like we were made for each other. We fall. We fall fast in love with each other and, together, in love with theater again and again. For the next few weeks, we fill our young lives, not just with each other, but with friends, and with hard work on the depth and craft of the art we are in love with.

We spend our last night at the program together, making out, feeling each other up, pining for the lives we want to start, for ourselves and for each other, but we don't have sex. (That will happen when I visit him in California during the holidays.) We promise to stay in touch and we do. Writing letters and running up our parents' phone bills. Somewhere in there we admit to the ridiculousness of it, that we could know real love at sixteen. We admit to the ways in which this love has blindsided our single-minded launch toward creative lives. Somehow, verbally or telepathically, we promise to keep each other free. We promise to support each other's desire to be artists. We promise to love each other but not to get in each other's way. I met my boy in eyeliner about fifteen years before it would have been convenient. Not English, but close enough.

♕ ♕ ♕

My drag pal, Vinsantos and I met for our first proper kiki in 2004 at a bar in my neighborhood. We cackled and bonded, talking about our hopes and our husbands, and he matched my two drinks with four. When our night was over, I suggested he hail a cab to haul his drunk ass back to his far-flung neighborhood.

"Pffft!" he said, doing a jazzy dance move to hide the fact that he couldn't walk a straight line. I tried to snatch his keys. "No-nooo Miss Thing." He waved away my attempt at common sense and swayed toward his car. "Why don't you drop me off at my place?" I suggested, to at least keep him from driving all the way home. I would invite him up (*One more for the road?*), make him a nice cup of tea, and maybe he'd crash on my couch. It worked. Vinsantos found Doris Day parking in front of my building and followed me up.

"Where's Mr. Holesome? Where's *huhhh*sband?"

"Working the door at Sugar."

"She better werq! The door." Whenever the queens or I throw Marc a "she," "her," or "girl," he catches it with love and tosses it back.

Vinsantos kicked off his shoes and stretched out on the couch. When I came in with the tea, he was already passed out, a sweet little tattooed angel. *Phew.* I congratulated myself just as my ghoul-friend suddenly came to, a jump scare at the end of a horror movie. *Gah!* Then he looked around our living room, drew a circle in the air with his index finger, and proclaimed, "Fiercingtons!" before falling back, out cold. In a moment of drunken hyper-sanity, Vinsantos stumbled on a drag name for Marc and me to share, that spoke to our place together in this queer family. From that moment forward we were The Fiercingtons.

♔ ♔ ♔

About ten years ago Marc and I went to see the legendary New York queen Joey Arias in *Arias with a Twist*. We went backstage to thank and worship the diva, with whom I had performed at a festival a few days before, my Fiorucci-boutique-teenage-dream come true. There, mid-conversation with Joey, was none other than icon and actress Debi Mazar in all of her 1960s-Barbie perfection. She introduced herself, adorably, needlessly. When I introduced Marc, she responded in the over-the-top New York accent that you would want her to have, "Ohhhh, he's cu-uute. How lawng have you been married?"

We dodge this question because we don't celebrate our actual wedding anniversary and neither of us could tell you how long we've been married without looking it up, which we always have to do when we need the date for immigration or tax purposes. The fact and act of our marriage was the result of Marc's Canadian-ness and the necessity that we earn him the status of "resident alien" to keep ourselves legally in the same country. A marriage, but not a wedding. The whole thing arose out of love, but if he had been American, I'm not sure we ever would have done it. What we do celebrate as our anniversary is the day we looked across that crowded theater lobby in Chicago: July 12, 1987.

When we had been in love for half our lives, in 2003, we finally celebrated. I wore a burgundy charmeuse bias-cut tango gown by Mr. David, and we listened as a gathered community of blood family and chosen family, most of them queer, said the kinds of nice things people usually only say about people after they die. And then we actually enjoyed the party.

I hem and haw at the "how long have you two been together" question because I never feel like the straightforward answer fits who I am, who we are. The answer that does fit is just too complicated, bespoke, time-consuming. Marc never balks, and answers succinctly and proudly that we met when we were teenagers, happy to leave the querent's questions unanswered or assumptions intact. I love him for it.

I think it's different for me, a woman, a feminist, to tell people she's married to a man she met when she was sixteen. If there is a type of woman who marries someone she met at sixteen, she is not who I meant to become. The story of a long-married woman does not appear, on its cover, to be one of liberation.

"Well," I said. "We've been together forever. Since high school."

"Awww. Like the Toledos!" Debi cried, beaming with genuine joy and respect.

About these Toledos . . . in the 1970s, two young Cuban immigrants moved from New Jersey to New York City and began their lives as artists. Ruben and Isabel Toledo, he a fashion illustrator rendering charming ladies in fanciful line drawings, she a couturier who learned her craft from her family's matriarchs, honed it as an intern to Diana Vreeland restoring items in the Met collection, and bloomed into a designer's designer. The Toledos are cool. Insider East Village New York City cool. And they met and fell in love as teenagers. They married, supported each other's careers, and lived child-free in a magical bohemian loft in full adoration of each other. *Yes,* I thought. *Like the Toledos. Not like a couple of squares!* Setting aside Isabel's too-early death from cancer in 2019, this comparison to the Toledos gave me an emblem.

Looking at photos of the Toledos, him with his pencil moustache, her with her center-parted curtain of raven hair, I am reminded of another couple whose marriage I seek to emulate: Morticia and Gomez Addams of *The Addams Family*. Both are, like me and Marc, hetero couples with a sense of queerness. The Toledos made their shared name in the gay milieu of fashion and kept roots in the queer-friendly downtown art world that raised them. The Addamses were "creepy," "kooky," queer. Not queer in the way we understand it now, but not exactly straight. And I have always thought the smartest choice in the writing of Gomez and Morticia Addams, the *queerest* thing about them, is that they are a longtime married couple who cannot keep their hands off each other. If we expand our meaning of "queer" to re-embrace its original meaning of strange and rare, the Addamses, the Toledos, and we the Fiercingtons all fit the bill. To put it another way, we are *culturally* queer.

Isabel Toledo said to lifestyle magazine *Kinfolk,* "In a relationship, you should never be a tree; you should always be a vine. Trees grow, but they topple. Vines? Well, pieces fall off, but it keeps going." This is uncannily close to a theory I bring out when conversation about Marc and me deepens past the "how many years have you two been together?" question. It works best when you can see me talk with my hands, but I'll try here. Our marriage thrives, of course due to a lot of hard work, but also because Marc and I are lucky. Lucky that we have grown like vines that move a little bit apart and then crisscross back together, rather than two parallel or diagonal lines. We are lucky to have spent our lives growing together, lucky not to have grown apart, lucky we adore each other. It's a monumental love story, one with its own plot twists, rocky parts, and cliff-hangers. It could fill another book, but not this one.

ALL THE
SEQUINS

"No to Spectacle," begins Yvonne Rainer's "No Mani-festo," and goes on to name all of the things she refuses: costumes, stage presence, acknowledging a relationship between the performer and the audience. Artifice. Written in 1965 by the choreographer and filmmaker, the "No Manifesto" haunts her as her most famous, least understood work (isn't that how it goes?) yet it stands as a crucial pillar of postmodern performance and choreographic practice. As manifestos do, it calls for transformation, in this case seeking to dismantle the outsize drama of Martha Graham and story ballets. Rainer and the rest of what came to be known as the Judson Dance Theater bulldozed the tired old structures of ballet and modern dance to build the foundation for an authentic practice of movement exploration, digging out a space for dance inside the experimentation that was happening across the contemporary art spectrum. By stripping away camp and artifice, Rainer (and many others) unveiled the subtleties of human movement and commenced a sophisticated inquiry.

My dance education at Bennington College was steeped in this ethos, and after my immersion in ballet, administered the same shock to my system as the one Rainer aimed at the culture of dance. "I'm seeing a real problem with the articulation of your spine," said my teacher Martha Wittman, softly, infuriatingly, after a week of technique class.

"Um, why do you shave your armpits?" asked a girl in dirty sweats on day two. I could come up with no good answer to this question I had never considered asking. She walked away and joined a group who side-eyed me in my shiny blue unitard and my hair snatched back in its tight ballerina bun. At Northglenn High, I had been an avant-garde artsy kid, but here I was an uptight dork. That first week I met Spencer Cox, a fabulous gay senior who spent his weekends in New York protesting with ACT UP. When I told him I was a dance major, he said, "But you're so clean."

Upon landing on this new dance planet, where few cared about body size or shape, where everyone actively interrogated the discipline's traditional values, where "interrogate" was something people did to things like "discipline," my body dysmorphia really began to disengage. Dance training at Bennington wasn't about being thin or looking taut or even about working better, faster, harder toward an ideal. It was about making something. At seventeen I still wanted someone to tell me how I was doing, to give me permission to make something only when they knew I would be good enough to pull it off. I had chosen this liberated institution, where your work was up to you and no one handed out letter grades, but I wasn't ready to experiment if it meant failure. There was a lot I wasn't ready for. I thought about my spine.

Fall of my sophomore year I took one class in dance but nixed my plan to major in it, ready to go all-in as a lit major with some philosophy to back it up. I took a class called "Topics in Ethics," where my teacher smoked cigarettes that smelled like burning hair and told me I had a "knack for Philosophy." I took Homer, where we ended the course by reading the entirety of *The Iliad* aloud, each student taking a chapter. Despite my living an approximation of my childhood boarding school fantasy, I hadn't found my groove. I fell in with a bunch of other lit majors I thought were my friends but who scoffed at me for being overly sensitive and, I would find out later, took bets on which of them could make me cry first. After I read my poetry aloud: "It must be a comfort to know that your real talent is dancing." As I approached the table with my lunch: "You know, you could be so skinny if you smoked." That was when I learned that queer intellectuals could also be bullies, no different from the boys in third grade.

Every January and February most Bennington students leave campus and take an internship somewhere, a great way to avoid heating the college during Vermont winters and in tidy keeping with its DIY ethos regarding curriculum. I had decided to spend the winter in Vancouver. In a new place again, I did what made me feel most at home and found the nearest ballet studio, which happened to belong to a sweet, high-strung Englishwoman named Nadya who taught Vaganova technique, the style of the Kirov Ballet in Russia.

It had been a big year. My time at Bennington had set out to dismantle the art form that had built me ("dismantle" another new word I would encounter a lot), and my parents' divorce had fractured my family. With my hands on the ballet barre, the piano guiding me through familiar steps, I was temporarily reassembled. I kept going to class, after a month of which Nadya invited me to be in her upcoming show.

Nadya had studied with Ninel Kurgapkina, a friend of ballet legend Rudolph Nureyev, and in the spring Nadya brought Ninel in to work with us. Ninel spoke only French and Russian and would yell at me to soften my hyperextended arms, which sounded like, "Rukhi! Oczhenstrajzna!" and meant "your arms are scary." She would dramatically put her hands over her face like she was hiding from my terrifying arms, and then peek from behind her fingers as I tried to follow her instructions and say something that sounded like, "Hchorascho, hchorascho" which meant "better, better."

Knowing this was my last fling with ballet, I could fully enjoy the campiness of the situation: the crazy yelling Russian lady obsessed with our technique, the nervous English lady obsessed with impressing the Russian lady and pining after "Rudi" (Nureyev), who would be in Vancouver on tour in *The King and I* and whom she hoped to entice to come to our show. It was *Waiting for Guffman*, ballet version. As I lightened up, the craziest thing happened. My ballet dancing improved dramatically. It was in Nadya's studio that I did my first perfect quadruple pirouette, which felt like one of those dreams in which you fly. Apparently, I had gotten out of my own way. In Nadya's show I wore fake eyelashes and a flouncy dirndl for a bouncy peasant pas de quatre from a story ballet in a big theater in front of a painted backdrop. With all those trappings, the ballerina part of me could die happy.

I ended up spending the entirety of 1990 in Vancouver, a needed break from Bennington, its dirty rich girls and shitty frenemies. The reason I had chosen Vancouver in the first place was because Marc lived there. We were still head-over-heels, bonkers in love even after two years of a long-distance relationship and seeing other people. We had never spent more than a week together, and it was time to find out what lay beyond our perpetual honeymoon phase. We found a studio apartment with splatter paint job (1990, honey) on the gayest corner in Vancouver and moved in, the only hetero couple in the building where "Everybody Everybody" and "Ride on Time" by Black Box blasted from the apartment next door. Marc had already been going dancing at the gay clubs even though he was straight. He was pretty straight-edge too, both of us serious kids who feared drugs and alcohol would crush our dreams and send us back to the suburbs. After a year in gray Vancouver—*Is it six a.m. or six p.m.?*—I realized why coffee, heroin, and suicide were so popular in the Northwest. Dance music helped sustain our will to live. We couldn't survive on Nirvana alone.

After my great breakup fling with ballet, I left Nadya and joined the Student dance company at Simon Fraser University. I landed a role as one of the Furies in an experimental production of *The Oresteia* called *The Electra Project*, which we nicknamed "The Ecclecta Project." No one said "no to spectacle" there, but the work was no less intelligent for it. I interned with a contemporary dance company after they blew my mind and broke my heart with a piece for six strong women in combat boots dancing to Vivaldi's "Stabat Mater." Maybe I was ready to make something. Maybe I wanted to be an artist and not just a dancer.

In the fall of 1991 I returned to Bennington, and double majored in literature and dance. I embraced the school's stripped-down and subtle aesthetic, knowing that I could make work from a different system of values later if I wanted to. I yielded to the loose softness being taught there, and it made me a better dancer. I found a sense of fluidity. I found my spine.

I cultivated a solid group of friends who treated every dining-hall meal as a fabulous dinner party. We were smart, occasionally snarky, but no one tried to make anyone cry. Really, it was a workshop on how to talk. As such, the master teacher was our friend Jason. A few years older than all of us, Jason was out and gay and had spent some years in New York before college as an activist and professional actor. We all knew his origin story, a good one. He had trained extensively in theater preparing to perform Shakespeare but found himself at an audition to play a California Raisin dancing to "I Heard It Through the Grapevine." His realization that he *really wanted the job* sent him running away to college.

Jason riffed on famous Bennington alum Carol Channing, telling made-up stories of slutty behavior in her unmistakable voice. "Well, of courshe the Williamsh boysh knew we were *eashy*. Those roomsh on campush they call 'card roomsh'? They weren't for playing *cardsh*! That'sh where they used to *fuck* ush!" He also made up a voice and persona for Chita Rivera, telling stories of being a "Broadway hoofer" and how "that fucking cab driver BROKE MY LEG. But I'm still DANCIN'!" It preceded the SNL "I'm FIFTY" sketch by decades and surpassed it.

Jason's AIDS activism had plunged him into a young adulthood I couldn't imagine. From him, I first witnessed the gallows humor that grew in the gay community during those years like a super-bloom after a devastating wildfire. He held the table rapt as he told us about his visit to the AIDS Memorial Quilt, which the rest of us were planning to see on its upcoming tour. "It is one of the most stunning, tender things I have ever seen. I was weeping. *Weeping*! Then, as I'm leaving, this attendant appears out of nowhere like a ghost, puts his wasted face two inches from mine, and hisses 'REMEMBER THEIR NAMES!' I mean, as if I could forget. *Queen*, I came to see the quilt." A ghoulish denouement played for comedy. A way to hold, share, and release unbearable horror. As I set out to visit the quilt myself, Jason grabbed my arm, fixed my gaze, and stage-whispered, "Remember their *NAMES*!"

Our friend group ran to see *Paris Is Burning* the moment it came out, making a special trip to the movie theater an hour away in Albany. We all wanted to turn right back around and watch it again. "All wrapped up in LaBeija" became our shorthand for any kind of intense focus. "Sorry I missed you guys at the party. I was in the library all wrapped up in LaBeija." LaBeija in this case meaning writing a paper on Tolstoy or trudging through Kant.

That year I also watched *The Times of Harvey Milk*. The people I admired at school, Jason, Spencer, were the contemporary versions of the characters in that true story. The flicker of a thought that I should move to San Francisco became an urgent flare.

Things had continued to work so well with the boyfriend that we made that move together. Marc and I shared our first apartment in the Mission with a difficult housemate. He was a twenty-two-year-old white guy from Santa Cruz who identified as queer but mostly had girlfriends. He shrieked at the news every day from the couch, shrill as my old ballet teacher Marcelle. I took this as a kind of fire drill that meant that I had better try to keep up, and I did try. But every time I managed to form an opinion, he helped me convince myself I had no head for politics, that I was too burdened by my privilege to get any of it through my thick, pretty skull. He didn't care about fashion or fiction or any of the things that made life worth living for me and always won arguments because everything he cared about, he knew a lot about, and everything I knew a lot about, he didn't care about. A shrewd tactic. I had been taught to consider both sides, but if I considered the wrong side in front of him, he deemed me "ignorant."

My college professor had told me I had a "knack for philosophy," but my housemate countered that my ability to see gray areas was too problematic for rigorous theory. Before Rebecca Solnit invented the word for it, he "mansplained." He mansplained bell hooks and Judith Butler. He mansplained my own identity and my own position. By grappling openly with my privilege, which is what I thought I was supposed to do (as I struggled to scrape together enough money from my two retail jobs to buy tampons), I laid myself open, gave him an opportunity to take me down. He saw my weak spots and exploited them. "Well, you're a straight girl" he'd say, a phrase that invoked his queerness to eclipse my femaleness and revoked my right to a perspective. Another smart, queer bully.

In the hindsight of maturity, I think he did it to make himself feel better, to quell doubts about his right to his own pain as he sat at his own particular intersection of privilege. He, I found out recently, is now a therapist. *Of course he is. Heal thyself, honey!*

People have the right to grow up. I wish him well. I really do.

Twenty-five years later, in 2017, I found myself in a public conversation with *the* Judith Butler, who as a child dreamed of becoming either a philosopher or a clown. "How did you become a theory queen?" Judith asked me. I swooned, and then thought, *Well, there was this sad clown I used to live with, who used to mansplain your work to me* . . .

In the mid-1990s, I realized after a few years in my dream city, that I had emerged into a dance world immersed in that same "No to Spectacle" aesthetic, of dancers performing in sweats and ignoring the audience, of declining any sort of artifice and deeming loose, noodly movement the most "authentic." Though this aesthetic of refusal had ushered in a vital change for the form and its practitioners, after being submerged in it, I started to get sad. I missed artifice. I needed spectacle.

A few years later, the documentary *The Cockettes* illustrated my epiphany as an early member described the rift between the Kaliflower commune and the Cockettes. "All the plaid shirts went over there and all the sequins went that way." I had to leave the plaid flannels and go find my sequins.

I stopped feeling pressure to conform to the plaid shirt "No" aesthetic and began to zhoosh up my dance with drag. The queens at Trannyshack emboldened me to try things on the "legit" dance stage that the Judson artists would have hated. Shortly after college I had discovered writer Wayne Koestenbaum and his singular book *The Queen's Throat: Opera, Homosexuality, and the Mystery of Desire*. His was theory that had fun with itself, skipping and twirling through fields of what I loved or didn't know yet that I loved. He introduced me to Maria Callas, and I received the Callas box set for my birthday. Along with the greatest hits of the opera aria canon, it featured an unexpected prize, an interview to which I listened incessantly. The rhythms of Callas's speech, its hauteur, clarity and authority, begged to be lip-synched. I was on a dance floor with Kevin when lightning struck.

"I think I wanna make a dance piece where I lip-synch to Maria Callas! Do you think I should?" I yelled over some remix of "Sing it Back" by Moloko.

"Are you asking me what you should make? Why are you asking me? Of *course* you should make an opera drag dance, Mary!" he shouted.

The Callas piece would mark a turning point. The seed was the lip-synch, but I also needed to embody "La Divina" through dance. So, starting with photos of her, I amassed a collection of poses and facial expressions, stringing them together as expression and punctuation, animating the cadences of her conversational voice. The piece needed the context of Callas's singing voice, but simply dancing to an aria seemed too one-to-one. Marc found a piece by experimental composer Christian Marclay that overlaid several Callas recordings to atonal, witchy effect. *Perfect.* I stretched and repeated a vocabulary of iconic operatic gestures, some culled from photos, some imagined: Medea stabbing, Tosca dying, Callas taking a bow. I had a dance.

I chose the piece as the closer for my first solo show, which presented a problem: how to make the quick change into Callas drag after three other pieces? The project of marking my face with the diva's specific signifiers—heavy black brows, perfect wing eyeliner and blood-red lips—was not something I could do quickly offstage, nor could I keep the audience waiting. The problem and its solution became a signature in my performance work. I would turn the preparation into a dance; I would place the makeup ritual onstage. At first I thought of a two-way mirror, which would allow me to see myself while revealing the process to the audience, but with the instruments available, lighting it was impossible, so I made a choreographic choice. I added an assistant.

A young man in a black suit stands holding a large mirror at my eye level while I sit on a piano bench with my back to the audience. For the two-minute duration of the aria "Vissi d'Arte" from Tosca, *the assistant oscillates the mirror as slowly as he can, so that one side of the audience or the other can always see my process but I never lose sight of my own reflection, allowing me to complete my task, eyeliner first, eyebrows next, and on the aria's very last notes, the lipstick.*

I was finally making the art I was meant to make and not what I thought I should be making. I ended up performing that piece for a decade on many stages, including six years later for the seventy-fifth anniversary of Bennington College, locus of my creative identity crisis, my spinal reckoning. Drag artifice led me to my own version of authenticity.

The Callas drag experiment was one of the mothers that spawned my career. She revealed femininity as the through line in my artistic practice, a theme that could undergird my life's work as a performer and choreographer. This line of femininity is a magnet to attract everything else in my philosophical and experimental toolkit: gesture, specificity, camp, the body, role models, glamour, humor, pathos, unapologetic queerness . . . Realizing that I could organize my life's work in relationship to the examination of femininity was a huge relief. Suddenly and sensibly, I had something to link it all together, a "One Thing," an area of expertise.

Over the next two decades I would create not only dances and drag numbers, but every conceivable combination of the two, every kind of drag dance experiment: choreographic provocations, video meditations, durational installations, multimedia fantasias, and cabaret extravaganzas. I would take them to major museums, queer historical sites, city hall, and Gay Pride. Since this realization I have rarely been without things to say or ways to make art.

As a drag artist I practice this fluidity called femininity, and in the midst of it all, I also do feminism. Drag is, for me, ultimately a feminist practice.

The foremothers who did the work of dismantling and rebuilding the terms of dance performance made it possible for

me to be who I am. My own path followed theirs, and then
went meandering, winding, and circling back around in ways I
never saw coming. Yvonne Rainer said "No to Spectacle" so that
I could say "yes" to sequins.

PAGEANT II:
THE READING

My friend Karl is always good for an honest read: of people, of books, of situations. On this particular day in fall 2003, he was reading my tarot cards. I was wondering how I was going to pull off this drag pageant thing and, upon casting that question into the space between us, had pulled Death, The Empress, Wheel of Fortune, Judgment, and then The Sun. He looked down his fine freckled nose and fixed his serious, light-blue eyes on the cards. He took a pause.

"Girl, I have never seen so many major arcana in one reading. Okay. You're going to let go of something. This is a good thing. You probably need to, and then, well, you're gonna rule."

I was working on "fierce" and here was "ruling." Fierce and ruling, the two classic drag queen qualities. I was ready. In a sense I had been working toward this my entire performing life; even playing dress-up as a little kid had prepared me for this. There was a lot, however, that could hold me back—things I had implicitly been forbidden to explore as a professional dancer coming of age in the postmodern era. Maybe the Death card wanted those rules to die. Maybe I had to let go of the rules of serious art, of postmodern dance that had been hammered into me over the last few years of my professional life. Rules made up by people who cherished some unattainable ideal of neutrality, people who told me I had too much "attack," that my face was too expressive and that I was too theatrical, that I was too connected to the audience. Now I could say "yes" to theatricality, "yes" to trying to impress the audience, "yes" to costumes, to pop and camp affect, to cheesiness and silliness: yes yes yes!

PARTY'S
OVER

I arrived in San Francisco fresh from college in 1992, an artsy version of Mary Ann Singleton from Armistead Maupin's *Tales of the City*, full of hope and pluck, looking for My People. But the city to which I thought I was moving was half hollowed out. That's how it always goes, doesn't it? When you arrive at a place you've been dreaming of, everyone there will tell you it's *totally over*. But at this time, and in this place, it was pretty much true.

After seeing *The Times of Harvey Milk*, as anyone who moves to San Francisco should, I wanted to live in the Castro, but couldn't afford to. The Mission would have to do, or as my landlady called it: "Lower Noe Valley." That was when old white people were still scared of the Mission and there was only one café on Valencia between Twenty-fourth and Sixteenth Streets. The first time I walked to the Castro, I pretended I lived there, practically skipping down the hill from Twenty-Third Street: *I love the gays and the gays love me! Hello my people! Hello everyone!* Through my twenty-one-year-old eyes it looked like the set of *The Umbrellas of Cherbourg*, candy-colored and coordinated; but in reality, Castro Street circa 1992 was pretty fucking intense— dark and sad and depleted by AIDS in a way my innocent self could not comprehend.

The street that to me seemed so full of potential was, to its longtime residents, a remnant populated by the walking wounded. Had the streets really been like they were in the Harvey Milk documentary—thronging and throbbing with gay life, gay liberation, and the pursuit of gay happiness? Castro Street circa 1992 was trying to put on a brave painted face, trying to muster a reason to get out of bed. Castro Street was the grieving widow who still has to make breakfast for her kids and see them off to school without sobbing and then keeps herself occupied by making them Halloween costumes.

And girl, did she ever! That first Castro Halloween was everything. Was there Scarlett O'Hara via Carol Burnett wearing the emerald velvet gown with the brass curtain rod still in it? Of course there was. Were there undulating umbrellas lit from within and festooned with iridescent fabric making perfect jellyfish? Castro Halloween made that shit *up*! A giant Easter Island statue? Oh yes! An entire drag bowling team chanting a cheer with choreographed bowling moves? Check! Strike! An entire flock of Carmen Mirandas? Who can stop at just one? The Castro turned it out on Halloween of 1992, and she schooled us children.

We, that era's children, the Gen Xers, had emerged into a terrible recession to start our adult lives. My artsy college had prepared me to make dances and write essays and think critically, none of which, not even the critical thinking— especially the critical thinking?—had prepared me for reality. Capable Mary Ann Singleton from *Tales of the City* with her typing skills I was not. But on one of my jaunts through my favorite 'hood, as I breezed past the soap shop with the bubble machine and the beautiful bald girl working there, past the queer bookstore A Different Light and Condomania, I spied a help wanted sign in the window of the most charming little shop where an artist and his boyfriend sold Japanese paper and lovely things made from it.

I love things Japanesque! I love the gays! I got the job! They liked me! I couldn't possibly have guessed that, as it was mid-October their only reason for hiring me was their impending need for my trained hands for the holiday season, and the fact that I was thrilled to work for seven dollars an hour. Liking me had nothing to do with it.

The store was not actually a room but a sliver of the entrance hallway to The Patio, the nineties answer to a 1970s fern bar. Or "The Central Perk" cafe from the TV show *Friends*, but gay. At the paper store I learned how to fold origami cranes and to wrap gifts flawlessly without using tape (a skill that endures and never fails to impress). I also learned that not every gay man in the world is utterly charmed by me. Go figure! I tried my hardest to impress my boss, Han, but he was having none of it. Through his placid veneer he showed a layer of contempt that seemed intentional. You could smell it in the heinous cloud of cigarette smoke that sometimes billowed from his little one-man artist cubby behind the counter. But his work—the cards, photo albums, and picture frames—did what art should: it reminded people that beauty, even in the midst of plague and economic recession, was necessary. Jerry, Han's boyfriend, did the bookkeeping and carried a persistent, profound, and contagious discomfort. Neither of them seemed thrilled to have me around.

The only other employee was Rand. He was the first hippie spiritual queen I ever met, a faerie steeped in all things woo from a variety of traditions: Buddhism, Santeria, Native American ritual, and even mystical Catholicism. Who knew Catholicism could be mystical? He affirmed my hunch that Saint Teresa of Avila was one of the more glam saints. I had never met anyone spiritual who also appreciated the camp of it. The Colorado Christian girls I grew up around were sanctimonious bores, and the Wicca converts I met in college were dead witchy serious.

Two weeks into the job I cut my finger really badly at home, slicing a bagel with a cheap, dull knife, and Rand brought me a rose so that Saint Teresa could help me heal with her flower power. Han worried that if the patrons saw me wielding an X-Acto with a bandaged finger, they would think me incompetent (which I was actually), and he banished me to his cubby at the back of the store.

I think one of the reasons Han and Jerry hired me was so that Rand could have more time off to care for his dying partner, whom he never talked about. I couldn't guess the magnitude of what all of these guys had endured. I pretended to know in theory. Twenty-one-year-old white girls from liberal arts colleges know a lot—in theory. Maybe my hopeful presence was a nuisance, but more likely no one thought much at all about my presence. I was there to help sell holiday cards and wrap boxes, that's all.

By 1992, everyone had lost so many and so much. I guess I had assumed the worst was over at that point, but no. Was the worst point 1981, when no one knew what was going on? Or was the wasteland of 1992 the worst of it? Unsurprising relentlessness. Daily grief. All of it was the worst. Those just five years older than I had been forced to grow up five times faster.

The first time a very ill man came into the store shocked me. I had seen photos of gorgeous young men ravaged, but even at Bennington where so many students and teachers were queer, I never saw anyone get sick and die. Now I realize my whole college faculty must have been grieving, but only shared the briefest glimpses of what they were going through. Their business as teachers of college students was to instill hope, to convince us and our parents, who were paying so much money, that our liberal arts educations were worth something, that there was a future into which we would emerge.

My college friend Eric had just graduated with me and moved to San Francisco, too. We weren't super close, but he was dear. He came into the store every so often, once to do me the honor of waiting until he was with me to take his new copy of Madonna's *Sex* book out of its platinum wrapper for the first time. We *oohed* and *aahed* and giggled over Madonna and her audacity, guiltlessly loving her sexy appropriation and elevation of queer culture.

I had suspected that maybe Eric was sick our last semester at school and I wondered how long he had known. He had been the first person I laid eyes on when I got to my dorm at Bennington at age seventeen, shell-shocked from my parents' bitter breakup mere weeks before, intimidated by all the sophisticated rich kids and lonely as hell. I ran into him in the hallway before I got to my dorm room door, and he gave me a sweet smile and an authentic handshake. Eric was cool but not intimidating, one of those blessed people with nothing to prove. Thick auburn hair, sharp cheekbones, red lips, earnest eyes, and an overbite that could have him playing a much prettier Freddy Mercury. He was always skinny, and when I saw him in San Francisco, he was impossibly more so. For his senior piano concert at school, he wore a 1960s vintage ladies' black tunic and pants trimmed in jet beads and no shoes. On skinny Eric it was the pinnacle of chic, which with his bare feet lent perfect levity to his concert of Stockhausen-esque compositions. He had style. Why the fuck did he have to die? There was no one like him. Yet we lost so many like him.

The paper store turned out to be an awful place to work. My seven dollars an hour often depended upon me spending eight hours alone with no break and no key to the shop, so in order to use the bathroom or take a lunch I had to ask the sullen girl at the jewelry store across the hall to watch our shop. Like Han and Jerry, she was over me too. When I brought up the issue of the bathroom and key with Han, he inhaled a drag of his horrible cigarette, exhaled with a sneer, and informed me that if I were in his home country I would be working backbreaking twelve-hour shifts in a factory, so I really had nothing to complain about.

And I shut up because I thought I was lucky.

Mid-November found lucky me hunched over the counter on a too-high stool, folding origami crane after origami crane—for long life and good luck—to a soundtrack of new age pan flutes and babbling brooks, holding in pee and holding back tears while the Castro gays remarked how peaceful it must be to work a job surrounded by such beauty. A rare customer would hover, proclaiming my wrapping neither good enough nor fast enough. If Han and Jerry had helped me figure out that not all gay men adored me, I learned then, with some micro-managing queen standing over me, that sometimes the feeling was mutual. Still, the overwhelming majority of delightful folks, plus Rand, helped quell my fantasy of tossing a match through that door and walking away.

Three days after Christmas, I arrived at work and Jerry both greeted me and fired me in one fell swoop: "Don't bother to take off your coat." He offered something about my having asked for too much time off, but I think letting me go after the holidays was their plan all along. I turned on my heels and walked out the door down Castro Street in the rain, furious, but feeling lighter, happier, literally quite *gay*.

DON'T GET
TOO COMFORTABLE

L ittle did I know, at the exact same time I toiled at that wretched paper store, a divine being was working at A Different Light bookstore only a few doors down. I can divide my life into two halves: before I saw Justin Vivian Bond perform and after. It was the mid-1990s when I first saw Mx. Bond, in her duo Kiki and Herb. As soon as I saw that face, that fluidly relaxed but totally commanding bodily presence, I was there for whatever happened onstage. Like with the album covers of my youth, whose surfaces lured me in before I heard a note.

"Land" by Patti Smith shimmered freshly in my mind. I had just discovered it, a twenty-something catching up on queer classics. Vivian seemed to divine the particular way in which I needed to hear this epic. Having changed the name of the song's protagonist, "Johhny" to "Herby," for her musical partner Herb, she raced up the first arc, a nightmare of school-hallway sexual violence. She conjured an incarnation of collective rage to rise up and fill the room.

"UrrrrrUUUUHhhh . . . startedcrashinghisheadagainstthel ock-AH, startedcrashinghisheadagainstthelock-AH . . . started laughing hystericall-YYY, and suddenlyyyy uuuurrrhHERBY had the feeling, he was being surrounded by . . . Horses! Horses!

Horses! Horses!" I was swept up in the full gallop.

Vivian Bond's presence was like a missing piece, something I had been looking for and didn't know I needed. I had been spending a lot of feminist energy critiquing the concept of "hysteria," knowing it was one of my frequencies but afraid of it: too close to home. I cry so frequently, easily, and deeply that had I been born a few decades too early I might have been labeled "hysterical" and put in what Bond-as-Kiki would later refer to as an "institutional."

Here was this genderqueer femme person fully embodying hysteria, that feminine brand of rage, but keeping a layer of humor intact the entire time. Her performance held reverence for Patti Smith's holy poetic incantation while also holding the ridiculousness that so often lurks in art, in poetry, the question, "Why *Horses?* Well, why *not* horses?"

Vivian was Patti and Johnny and also neither. Vivian was singular. Vivian was everything. I was quenched, lifted up, wrung out. This was one of the souls in the world who would teach me what it is to take space, to step forward, to speak up.

I went to that show with Marc and a friend from his job at the record store. Marc instantly understood what I saw in Vivian, which probably served to further cement our love. If he hadn't understood, we may have lasted, but it might not have been the same. The guy we brought along ran an indie rock label that specialized in the kind of music that was later labeled "twee pop," a kind of anti-spectacle, anti-rock by people who were uncomfortable in the spotlight but needed attention anyway. The apex of twee pop was the Scottish band Belle and Sebastian, whose song "Fox in the Snow" Kiki and Herb cover to perfection on their Christmas album *Do You Hear What We Hear?* Our friend was not into it, showing himself to be more of an anti-spectacle, plaid flannel person than I thought he was, in love with music but ill at ease with this level of emotional expression. That show gave me a little window into a way to find my people. My people are those who appreciate Vivian Bond. I am now lucky to call this role model a friend.

Vivian says she likes to "keep it pretty, keep it shallow, keep it moving." Well, it's only shallow before you start to wade in. Soon you're caught in the current and swept away, sometimes over rocks and down waterfalls, sometimes into glassy pools. Vivian moves you from irreverence and into serious depths and real vulnerabilities.

I know I have told a lot of stories of performative triumph in this book, but really it's not always thus. I'm not one to court disaster by entering the stage space intoxicated or woefully unprepared, so my worst stage experiences (besides the time I dropped into the splits, and heard a big "pop" sound, which was my *hamstring*) are less spectacularly bad than generally mediocre, "*meh.*" Technical difficulties can often (but not always) tank a show, as can obnoxious or rudely inattentive audience members. In these challenging onstage situations, I silently repeat the mantra *WWVBD: What Would Vivian Bond Do?*

One case was more like "what would Kiki do?" Kiki DuRane, the unsinkable character who made Bond famous, is an octagenarian, hard-drinking cabaret singer who says whatever is on her mind. Kiki gets "perturbed." Kiki becomes unhinged.

It was 2005, a night at the 'shack called No More Words, the theme of which was "no lip-synching allowed." Basically, experimental dance. This guy in the audience is standing right up against the stage, with his back to it. Talking, talking, talking. Squawking, really. Over the sound system at the Stud, no mean feat. I watch from the sidelines as he keeps on squawking over each artist and their hard work.

Hmm, I think. *You're free. You're not at the Opera House. You're free to stand against this stage with your back to it and squawk over the show. Well, with freedom comes possibility.* I hop onstage to perform a strenuous, tightly choreographed-but-gonzo ballerina number to "Close to the Edit" by Art of Noise. Miss Thing is still squawking.

I see my window. I consider the precision of my training. I do an epic *ronde de jambe*, known to the martial artist as a "roundhouse kick." I just *graze* his forehead with my toe. He goes full Marsha Brady. "Owwwwwwww. My NOSE!" And I'm like, *Girl, please. If I had wanted to kick you in the nose, believe me, I could have. Do you know what some of these people have gone through in order to drag themselves up onstage for you tonight? Do you think queens rioted at the Stonewall in 1969 for your freedom to ignore their daughters and granddaughters?*

To quote Kiki, "I snapped." The only real punk thing I've ever done.

I invoked a proper WWVBD during my one-woman show *The F Word* in 2017. The *F* is for feminism. And Fauxnique. In the tradition of artists like Bond, the show moves through the territory of raucous drag cabaret into places that feel more vulnerable, that require a generous exchange of attention. One night an audience member was just a little bit too participatory. At first it was great, her responding to my every punchline with "Werq!" When she met every *other* line with "Woo!" it got to be a lot. I located the chatty Cathy, the Woo! Girl, just as I launched into an earnest moment, in which I sang live, offering a tender rendition of "Boys in the Trees" by Carly Simon, which has since entered Vivian's own repertoire.

Miss Woo! and her companion tittered and tee-heed just two feet from me as I struggled to maintain the soft, steady focus the song required. I can carry a tune, even offer a styling, but I feel more naked when I'm singing than when I'm actually naked. I had to uphold an arc of serious energy, and feared it might collapse under the weight of all the "Woo!" I took a deep breath and summoned Vivian's authority. *WWVBD?* I thought. *Another sort of "woo." The magick kind.* I considered the luxurious power of my position. I adjusted my flower crown. I held my goddess space. When I finished the song, I addressed the titterers with my glamour gaze.

"My darlings," I said into the microphone, "May I ask you a question?"

"Omigod! Yaaaaas Queen!"

"Are you two on mushrooms?"

Their big, tight smiles softened as they looked at me, then at each other, unsure of what to do and then shook their heads. The guys sitting next to them mouthed *thank you* and did the Faerie/Beatnik/ACT UP snap-as-applause.

"Look at me. I'm gonna need you to read the room, and stay with me. I'm giving you a lot of myself."

"Okay."

"Thank you." The show moved forward with me at the helm and in control.

Vivian Bond is a master of the stealth read: the heckler never knows what hit them and ends up reintegrated into the audience flow as if nothing happened, not chastised, but not likely to misbehave again. Where a lesser performer might risk exacerbating the situation, drawing energy away from the audience's shared vision and experience, Vivian wields the disciplinary magic of Mary Poppins. She restores balance. When I see Vivian perform, after being swung around and dragged through my emotions, shown things I didn't know I had been ignoring and reintroduced to parts of myself I had forgotten to embrace, I find my balance again as well. I remember that balance is motion, and Kiki's motto is the one I repeat: *Don't. Get. Too. Comfortable!*

HAGEN
& SIMONE

"Happy Birthday, Mary!" said Kevin, the year I turned twenty-nine, in 2000.

"Thanks, Mary!" I replied with our favorite pre-Stonewall gal-pal pet name.

"Um, I hope you don't think it's weird," he said as he handed me a package. He widened his big eyes, clamped his hand over his mouth, and reared his head back in mock fear, but his pose bore a touch of real concern.

I felt the package Kevin handed me, wrapped in his signature way: an envelope made from glossy magazine pages sewn together on the machine with a zigzag stitch.

"Oooh, it feels like—"

"—clothes." He couldn't wait. "It's clothes. Oooh! I hope it's not too intimate, but I saw it in a window and it looked—"

"Omigod! Shush, Mary. Just let me open it!"

In the home-sewn envelope (so fun to open by pulling the thread out, like an old-timey cloth bag of flour: zip!) was something fabulous, the fabric shiny greenish-gold brocade with a matte turquoise pinwheel pattern. Unfolding it revealed a pencil skirt. Kind of psychedelic Jackie Kennedy. Prim weirdo glam.

"Wow! I LOVE it." I did.

"Oooh, I hope it fits! Here, give it to me a sec. C'mere."

He stretched the waistband taut, stepped up close to me, and carefully wrapped it around my neck, so the two sides of the waist met in the back.

"Wow. Perfect." Kevin handed the skirt back to me.

"Wait, what did you just do?"

"Oh, girl, you don't know that trick? If the doubled-up waistline fits around your neck, that means it'll fit your waist!"

Add one more item to the long list of Kevin's helpful household hints. I ran to the nearest bathroom and tried the skirt on my body just to be sure, but it wasn't necessary. Vintage brocade with no give whatsoever, and it fit perfectly. Without knowing my dress size Kevin had seen this skirt and had been able to translate it onto my body. And somehow he knew that it would be not just my style, but the style I was trying to cultivate, not just what I would wear, but what I hadn't yet realized I wanted to wear.

After the skirt, and him getting me addicted to performing at the 'shack with our Mormon missionary number the year before, the next logical step was for us to form an official duo.

"Are we moving too fast?" we often joked, as if we were a couple planning a wedding after a truncated courtship. We thought *"Probably"* followed by *"Why the hell not?"* and jumped into an art marriage. We looked to current and past duos for inspiration: Lucy and Ethel, Gilbert and George, Nichols and May, Kiki and Herb, Abramović and Ulay, Laverne and Shirley . . . We looked to drag, dance, theater, fashion, the ridiculous and the mundane, for our inspiration.

The drag club gave us an audience who understood us and a laboratory in which to work, but immediately we began to think about expanding, creating performances to play on stages in the world of dance and theater where we had initially met.

Our first opportunity happened to be a spot performing

in store windows as part of something called the Retail Dance Festival, and we snatched it off the hanger. The festival's name, though clunky, enticed us nonetheless as an ideal showcase for us, shameless fashion fans in the often fashion-averse world of dance. We signed up, and with our creative brains cracked open from going to see so much smart drag, began assembling the pieces of our performance. We had one problem: our duo had no name of its own. We could have chosen our last names and left it at that, in the spirit of our inspirational duos, but we wanted a little twist on the theme, something a little more designed than the last names we happened to carry. And then we tripped over it.

As we walked home from a night out with Karl, we mused on divas, as was our habit. The conversation turned to Kiki and Herb, how no one but no one could command a stage like Kiki, and how Patti Smith's "Land" had just opened up for us through Kiki's interpretation. We all agreed that though no one but Patti Smith could *be* Patti Smith, Kiki's rendition of the song added layers and dimensions that Patti hadn't expressed. We imagined "Land" as a standard, a new barometer for diva greatness, and longed for more interpretations.

"But now I think I need to hear everyone do it, just to be sure," I said.

"Of course, we really need Yoko to do it," said Kevin.

"Dying to hear that," I said.

"And Dolly," said Karl.

"And Bette," I said.

"Ooh! And Nina!" said Karl.

"Which one?" I said.

"Hagen *and* Simone!" said Kevin. As if it were obvious. It was now.

And just like that Kevin and I had our name. Hagen & Simone. It did everything we needed it to do. It even nudged the Nina Hagen fandom I'd shared with Frank in high school.

Neither of us would be Hagen, nor Simone. *We* were Hagen *and* Simone. Except neither Kevin nor I could resist the swooshing graphic beauty of an ampersand, so it would always be Hagen & Simone.

For our Retail Dance Festival performance, we asked an acquaintance who owned a vintage shop if she might lend us clothes and allow us access both to her window on Valencia Street and to the window's special feature, an automated rotating platform. She hemmed and winced at the platform request, but somehow Kevin talked her into letting us climb upon her fragile, cherished prop. I have tried to study and learn from Kevin's graceful designer's talent for relaying the value of an idea to a skeptic, as if letting them in on its magic, often convincing them that his idea was theirs all along. It's an art by itself. Kevin values a great design decision over the right to lay claim to the brainstorm that birthed it.

Dolls and mannequins, robots and zombies, all of those creatures of the animatronic or reanimated uncanny, are classics in the drag oeuvre, and even now after having seen decades of shows, still my favorites. Since it took place in their natural habitat, our shop window piece demanded that we portray mannequins. We found a ready-made camp soundtrack in a cover version of Kraftwerk's song "Showroom Dummies" by a German electronic musician cribbing a cumbia style and calling himself, in this context, Señor Coconut. On the slowly rotating platform, we would perform a striptease imported from the uncanny valley. The moves that removed our clothes happened during the time when we faced away from viewers on the street, rendering our position changes imperceptible, and as we revolved back around into their line of view through the window, we appeared stiff again, thus giving the impression of our clothes weirdly falling off without our doing anything. Once we were down to nerdy white underwear (which would become a Hagen & Simone touchstone) we experienced the awakening that animates any good mannequin narrative. We broke out of our corporeal strictness and ended our performance in a kind of libidinal chaos, one of us wielding a sticker tagger, the other a price tag gun, covering each other's bodies and unsexy underwear in tiny signs of cut-rate value.

Our next opportunity, in 2001, landed us on a mixed bill with two other choreographers. This show demanded that we step out of our short-form practice and produce twenty minutes of material, which seemed like a lot at the time, so to ease a task that could have overwhelmed us, we wrote all of our ideas, from theme to costume, on scraps of paper and threw them into a bowl, mixing them up in different combinations. I still use this technique all the time, a variation on chance operations that takes the heavy labor of decision-making off the table and drops you right into creative action. We knew we were both compelled by clothing as content, not only as costume, and from there the ideas cascaded into the bowl: crisp white shirts, red thread, buttons, needles, squares, scissors, shadow-play and nudity. Without much processing, we had more than enough material.

Out of our paper jumble the image of crisp, white, oversized shirts held multiple possibilities. We bought three shirts at Thrift Town and buttoned them together into a monster shirt with a giant neck and six sleeves, creating a dance around all of the ways we could share them. We called it the "shirt tango." We ducked into and out of the shirt configuration, devising a hyper-detailed, exact choreography of gesture that delighted us both. The fact that Kevin and I are almost exactly the same size— down to our feet—made it possible to push acts of unison into the territory of twinning, an auspicious design option for a duo. In this case the three shirts buttoned together also hinted at the kind of tether shared by twins.

The scissors glistened with possibility and symbolism as props, suggesting danger, vulnerability, and transformation. The three shirts morphed into a tent under which we created shadow puppets with the scissors and a flashlight. At one point we created a kind of shared umbilical cord as one of us stitched thick red thread into the shirt of the other and pulled it long and taut. At another point I wielded the scissors to cut one of the shirts off of Kevin's body and then finally to snip off his tightie-whities, predating the Yoko Ono "Cut Piece" tribute we would bring to the Stud stage a year later. The piece was charming, inventive and tight, a good start to our project of bringing drag aesthetics into the theater.

👑 👑 👑

Our friendship deepened as we uncovered affinities, what made our lives worth living: art, fashion, books, beauty, food, dancing, people . . . We learned as well how our personalities had been forged by past challenges, our problems not identical, but the outcomes shared. We grew to appreciate in each other those obstacles each had to overcome to reach the place where we met. If Kevin and I first bonded on our Chicago tour five years before, we cemented it bit by bit with all of the little moments we spent together in creative partnership. Often these moments came while walking down the street or yelling over loud music on the dance floor. I remember one conversation in particular happening in a car, as they so often did in my high school years with Frank or Lawrence. Or maybe my memory has placed Kevin and me in a car because the conversation felt like one of those high school moments where we forge our identities, the type of place that, as adults, we tend only to revisit in times of crisis.

I remember us confirming what we already knew about each other: we were people-pleasers. Kevin, the good boy from a working-class home, the responsible one who had consistently held a job since the age of fourteen (one at a donut shop where he had to get up at three in the morning as in the commercial:

"Time to make the donuts . . ."). He who always delivered the birthday, Christmas, and Mother's Day gifts on time, and went beyond expectation in selecting their contents, like with that skirt he found for me. Late to come out to the world as gay, and later still to his born-again Christian parents, he stalled his own rebirth as a queer adult, knowing that if he came out to them, they would certainly condemn him to hell. They couldn't possibly understand the magnitude of the sacrifice that he made in doing that.

I felt spoiled by comparison as I always did, but he never said I was. I felt I had to be all things—the pretty one, the smart one, the funny one, the good one. Being the fuckup was never an option for either of us. On that day I think I told him about the self-image issues, about being under the microscope of adolescence and in the fishbowl of ballet at the same time. About the eating disorder, my first diet and hating my body. Hating myself. Hating the nose on my face, and the quiet corroboration of that by my parents. That I could be and should be "fixed." The nose job at sixteen. And then the weird shame spiral of the girl-who-hates-herself-for-hating-herself.

We both tried to be perfect for our parents, who had sacrificed so much to give us the lives we led. We were charming and accommodating, accomplished and helpful. And underneath that we were also sad and tired. This same commonality I had found with Frank and with Lawrence—inspiration, aspiration, and exhaustion. Our time in that car, if we were in a car at all, must not have lasted long. We were busy. If we had borrowed a car that day, it must have been to do some of the endless list of show-production errands. We must have found a magical and concise way to communicate all that we needed each other to know. All I know is, after that day we came away with a kind of shorthand. We had a tether, a common thread, just like in the dance we had made.

♔ ♔ ♔

Meanwhile, the creative machinery kept rolling along as we delivered drag numbers to the stage at the Stud. I couldn't get enough of performing at the 'shack, and my drag persona Glory Holesome found her way onstage practically every week, often with Kevin who, after his debut as Celine Solution at the Faux Queen Pageant, had become Falsetta Knockers. When Heklina offered me the chance to co-host Trannyshack for the first time, in 2003, I nabbed it, and with it, my first opportunity to choose the evening's theme. Having been inspired in the past by The Steve Lady's number in which she played a giant Barbie, by my own childhood fantasies of my toys having parties while I slept, and by our recent mannequin number, I wanted to see a whole evening of drag performances inspired by toys. Welcome to "Glory Holesome's Toy Box."

For the opening number of my co-hostessing debut, Falsetta and I would perform a duet to Roxy Music's maudlin song "In Every Dream Home a Heartache," one of the handful of creepy pop paeans to sex dolls. We would reprise the idea of eroticism between inanimate objects that we had evoked with our store window number, but this would also hint at "kai kai," slang for sex between drag queens. Though sibling-like in our personal relationship and never sexually involved, as drag queens Kevin and I loved the idea of kai kai as it was somehow one of the only acts capable of scandalizing our otherwise un-shockable drag cohort.

I would play the unglamorous, iconic first-aid practice dummy known as Resuscitation Annie and Falsetta would embody a cheap vinyl sex doll, the object of my kai kai affection. I already had Annie's mangy blonde wig stuffed in the bottom of my drag box. Her dorky blue sweat suit materialized instantly on the front rack of the first thrift store we walked into. The sweat suit, plus a bald cap over my hair with the wig slapped askew over it, my entire face covered in a thick layer of unblended, un-contoured pancake makeup, and I was done.

Falsetta's look, equally iconic, was not so easy. Kevin immediately went to one of those dodgy shops on Polk Street and bought a cheap inflatable sex doll, thinking that we might construct a costume out of the materials. But as soon as we got her out of the box, we found it would be impossible, as she was far smaller than human scale and her cheap material, though plastic, was not at all elastic. So, as he often does, Mr. David saved the day, this project just weird enough for him to agree to at the eleventh hour. David knew he couldn't construct anything wearable out of the doll we had already bought, but he took her anyway as inspiration and set to work, producing a beautifully hideous concoction out of peach-colored PVC. He actually did salvage the parts of the doll that he could, cleverly attaching the inflator nozzle to the back and sewing on her pink private parts in all of the right (or, really, wrong) places. Though Mr. David has the skills to make a PVC unitard look like a second skin, this one was ill-fitting in a most specific way, the seams perfectly imperfect, the whole thing making Falsetta look stiff and uncomfortable, like a "real" cheap blow-up doll.

Falsetta starts the number slumped and draped in my lap, Kevin using his expert physical theater training and rigorous focus to appear lifeless. Between the lines of the Roxy Music song, its blank, morose delivery well-paired with my vacant dummy countenance, I blow into the inflation tube on Falsetta's back. She comes to life little by little, lifting her body and then stopping in an intricate choreography of imaginary shared breath. She pops up completely only at the last minute for the long guitar solo that ends the song. Falsetta's one prop is a toy blow-up guitar strapped across her body, which I kneel and inflate in imitation of David Bowie and Mick Ronson's infamous seventies guitar/fellatio insinuation. The part of Falsetta's look that everyone sees at the last moment, the real punch line of the number, is the part that's always most disturbing on a sex doll (even on today's

high-end Real Doll). Not her sex, not even her blank stare. Her mouth.
To create that uncanny cavern of the blow-up doll orifice, Kevin's
design mind births a brilliant solution. When Falsetta stands, she
reveals the Pepto-Bismol pink plastic maw we managed to salvage.
In order to support it, her mouth, which hangs open the entire time
she is onstage, is stuffed with a female condom. Disgusting.

For the 'shack's semi-annual Duets night, Falsetta and I devised a Peter Pan and Tinkerbell number, me in a rare drag king appearance as Peter Pan, and Falsie as Tinkerbell. We also featured our friend Mike, a big adorable Texas boy as a beefy blonde Wendy, nude under a see-thru nightie.

Our song is "You've Got a Friend," the scene opening with
Wendy leaning on a mimed windowsill mooning over Peter and lip-
synching Carole King's sweet, sincere vocals.

For my entrance as Peter Pan, we mix in the James Taylor
version old-school style onto a cassette, by pressing the pause button
and changing the record, creating a clunky soundtrack that gives
the impression that so many Trannyshack performances gave, that
of earnest community theater. Wendy and I scarcely have a moment
to strike up our romance before Falsetta-as-Tinkerbell stumbles
onstage, drunk and tearful with smeared mascara and a heart tattoo
bearing the name "Pete." Tink removes a handle of gin from a paper
bag, takes a swig, clobbers and knocks out Wendy with the bottle, and
then pukes into the bag. Kevin uses split pea soup as Tinkerbell's stage
vomit, and for her voice we mix in the Carole King version of the
song again, this time sped up from 33 to 45 rpm so that she sounds
like the amped-up angry fairy she is. The number ends with Tink and
Pete spitting in each other's faces until Wendy comes to, takes off her
panties, and stuffs them into Tink's mouth yelling "Die fairy, die!" so
she and Pete can live happily ever after.

After that dark ending, Falsetta and I hung out at the club for the rest of the night with each other's spit lingering on our faces, mine with the bonus of Tinkerbell's split pea soup puke. You've got a friend, girl.

For the next duet night Kevin and I continued to revel in drag's possibilities for twinning.

Donning complementary black-and-white looks, we trade lyric lines in a sassy indie rock song about the easy come/easy go travails of modern love. We lob our lip-synched words of mounting frustration at two cute, slight boys, culminating in our grabbing them by the fronts of their shirts, each of us picking them up with one hand, the scoundrels terrified and squirming in the air above the heads of the audience. The boys are audience plants being secretly lifted from the ground by two sturdy guys who blend into the crowd so as to create our illusion of the superhuman strength of women scorned.

For our next twin adventure, "Tired," we presented ourselves as a conjoined creature in kinky nurse drag. We wore shabby blonde wigs (the one I had worn as Resuscitation Annie having a twin of her own) and turned some leftover white shirt collars into nurse hats. We covered our nipples in red glitter and threw on shiny red panties from the dollar store and, standing side by side, bound our inside legs together (my right and Kevin's left) with wide red elastic. To finish the look, we shared a pair of white patent leather lace-up stripper boots on our outside legs and a pair of red low-heeled Mary Janes on our inside feet, becoming a lumbering creature only able to move our one big middle leg in unison and our two outside legs in an off-kilter cannon rhythm. In the Studio we experimented with the movement potential of our strange setup and discovered that the limitation was generative, as limitation often is. We found that either of us was able to shift weight onto the outermost leg and hoist the other onto her hip so the top, boot-clad leg could fly into the air. The maneuver, which seemed impossible, thrilled me to a squeal the first time we accomplished it, and also felt surprisingly secure. This somehow seems like a symbol for our friendship—the generative power of obstacles, the physics of togetherness, the alchemy of trust.

When we performed "Tired" as a piece in a theater, the size

and sight lines of the space allowed us full use of the floor, which we did our best to exploit.

Performing backward rolls from upstage with our middle legs banded together becomes a weighty, ponderous process that we milk for comedy. When we arrive downstage, we maneuver ourselves to face the audience and, flopping onto our backs, cross one high-heeled boot over the other to reveal red electrical tape on the soles that we've fashioned into the shape of lips, turning our boots into faces. We've recorded lines for our puppet-boots to recite, based on annoying excuses that fall from the mouths of our flakiest friends.

"Oh gurl, I'm sorry I missed your show, but I got home from work and I was so tired."

We add a retort that we wish we had license to use on those deadbeats, in the snappy thirties Hollywood vocal style we love.

"Why, you can say that again, Mary; you are tired." And then an "I never" gasp for the offended shoe.

The song we use is "Entertain Me" by Soft Cell, an anthem to the seen-it-all, done-it-all jadedness of clubland. We premier the piece in a queer dance festival, where we think it will be well placed, but where it just doesn't land. The audience is much more sincere and far less campy than we had assumed. They don't get us. Back to the 'shack we go, where we know our people will eat it up, but a problem remains. How to do a version on that tiny stage?

The perfect placement came soon in the form of "Tired Night," a theme the 'shack dragged out once a year, a kind of purging of all of the overdone, overexposed, super-trendy or tacky things that people secretly loved—the lines between love and hate, genius and stupid, tired and treasured always as smeary and smudgy in the drag club as a good smoky eye makeup look. On this night a smarty-pants art queen might lip-synch to Celíne Dion's "It's All Coming Back to Me Now" or the insufferable electronic dance music cover of the perennial prom ballad of our youths, "We're in Heaven"—a giddy groan-fest.

Though our "tired number" was not really a *tired number*,

but a number on the theme of being tired and wanting to be mean about it, it fit right into the evening. Having nixed the rolling on the floor part and perched ourselves on barstools for the shoe puppetry, it also fit onto the stage. Afterward, Heklina looked at us in mock horror and called us out: "That wasn't tired. It was fierce. Too fierce! Too Fierce!" she faux-scolded, wagging her Lee press-on in our faces.

With that we were ready to head full gallop into our next project, which would be a big one: *Future Perfect*, an evening-length work focused on the concepts of style and editing, taking its text from legendary fashion editor-in-chief Diana Vreeland's memos to her staff at *Vogue* and from William Strunk Jr. and E.B. White's *Elements of Style*, the tiny gem of a style guide for writers. We used our heady inspiration to create a comic blend of scenes: an adagio of modeling poses and gestures culled from classic *Vogue* spreads performed in our now signature white underwear to a tune from one of Bach's *English Suites*, a love duet based on hyphenated words, and monologues about how our propensity for good grammar or fashion editing had abetted poor decision-making. We realized early in our studio process that our piece needed two additional characters who would function as authorities and arbiters to assist in the journeys of our every-man and-woman, a Vreeland and a Strunk/White to guide us from on high, rendered on two video screens. Glamamore was the natural fit for Vreeland, the fact that her alter-ego Mr. David had already signed on to create costumes notwithstanding. Glamamore owned the role, recreating the hairstyle, the makeup, a chic gray and red wool skirt suit, and most importantly Vreeland's singular combination of hauteur and grooviness. Actor Richard Louis James played Strunk/White as gruff yet lovable, with just the right amount of authoritative gravitas as he laid down the grammatical law.

It is a testament to our love for each other that Kevin and I are still friends after having spent so much creative time tied, bound, and strapped together. When the time came to cue up the music, answer the door buzzer, or take a sip of water during those urgent studio hours, we scooted across the floor as one unit in whatever getup we had concocted, only going through the formality of casting off our shared garments for bathroom breaks.

A filmmaker friend hired us to dance in a music video. She would film us underwater and then photoshop out all of the bubbles from our noses and mouths so that we looked like we were flying through air. We arrived on the set, which was the swimming pool of a backyard in Palo Alto, on a sunny but crisp March day. The film crew greeted us from the pool, all of them in wetsuits.

"H-h-h-h-hi you g-g-g-g-guys," said the filmmaker.

"P-p-p-p-put your st-t-t-t-uff inside." The homeowners thought the shoot was a day later and had neglected to turn on the heat in the pool.

"It's n-n-n-n-not th-th-th-that b-b-b-bad," she sputtered out from between her bluish lips.

Hoping to make swift work of the shoot, Kevin and I talked through the choreography once more before getting into costume, and then tried not to think too hard before plunging into the pool. As soon as I hit the cold water, my brain shut off. We had about four minutes in us before we would have to get out and warm up. On the first round, we discovered that the hot tub, which was only a few degrees warmer than the pool, actually warmed us. For a minute. After the second round of filming, we started losing heat fast. In order to warm up we had to get out of our freezing costumes and into a hot shower, but realized that if we each did that, we would quickly exhaust the hot water, and whoever had to wait would end up freezing even more, so we stripped off our clothes and sat naked in the bathtub together like toddler siblings with the steaming shower running over us.

Kevin and I came to know each other in that way only

dance partners or lovers can, becoming familiar not only with friend-level likes and dislikes, but with the relative heights of our pelvises, the smell of each other's breath after three cups of coffee and not enough water (not to mention fake pea soup puke), the smell of bodies after three hours of dancing, all of the small physical manifestations of frustration when the going is tough, and conversely, the bodily joys of the breakthrough.

Intimacy, especially without boundaries, certainly can breed contempt, to paraphrase some cynic, but as a person who thrives in loving friendships, and whose work relationships are almost all friendships anyway, intimacy is air and food and water to me. But in all of my intimate relationships I have found that civility, even formality, is the glue. Though sometimes catching a whiff of each other's farts and BO was unavoidable, Kevin and I tried our best always to value respect for each other above all. After the intense periods of intimate studio work concluded on the last night of a show—the daily phone calls, the shared fears, frustrated tears and loopy tech-rehearsal giggle fits—we would look at each other fondly over the last post-show drink and say, "Talk to you in a week, Mary. Maybe two."

When it was great, it was great, our two wildly different sets of skills complementing each other, each giving the other what we were missing and together giving the process and project what it needed. Kevin would come in prepared with a scene in mind and begin to stage us in it, and later I would go into a corner and conjure some dance moments through improvisation. We came up with some amazing stuff, and it is still a mystery how we did it. Performance creation, image-making and choreography are like that, processes that exist in a universe of their own logic, sometimes with a kind of postpartum amnesia setting in when the work is done, the memory of labor pain fading away.

But as in any relationship, sometimes we struggled to understand and appreciate each other's way of thinking. Kevin is not only a talented performer and actor, but also a painter and graphic designer who minored in math. As such, he possesses one of those minds that thrives on matters of space. He can conceive of a space from all directions without having to be in it. Kevin is all about precision, making a choice and committing to it, honing and whittling the joints so that it is seamless, trimming the excess so that it's tight. Though he is an expert talker in the relaxed flow of party conversation, he is not fond of improvisation in the theatrical context.

I too cherish precision and derive real joy from the practice of editing, but I have to arrive at the thing to be edited through physicality. It isn't that I particularly love to improvise in the dance studio, but rather that I must. I don't know what I want to do until I try something. Thus, I can be an infuriatingly flexible decision-maker, especially when time is of the essence, which, in the dance studio, rented by the hour, it almost always is.

It began during a two-week residency in one such dance studio: Hagen & Simone's decline. Our assignment at the end of the two weeks was to show a ten-to-fifteen-minute sketch of a piece. The residency prided itself on being a crucible of low-tech, low-stakes creative exploration. That said, the "showing" was really a show, to which the paying public was invited. *No pressure, really*. I was free and easy about it, excited to experiment and show whatever we came up with during the luxurious stretches of subsidized time we were granted in our new lab, comfortable with the possibility that our showing might fail a little.

Meanwhile, Kevin was all in to make something as brilliant as possible during our precious two weeks, sure as they were to fly by. Thinking of the audience, Kevin kept in mind that they were paying for what we delivered and deserved our best efforts. I imagine sometimes my looseness seemed lackadaisical to him, and I know also that sometimes his intensity inclined me to tense up, inhibiting my best thinking. Because he always came to the Studio prepared with a vision of what would look good, and it always did (like that spot-on pencil skirt), his vision often won out. My tendency toward "I really don't know if this will work, but let's try it?" often consigned untried material to the cutting-room floor. In Kevin's mind, two weeks was not enough time to fuck around, but in my mind that was precisely what those two weeks were for.

We ended up producing something strange and funny, which we called *Help Wanted*, and hoped to turn into an evening-length piece. Meanwhile, we were invited to create something for a festival at one of the bigger contemporary art centers in San Francisco. For that we made a whole other piece, for ourselves and twenty-three dancers, called *The Excused*, a meditation on the lines between civility and etiquette and what it means to be American. The process was like a big party/workshop/team-building exercise, and the performance opportunity was unprecedented. In the middle of the process, though, I landed another once in a lifetime chance, to perform at the Coachella festival with a musician I admired. This would take me away for a week at a crucial point in our process. I went. But in so doing broke our vow not to take each other for granted.

Kevin was understandably peeved, as I had fled and left him to care for the fledgling. That baby, our show, made under duress, though at times stunning (it's hard not to love the spectacle of twenty-three people moving in unison), came off to me as prissy and overdetermined, heavy on explication—too much telling and not enough showing. We completed the assignment and earned a solid C. Our biggest venue yet, but not our best work, which still stings a little.

After *The Excused*, we took our usual post-process week apart and then met up on a sunny day in a park. We both knew what was coming, but Kevin initiated it: we were breaking up. We both cried, having to mourn even though both of us knew it was for the best. We both knew, even before that moment, we wanted radically different things. I had been ready to settle down and keep making art babies, to move through the difficulty and start planning for the future so we could build something bigger. Kevin wanted to be free to be in other projects, to see other people as it were; and indeed throughout our creative relationship he had been working a lot as an actor—shining brighter in each role, and it was time for him to focus on that. And he, unlike me, found that being the one responsible for a project snuffed the spark of joy for him. He was content to lend his voice and talents to an ensemble, letting the director take the credit—and shoulder the burden.

I had a bigger ego in that department, having realized over the years that even if I didn't always know in the thick of the process what a work would become, I wanted my name on it as its creator. I'd learned that laboring as so many actors and dancers do, under the guise of collaborator only to watch the choreographer or director take the credit, filled me with resentment and shut down my creativity. Kevin suggested that I focus on the solo artist path, that I free myself from our literal and figurative tethers.

But there was something besides creative differences, which Kevin brought up in the most loving way he could, another reason for his ending our working relationship. "Mo . . ." Kevin said, choking back tears, this moment too serious for him to call me Mary. "I . . . I can't be around you when you're beating yourself up. It's too hard. I can't work; I can't live with that in the room. I love you, but I just can't."

That ancient issue, my self-loathing, still occasionally seeped, still does seep (seldom, but still . . .) like a toxic sludge into my otherwise healthy source. In the thick of a process, I sometimes revert back to that dysmorphic thirteen-year-old. As we reviewed video of *Future Perfect*, my demon, fully revealed by the garish floodlight of editorial focus, snarled and snapped. *Look at you! Why would you be so insane as to put yourself in this position, on a stage for everyone to see? The camera adds ten pounds!* My demon feeds on video.

Even then, over fifteen years ago, video was an important performance-making tool. Now that everyone walks around with high-quality video cameras in their pockets, what is for me an excruciating step in the process has become essential, even threatening to replace the magic of live experience. I know I'm not alone in my terror of watching myself. Actors who can't stand the sight of their faces or sound of their voices are legion, and if a trigger exists, an understandable one would certainly be seeing oneself on video in the bra and white granny panties that were my costume in *Future Perfect*. But the actors we hear stories about have directors and editors to do the close watching for them. Someone like me, who insists upon being both creator and performer, has no such luxury. Ultimately, I had to put on my big girl panties and be willing to watch myself dance around in them. After all, I chose them. The anything-goes playground of the drag club had helped me vanquish enough of my body dysmorphia to say "fuck it, if the piece calls for a costume of white granny panties, be bold!" But the voice that dominated my internal dialogue after the piece was finished was one that desperately wanted everyone to like it, to like me, who feared that all our hard work might have been in vain. My fear response tried to protect our collaborative work by subjecting Kevin to my ridiculous self-denigration, but my comment undermined all of its ardor. I had called our baby ugly.

We two perfectionists had named our piece *Future Perfect*. Our shared issue had even provided material. One of the moments featured me attempting to refine a ballet arabesque while Kevin circled me, writing notes on a clipboard, sticking gold stars on various parts of my body.

I have since learned that there are two brands of perfectionism, one more functional than the other. Kevin's brand pushes him forward: he prepares well, works diligently, often obsessively, and takes real joy in a job well done. Mine is the more crippling brand, and I have learned over the years

that its unmanageability mutates like a virus. Seeing this kind
of perfectionism in other artists reminds me again and again to
silence my self-critical remarks at crucial moments. I have learned
to fake it till I make it (a recovery slogan, as perfectionism does
hold its own in the league of addictions). I once commended an
artist on a performance she had directed. It involved dancers not
only moving, but singing and speaking, to gorgeous effect. She
responded, "Are you sure they didn't sound like shit?", swiftly
fouling my experience of her work and making me feel sorry for
her performers. I vowed never to perpetuate that kind of thing.
If I can't actually stop hating myself, I can at least stop telling
people I do.

It was one thing for Kevin and me to talk about my issue
in a car, or a bar, a space reserved for friendship. It was another
thing entirely for him to see the demon in action, spewing her
version of split pea soup vomit all over him. I thought I had
hidden her relatively well, but no. She had poisoned the Studio
and threatened to drive away one of my favorite people in the
world.

The paths of art and showbiz history are littered with
the wreckage of relationships bulldozed by projects, from the
masterpiece to the disaster-piece. I am sure there are great artists
who consciously sacrificed relationships, marriages, friendships
for the sake of an object or film or book we now cherish. Kevin
and I could have gone on making good art together until we
hated each other. He could have dumped me as a friend like
Frank had, philosophical difference trumping creative kinship.
He could have ended our working relationship with some
version of "it's not you, it's me" and everything would've been
fine. Instead, he stood strong through his tears and, like the good
improviser he didn't think he was, said "Yes, and . . . yes and
here's the thing. It's also you." Kevin took to heart the deep sense
of civility we had always valued in our work and our relationship
and acted from there. His words, his willingness to take action

by speaking them, helped me see that my habits of self-loathing were also actions, actions with consequence. The consequence was that Hagen & Simone had to end. Kevin and I realized that our friendship was more important than anything we might make in the Studio. Our friendship was the higher calling. But because he was one of those few close enough to have seen me in its deepest thrall, Kevin was able to help me stare down my monster, and in a sense we threw Hagen & Simone to her as a sacrifice. By giving me the gift of information, Kevin gave me tools to vanquish the monster and go forth on my own creative path, proving himself a brave, true, and lasting ally. You've got a friend.

PAGEANT III:
YOU'RE A BUTTERFLY

Kevin and I had been obsessed with the soft rock hits of the seventies. We walked down the street after drinks one night with Karl in 2003, singing a medley: "Sometimes when we touch, I think the honesty's too much/If a picture paints a thousand words, then why can't I paint you/I have a name, I have a name/Butterflies are free to fly. Fly away!" *Oh my Goddess, yes. That was it!* "Someone Saved My Life Tonight" by Elton John. Tribulation, transformation, redemption, liberation—it was all there. My pageant number danced through my mind in the form of a pop song-length ballet.

I knew from the beginning that my pageant number must involve ballet. Drag had gotten me back up on my old pointe shoes and allowed me to reclaim my training. I realized, through performing in drag as a fake ballerina, I really wasn't as bad as I had thought I was when I put the killer satin slippers away for what I presumed would be the last time.

I also knew I wanted to debut a new drag name over the course of my act, a risky maneuver. One queen had tried it and failed—spectacularly and splendidly—but still, it was considered a curse. I decided to go for it regardless, assuming there was no way I would win. Besides, I was over my name and had found one that fit me much better.

Not everyone sticks the landing with their first drag name. Many a queen has called "Do-over!" I didn't expect to fall hopelessly in love with drag and find a deep, long-term relationship. I didn't know until I was in it. I named myself Glory Holesome without considering the future. At the table in college, Jason used to sing Laura Brannigan's "Gloria" as "Glory Hole," with the same alto lady-power bravada. We loved joking about glory holes. In the middle of the AIDS crisis, when I was in college, the glory hole represented the dirtiest, most hedonistic aspects of gay culture, the things that terrified both the religious right and the assimilationist gays. And nice girls like me. My taking the name Glory Holesome showed that I had enough knowledge of gay culture to be cavalier about claiming an aspect of it, but the reference to wholesomeness admitted that I had no business claiming the first part. It telegraphed that even though I knew *of* glory holes, I did not know *from* glory holes.

Kevin found my new name. He stumbled on it during a trip to see his family back East, driving by a strip mall. *Fauxnique*, enticing the eye to a fancy sign in the cluster of boring businesses. He called immediately.

"Too bad you already have a drag name."

"Not anymore I don't!"

Fauxnique was too good. "Faux": French for "artificial." My real name, but fake, and very close to "Faux Queen."

"I'm going mild for it, Glory Holesome," said Heklina. "Going mild was the opposite of "going wild." She thought Fauxnique sounded "like a cleaning product." I thought, *Perfect*. Marc said it was a keeper because it has both an *X* and a *Q*, the most glamorous letters. *Even better*.

I also loved the provocation "faux" offered, troubling my identity as a would-be "real woman" with the idea of the "faux."

Most importantly, Fauxnique speaks to artifice and authenticity, and authenticity through artifice. The culture portrays drag as frivolous fun, but it is also serious art in extravagant disguise. Claiming the fakery emboldened me in the same way that drag itself did. If I proclaimed that this was all fake, it let me and my audience off the hook and left space for surprise. The name was a tactic that would work in multiple situations.

♕ ♕ ♕

Fauxnique allows me to play with ideas of belonging or feeling like I don't. It evokes the feeling I had when I realized that the pretend-neutral version of authenticity espoused by the post-Judson contemporary dance world was not mine. Fauxnique articulates the authenticity I found in drag.

♕ ♕ ♕

Changing the drag name fit with the transformation theme of my pageant number.

Any good character has a backstory, so I wrote a mythology for this new drag queen I was creating. "Fauxnique" would be a tragicomic figure. She would be a refugee from Fauxqueenistan, a made-up, vaguely Slavic country (some of my own people were Czech), at war with neighboring Dragzakistan. Hers would be a familiar story of an immigrant leaving the squalid certainty of her place of origin for an uncertain, but aspirational, future. She would also be slumming it: a prima ballerina in her homeland now reduced to performing at a tawdry drag club. Drag and camp always love to denigrate themselves—think John Waters proudly taking up the nicknames "Pope of Trash" and "Prince of Filth." A faux documentary would set the stage onto which Fauxnique would emerge at the end of her rope, exhausted, ready to end it all, anticipating more humiliations, and then she would emerge triumphant.

"Girl. Get your ideas out of your head and work them out. Now," urged Putanesca. Always the mother, Putanesca was there to fulfill a valuable role, to remind me of the obvious: if this was going to happen, I had to actually do it.

I couldn't wait to grab Mr. David and delve into the costume plan. We would make ample use of the reveal, with me entering in some kind of cocoon-like dress, naturally. I had just seen the documentary on Yves Saint Laurent, and was really into the weird crocheted and beribboned concoction from his legendary 1965 collection, a wedding gown with a hood that made the prospective bride look like a giant dildo cozy. Of course, Mr. David was totally into that bit of inspiration, and rendered it in oversized proportions, with a forty-inch hula hoop sewn into the hem for the first of several big reveals . . .

"Mary," said Mr. David, also fond of that archaic term of endearment, "you still need a swimsuit."

"I know! Okay, maybe Fauxqueenistan is near Siberia, and I need a hat and muff to go with the swimsuit look."

"I don't *mind* that," said Mr. David, waving his Nat Sherman, a half inch of ash dangling dangerously from the tip. This is what David says when he really likes an idea. "And they need to be ginormous! But your swimsuit will be *nothing*. A piece of elastic across your nipples and one across your vajay and one down the middle attached at the neck to keep it all in place. Your swimsuit will be exactly *five pieces* of two-inch wide black elastic! Oh, that makes me so *happy*." Mr. David loves math. "I'm gonna make you a ginormous muff to hang off your arm, Mary, big enough to cover your whole front. Then you'll open your arm and reveal your swimsuit which will be *nothing!*"

Fauxnique would enter the swimsuit competition unsmiling and Slavic and proceed to reveal an aggressively uncovered lady body to a mostly gay male audience. *Swimsuit competition duly subverted. Check.*

"Oh, oh! And let's cover me in a light dusting of fake snow!"

The collaborative nature of the pageant did not begin and end with costume design. The culture of the 'shack was both collaborative and competitive. The weekly Tuesday club was itself a kind of competition, a community of artists provoking and one-upping each other, each queen outdoing the last, but also there to offer you her eyelash glue if yours fell out of your purse. Perhaps because it grew out of this community, or because it began as an undermining of the pageant idea, the pageant itself was no different. I enlisted the help of fellow competitor Mercy Fuque, and she enlisted mine. I would help her with choreography, and she would help me with video. We made our mockumentary, emulating the somber tone of early 1990s BBC News docs on the Balkans. I had an English actor friend narrate it. His instruction was to slowly transform his delivery from somber narrator to showy emcee, his last words functioning as an introduction, using my new drag name: "Ladies & gentlemen, Fauxnique!"

The list of contestants included, besides me and Mercy Fuque, who was going political with her number, queering the Columbine tragedy to the song "I Don't Like Mondays," were Helium Heels, Kitten on the Keys, Buttlicka of Guerneville, and a queen who simply called herself Snatch.

Buttlicka of Guerneville worked a fright drag look, with a long, matted hairdo made up of at least four wigs, huge fake buck teeth, and novelty nerd glasses that magnified her eyes about five times their normal size. She pulled no punches, regularly turning out epic numbers on Tuesday nights at Trannyshack. For a Michael Jackson-themed night she chose the song from the movie *Ben* for which she built a huge wig with a little door that opened to reveal a cage with a live rat in it. Another night she fisted a giant disco ball full of chocolate pudding to the tune of "More More More." As far as I was concerned, Buttlicka was the one to beat or, um, lick.

THAT'S
PROBLEMATIC

I've always admired those girls who came from families with a lot of brothers. They always seemed so cool and resilient. The girls who played sports, the ones who were good at math and science, who dug out space for themselves in the trenches of male-dominated professions. The STEM girls, the volleyball girls. The real feminist warriors. I became a dancer, the femme-y opposite of a feminist trailblazer. Though dancing ballet gave me a kind of athleticism, and taught me to be hard on myself, I depended on criticism from teachers, which was really just approval-seeking. None of this led to real resilience.

I eventually accepted the fact that I cry easily, but I desperately wanted some Teflon cool. I wanted the bullying comments of kids at school, or just all the *feelings* I felt every day, to glide off of me so I could move forward. I wanted to be able to stand against a razzing from my aunt or grandfather without getting upset, but I never could. My mom tried to toughen me up to no avail. I stayed soft and porous.

When I entered the drag scene, I was suddenly one of those women. I found myself in a male-dominated profession, with my family of drag sisters cast as the rambunctious brothers I never had. The 'shack was an irreverent zone with space for everyone but no place for preciousness. Though I have described these queens as kind hearted art mamas, they were also warriors. They had survived a plague, and humor had kept them alive. As one friend put it: "If I can't make an AIDS joke, it's not my revolution."

Heklina's refrain to me, apropos of nothing, or maybe the same way any ordinary person would say "take care," was "Please don't get AIDS."

"Bye Hekles!"

"Bye! Please don't get AIDS, Glory Holesome!"

If we happened to be on our way out the door together, she would say, "Hey, do you want to do the AIDS Walk with me this year?" Then we would start walking and she would say, "There. Ha HA! Hahahahahah!" Of course, any time Hekles rode her bike, she was on, you guessed it, the AIDS Ride. If she was stressed, she was "living on two T-cells and a prayer."

But the queen of the AIDS joke was Timmy Spence, or, "Tammers." As a longtime survivor who had practically come back from the dead, this was his right if it was anyone's. "Ugh," he would say, in his gravelly voice, "my AIDS is killing me! Oh . . . did I say my *AIDS*? Oh, sorry, honey; I meant my feet."

One night at the 'shack, when Tammers was co-hosting with Heklina, the San Francisco Gay and Lesbian Historical Society paid the club a special visit. Tammers took the stage and said, "Well, apparently the San Francisco Gay and Lesbian Historical Society is in the house. Now, I don't know why San Francisco *needs* a gay Historical Society. I mean, it's pretty simple: you come to San Francisco, you turn gay, you get AIDS, you're History." Followed by a long silence. And then boos. Too soon. Too far.

Tammers once did a drag performance in which she sprinkled a daisy with water she had been holding in her ass for an entire song. Years later the legend of this performance would travel to San Mateo County and threaten Mr. Spence's day job as a high school math teacher. But if Mr. Spence had been my math teacher, I might have become one of those STEM girls. Tammers should have had a drag daughter named Daisy STEM.

At the 'shack, performance was often something one pulled out of one's ass. Figuratively and literally. To commemorate our nation's independence, a queen called Deer slapped on some lipstick, threw on a cowboy hat, squeezed his thighs together with his cock and balls crammed between them and took to the stage to lip-synch LeAnn Rimes's version of the national anthem. On "Oh say does that star-spangled" she turned around and began to pull what would be recognizable first by its stars as a petite version of Old Glory out of her butt. On LeAnn's dipped high note on "Free-EEEEE" the entirety of the bandanna-sized emblem emerged, and then Deer waved it in the air with the wistful countenance of a proud patriot.

At Peaches Christ's "Filthiest Person Alive" contest, held before a screening of *Pink Flamingos* naturally, Renttecca pulled a pair of giant blue balls out of her ass to "Don't It Make My Brown Eyes Blue" and then held them up in front of her own eyes like a demented Little Orphan Annie, and then Raya Light squirted liquid into her butt, squirted it out into a martini glass, and drank it. Raya Light won, and has since retained her title as "San Francisco's Filthiest Person Alive." She hasn't rested on her laurels. I have since seen her up the filth ante by eating live earthworms onstage to "I've Never Been to Me." True feminist catharsis for me.

When I got deeper into the scene at Trannyshack and all the queens got to know me—and to know me is to see me cry—Heklina chuckled, "Aww-w-w-hahahah. You're so sensitive," as if I were something alien but entertaining, like a cat in a dress. Then she would say, "Well, like it or not, you're swimming with the sharks, Fish!" followed by her usual "ha-HA-HA-HA. Ha-Ha!" In fact, knowing I was a feminist, she took every possible opportunity in my presence to refer or allude to "fish" (that crude misogynist nickname old-school queens use). I figured the only way forward was to beat her to it.

"Heklina, guess what I had for lunch today?"

"What?"

"Tuna! ha-HA-HA-HA. Ha-Ha!"

Before the queens, my first gay big brother, the person who helped me get over myself and began to teach me the life-changing art of lightening up, was Rick. I met him when he started working with me at a semi-casual California Italian restaurant in downtown San Francisco in the early 1990s. Rick is handsome, "a poor-man's George Clooney," as he aptly describes himself. And charismatic. He ruled as soon as he arrived, having worked at Stars, an infinitely nicer place than ours, one of the famous spots that started the celebrity chef trend. His first day of training began and ended in five seconds with him saying, "Mmm-hmm, I know how to waitress; just tell me where you keep the sugar packets." And he took over like wildfire. Rick always said "waitress." "Waitress" really was where he started to pull at the tight seams of my newly constructed identity as a staunch feminist. Even though "server" had only just been adopted as the respectful, gender-neutral title for the thankless position we all held, I secretly dropped it for "waitress." "Waitress" felt campy and funny and fun, whereas "server" was part of a computer network. If strapping, empowered Rick could have fun being a waitress, maybe I could, too. As a waitress, Rick embodied the sassiness of the 1970s TV archetype, Flo, from *Alice*, making every exchange with his tables a vignette, complete with an authentically produced laugh track, but maintaining just enough formality not to get in trouble. He was also a money-making *machine*.

"May we have some ketchup?" the Witchita couple would ask.

"Oh my God!" Rick would exclaim, rolling not just his eyes, but his entire upper body, "Why does the *waitress* have to *get everything*?"

And then he would cackle, flash his gap-toothed grin as he handed them their ketchup, and they would empty their wallets, probably later telling all their friends back home how they had *gone to San Francisco and met this GAY waiter and he was kind of mean but also kind of nice and so handsome! What a hoot!* I could never get away with the shit he got away with. I tried and failed once, miserably. Rick overheard me and repeated my bit back to me. I was mortified. It sucked. I had bombed in my audition for the part of sassy gay waitress, so I left the role to him.

Once, I asked Rick to be a second pair of eyes for a grant application I was working on. "This is great," he said. "Did a *boy* help you write it?" Being friends with Rick gave him full license to make fun of everything about me in addition to the low-hanging fruit of feminism: my sensitivity, my seriousness, my good grammar, and my style, which at that point was going through a utilitarian phase. Post-collegiate and post-grunge, I was inspired by the minimalism of Helmut Lang, the audacious hideousness of Prada, and my own poverty. My hair was short— Mia Farrow in *Rosemary's Baby* short. I favored a tight-fitting long-sleeve crewneck T-shirt, a slim bootcut pant and a square-toe Beatle boot, all in black. Sometimes I wore a vintage men's disco shirt if I was feeling quirky. Dour to quirky was the range. The closest I veered into cute or sexy was when I wore a child's soccer shirt, which problematized the sexiness. I needed people to know that *I* knew that sexiness was problematic. Quirky.

Chris Kraus in *I Love Dick* calls quirky "that word that people use to render difficult and driven women weightless." At that point in my life (my early twenties) I was in a constant struggle with my own difficulty and drive, unknowingly unweighting my gravitas with quirkiness. When Mitzi visited during that era, she said, "Would it kill you to put on a little lipstick? Please? For Mommy?" I felt like, *yeah Mommy, right now it would* literally kill me *to put on lipstick for you.* When my mom met Rick, they tussled like long-lost siblings.

"Mitzi!" Rick said, pointing to a dress in a window we passed. "That would look so great on you! You should see if they have it in your size. What are you, an eight?"

"Eight?!? Fuck you! I'm a six."

They both hooted with laughter.

My everyday coat then was a knee-length quilted navy-blue thing with a Nehru collar. I loved that it covered everything and was casually formal. "What is this *coat*?" Rick asked. I was ready for a compliment on its simple elegance, perhaps a query as to whether it was indeed Helmut Lang (I was serving severity, though I couldn't shake my love of fashion) but no. "Very . . . Wife. Of. Mao!" He wasn't wrong. My ascetic style was a reflection of my desire to be taken seriously. Kind of a Communist revolutionary impulse to be completely honest.

One afternoon Rick and I were traipsing around and popped into a trendy boutique. "Put. This. On!" he commanded, in his mock-bossy way, waving a flimsy chiffon blouse at me. "Gah! Okay!" I replied, just to humor him. At that point blouses were still pretty unthinkable, as we had just come out of grunge and were heading toward the faux-futuristic Y2K-anticipatory late nineties, but in seven years chiffon and pussycat bows would be everywhere.

I came out of the dressing room, having pulled the delicate blouse on over the threadbare old sports bra I was wearing (I had come straight from dance class as usual). "You. Look. Amazing! . . . but what is this *bra*?" he scoffed. "Take. It. Off!" I did as I was told. This was Rick's power, the same power he used on the tourist couples at the restaurant whom he convinced to order the fish special and most expensive wine on the menu plus appetizers and dessert. His mock bossiness always gave you the out to say "Fuck you!" like Mitzi had, but mostly Rick just made you want to live a little! I came out of the dressing room in the sheer blouse with no bra, feeling pretty damn fierce.

"Oh. My. GOD! Look at your TITS! Who knew? I don't

want to see you in a bra for . . . How old are you?"

"Twenty-four."

"Eleven years!"

I had to admit, it was so much better without the bra. It was a runway look on a girl with short hair and small boobs, not an everyday look for sure, but a European look, a look that said, *These are my tits and I am not afraid of them, or of you.* The old sports bra immediately seemed like an affront. I thought of so many other outfits that would benefit from my new brave bralessness. Yes, the feminists (including me) might be going, *Wait, you let some guy tell you what to wear?* Yes. Yes I did. File under "gay men helping me enjoy my body." It's a big file. Besides, in our own way, weren't Rick and I honoring the seventies bra burners?

Decades later, with my drag queen-enabled sass, I attempt the same thing Rick did to me when I confront adorable young men in the gay bars about their own fashion choices.

"Jason!"

"Justin."

"Ugh. Right, sorry I can't tell any of you apart because you are all just a mess of facial hair. Justin, honey, you're hurting my heart. You are hiding the best years of your face under that *stupid beard*!"

JasonJustin (or BryanRyan) just smiles sweetly and heads to his next assignation with the next beard-loving gentleman caller. Scruff, Grindr, Growlr, or whatever comes next, wins the day. I don't have the fashion authority that gay men have over me. It doesn't go both ways.

After Rick helped shake some of the preciousness out of me, the drag queens worked on it a little more. One of the few times Heklina really whomped me too hard, we were backstage before a performance and panel discussion at UC Berkeley in 2003. I was excited to talk to college kids about my pageant win and work, about "expanding notions" of drag. I was warming up my body, ready to put in my headphones and hit my lip-synch one more time. Heklina looked at me in the mirror. "You know Fauxnique," she said, "you're only a token. *Nothing* but a token." She emphasized "nothing" with a little Baby Jane trill. I was shocked. "Fish" was ridiculous, but "token" hit me in a soft place. *Am I really?* I thought. *Do other people think so? Am I kidding myself that I belong here?* It was also a tender moment. I'm always most vulnerable when I am about to go onstage. And that made me mad. *She's trying to throw me off my game. Fucking bitch!*

It dawned on me later: just as I warmed up with jumping jacks and lip-synch for my role as Dancing Drag Queen, Heklina warmed up for her role as Bitchy Emcee with cruelty. I was her backstage scratching post. Nothing personal.

However, I think Heklina showed her true colors when she stuck up for me during another panel discussion, on NPR when a caller compared my Miss Trannyshack pageant win to "a white woman winning Miss Black America." Heklina offered a kind and measured defense of me and my right to do drag, which also served to explain perhaps the most essential element of the 'shack and its pageant: that it existed in part to poke fun at everything we hold dear about gender.

When queens said to me, "Girl, you're so *sensitive*," it was with a ping of amused recognition. I would learn that some of them are themselves extraordinarily sensitive. I would also learn later that many of them actively engage in a program of supported sobriety, a program that as far as I know, cultivates real empathy. Through those queens and their tough love, I have managed to get a little more resilient. I wanted to cry backstage at Berkeley, but I didn't.

Now I'm witnessing a generation coming up that is, even to me, unbelievably sensitive. I respect and love them, and there's also a part of me that wants to help them to get stronger. But, now just like in the nineties, everything is problematic, even resilience itself. I get it. Those whom the culture has asked to be resilient (trans people, people of color) have done enough extra labor. Maybe I can take up some of the burden. I am proud of the ways in which I have become stronger, because I was such a wimp—so privileged, so precious. Now I can laugh at myself. Sometimes. Sometimes is as good as it's going to get.

A friend of mine said that irreverence is a privilege. I think he's partly right. When I was a young feminist, self-effacement seemed like a huge risk. Irreverence pulls and pokes at what we hold dear, and when that feels truly threatened, maybe it's harder to laugh. But irreverence also comes from pain. Maybe if what we hold dear is constantly under threat there is nothing to do but laugh. Or maybe it has nothing to do with pain or privilege and it is just about constitution, like how some people can hold their liquor and some people puke.

My sweet, smart husband, a man so sensitive he tattooed Joy Division lyrics on his arm as an adult, was doing the convulsive silent laugh at the breakfast table. I was like, "What?" and he showed me his phone: Instagram videos of people falling down in truly terrifying and horrific ways. Ways that you just don't know if they were okay after. I almost threw the phone at his head. I felt exactly like I did when I was seven and saw the punk kid with the safety pin through his cheek on TV. Terrorized.

I think maybe Marc likes to laugh at people falling down because he started going to Brazilian jiujitsu in his forties. Maybe every time he trains he feels like those people getting thrown off of things onto their heads. He knows what it's like to get smooshed. Every time he leaves for class, I say, in my best Carol Kane voice, "Don't get smooshed!" though I know indeed he will get smooshed. If I interrogate the source of my joking, it actually does come from a fear that someone will break his beautiful face. I have to joke about it in order to feel better. However, when he had a motorcycle, I would never have said, "Don't get smashed." I simply said, "Please be safe." The stakes felt too high to play around.

But falling down *is* funny. Dropping pants is funny.

Embarrassment is funny. Taboos are funny. Difference is funny. These are places where drag loves to play. As the saying goes, comedy is tragedy plus time. How much time is the question, I guess.

In its specific time and place, the context of Trannyshack, irreverence was healing. I can't imagine what it must have been like for these queens to see so many of their friends die during the worst years of the AIDS crisis. Well, I often did imagine it. For a time, I used to obsess about the fact that if I had been about ten years older than I am, almost all my friends would be dead. I had just missed the ravages of AIDS upon the generation before mine. It was a terrible, maudlin thought, one I had no right to be having, but I did have it. It was no wonder they all laughed at everything once everyone stopped dying. Who has time to quibble about language when at the height of AIDS you went to twenty funerals in one month? Or stopped counting altogether.

Out of these ruins grew the drag clubs that welcomed me, where everyone joked about AIDS. Had these queens been made radically inclusive by the tragedy they had lived through? Was it why they welcomed me? The white, liberal arts-educated women in my dance world talked incessantly about inclusivity and community, but they never seemed to be able to manage it in the same way that the drag queens did. Unlike in the dance world, at the drag club I was surrounded by people who were different from me in all kinds of ways. I had friends from all over the gender map, with many different shades of skin; friends who were twenty or thirty years older than I, or many years younger; friends from other countries, who grew up speaking different languages; friends from radically different educational and economic backgrounds. We were living inclusivity and diversity, not just talking about it. Not talking about it *at all* actually, just doing drag together. Inside of that inclusivity and diversity the queens played hard with stereotype and context.

♔ ♔ ♔

In 2002, Phatima hosted a night—the one I talk about in my previous "Art Damaged" chapter, for which I clowned Meredith Monk in my legacy panniers. "Avant Tard," it was called, a name and theme that bore Phatima's unmistakable sticky paw-print.

There were multiple things going on with the word "tard" and its use in our particular drag community. First, few people used it, and seldomly so. Vivian Bond used it as an act of comic resistance in the guise of her legendary character Kiki. Phatima owned it. She also created a character called "Retarded Panda," which consisted of her lolling around the stage to discordant experimental music in some punk approximation of bear drag while holding a microphone half an inch from her mouth and munching on leaves. Phatima was an edgy provocateur to be sure, but the point of using the word "retarded" was not to hurl it at others like a schoolyard epithet, much less to denigrate people with cognitive difference. Nor was her intention simply to shock. She sought to defiantly redeem it, much like we had adopted "queer."

Second, the community around the 'shack welcomed every kind of outsider, including those at the edges of what we now refer to as neurodivergence. Phatima was genuinely bizarre and had undoubtedly been on the receiving end of every version of the word "crazy." By self-identifying as a "tard," she also parsed an important element of her particular brand of crazy; though she often staged spectacles of self-harm and punk nihilism, she didn't have a mean bone in her body. In creating a night of drag performance called Avant Tard, Phatima used the word to celebrate her own difference as part of her artistic inventiveness, and being empathetic and generous invited other performers to do so as well.

Third, this gesture was indicative of the gleeful reclamation of problematic slurs that reached an apex at that time in drag clubland. On any given evening inside the safety of the Stud, you might hear, lovingly lobbed between friends, the words "tard, hooker, slut, tranny, faggot." A gorgeous pair of stilettos would be "cunty," a hilarious and intricate performance "stupid," a perfectly made-up face "disgusting." In this context, to be a "tard" meant to lovingly crush and smear good taste, good sense and seriousness, and to do so with a sense of humility. Being an art-damaged queen marked you as smart, but "tard" was a swift way to knock the wind out of the self-seriousness of art with the wisdom of the fool.

I saw the potential for a kind of deep self-reflective power in identifying as an avant-tard, art-damaged queen.

♔ ♔ ♔

When I started college, the term "political correctness" came into common use. Dating back to the Russian revolution of 1917, it was revived by 1970s lefties to poke fun at their own overserious comrades. To my older friends on campuses in the early 1980s, it signified shared values. But my friends and I (class of '92) had already begun finding ways to let a little steam out of our own PC pressure cookers. A few years later, the drag scene created a liberatory generative practice for me around that release.

Maybe I had always been inclined to appreciate irreverence. Despite the fact that my grandfather's needling attempts at toughening me up drove me to tears, I could also see how undeniably funny he was, a great storyteller with that Southern arsenal of colorful descriptors for everything from delicious pie ("Ooh-ee! That pie's so good, makes a boy wanna slap his mama!") to an aunt's unfortunate looks ("A'int Maybelle was uglier'n a mud fence.").

The late, great San Francisco queen Nikki Starr reminded me a little of that grandfather, my Papa Tom, with some of her descriptive sayings: "Heklina, you could swallow a whole woman, still not look like one." But I wonder if who she really resembled was the woman who raised him, Mary Swagerty. Nikki, a Black trans woman and drag queen, drag mother to Heklina and Renttecca, in her own way did what Mary Swagerty and so many Black women had done: raised other people's kids, gave proper nurturing to neglected little white boys.

Once, Nikki's drag daughter Renttecca co-hosted a night at the 'shack called "Ebonica Hanukkah." A night of Black/Jewish relations. Yes, that happened. Irreverence. Playing with difference. Different times.

I lip-synched Sandra Bernhard's rendition of "Me and Mrs. Jones," in which Sandy, herself Jewish, embodies a blues-singing Black lady. Sandy, in character, encapsulates the night's theme with her comment: ". . . me and my Jewish piano player, you know how we people get along *so well*." The performance landed. Our crowd was also Sandy's.

I came backstage. "Gurl," said Nikki, looking up at me from her chair with her amber-colored Bette Davis eyes, "A truck could run over your face, elephants walk all over it, and you'd still never be as ugly as Sandra Bernhard. She's the ugliest bitch ever sat on a commode."

I usually thought Nikki's sayings were hilarious. But not this one. I was bummed she met this tribute to my personal goddess with such basic meanness.

The comment harbored the tangled rat's nest of tyrannical beauty standards that ensnared us all: Nikki, Sandy, and me. Nikki, a Black trans woman drag performer in a world that undervalued her beauty and her life, calling Sandra Bernhard ugly. Sandra Bernhard, who built a singular career inside the beauty fascism of Hollywood, had caught that meaningless and mindless epithet before: "ugly," a tired old pie in the face from the patriarchy. She had refashioned it and served it back with her particular brand of savvy panache, not unlike a drag queen, exalting and celebrating her beauty ("I have one of those hard-to-believe faces. It's sensual, it's sexual . . ."). And me, the treasured white girl who was told she was pretty, but still never quite pretty *enough*. Who finally found a fitting role model in Sandra Bernhard and acceptance among drag queens.

Still, if we take Sandy out of it, there was something comfortingly familiar in Nikki's tone, despite how terrible her comment was. It could have come directly from my Papa Tom: "commode," an archaic Southern word for "toilet." It would not be enough to say "ugliest woman in the world," which is really what Nikki was saying. No, the baseness and universality of the toilet is essential. As is, I hate to admit, the word "bitch." "Bitch" has never been my favorite and I have yet to reclaim it, although now that I am a showgirl of a truly advanced age, it is what my body says to me when I have overworked her.

"Bitch," my body says in Nikki Starr's gravelly Southern drawl, or in Gina LaDivina's mellifluous meow, "Don't even think about kicking your leg up to your ear today."

A bitch on a commode is funnier than a woman on a toilet. However, and I will never be able to communicate this properly, Nikki somehow managed to say what she said with love. The same way that when my Papa Tom called Aunt Maybelle "uglier 'n a mud fence," he always followed it with "poor dear." In the "poor dear" that coats the insult with Southern sweetness also lies the drag queen read. (Of course, anyone raised by Southerners knows that "poor dear" and "bless your heart" also often mean "fuck you.")

Did Nikki really adhere to such a colorless standard of beauty? Was she just staying agile, throwing tired shade around as a backstage warm-up, to keep the good lines coming, as Heklina had done? Or perhaps the shade Nikki threw was a curveball meant for me, couched in a compliment, the way another friend sometimes said to me, "You're very pretty . . ." with an implied *but you're not very smart*. Maybe it contained a secret message: "You'll never be a real drag queen. Bless your heart."

☙ ☙ ☙

In 2014, the word "tranny" officially became a slur. At this point it is risky for me even to spell it out without asterisks. But, like it or not, it is part of my herstory. In the late nineties and into the aughts, "tranny" had been a word for the community, practically nonexistent to outsiders. When I entered the drag world, the word, though transgressive, was so generalized and casual a term of endearment that people used it almost as one would use "girl" today—that is, for pretty much everyone in the scene, myself included. It would be disingenuous for me to erase that moment and the words those generous people used as they welcomed me into their family.

Trans and gender-nonconforming leaders Kate Bornstein, Vivian Bond, Jack Halberstam, and Julia Serano all discuss the word expertly. Their opinions, while some differ from each other, comprise cogent, respectful, and open-minded thinking on the subject.

In my memory, it was on *Project Runway* when Christian Siriano started using "tranny" so loudly and out of context that, as Aunties Kate Bornstein and Vivian Bond have said, "mean people discovered it." I remember watching Christian call some garment or model "hot tranny mess" and thinking. *This is going nowhere good*. It was ruined from inside the queer family.

A few years after Christian's use of the word as a compulsive utterance, social media exploded, amplifying the loudest voices and erasing historical context. It was also around this time that the larger world was waking up to the disturbing frequency of violence against trans people. Maybe this wasn't the ideal time to reclaim such a contested word. After Heklina decided to retire the name Trannyshack and rebrand her club in 2014, she penned an eloquent piece in the *Huffington Post*, followed by another in which Bond, Lady Bunny, and RuPaul all offered their takes on the subject, in favor of the freedom of trans people to use whatever language they choose. Uproar ensued.

I don't remember anyone getting quite as upset about the word "fishy." *RuPaul's Drag Race* took its sweet time to discontinue that chestnut. "Tranny" began as an edgy-but-cute nickname between trans women and drag queens, but "fishy," if you follow its logic, means "you look so much like a woman that your pussy smells like rotting fish." *Nice.* Of course, I know that most people who use "fishy" as a drag compliment haven't thought through this line of logic, and I can't waste my time fighting about it.

As for the t-word, Bond, Bornstein, and others—bighearted, deeply intelligent people who understand context—decided not to die on that hill and ceded the battle.

The antagonistic punk spirit that had managed to pull "queer" out of the slur heap was of another era. Queer Nation started amid strife and violence largely unimaginable to the current generation of kids who are proud to call themselves queer. The reclamation of queer was the work of irreverent people, anti-assimiliationists who were capable of making jokes through bitter tears. They are the reason so many kids refer to themselves as queer today.

I was once sitting in a bar with Vivian Bond, and they said some disparaging, off-the-cuff thing about "straight people," then turned to me and said, "You know I'm not talking about *you*." I said "of course I know," and I did. They didn't have to explain a thing. But I also exhaled a sigh of relief, because though Vivian didn't have to explain, and I was glad about that, I am so glad they did. I've never felt like *straight people*.

Around the time of Heklina's decision to change the name of her club, I texted Vivian about something, and V's greeting was, "Hi, Tranny!" Another exhale and also a giggle. With that comment it was as if Vivian had swiftly and skillfully opened a bottle of contents under pressure, or disarmed a grenade.

The first time I took a class at the yoga center where I was considering a teacher-training, I wasn't sure I belonged there. It was an earnest urban ashram, where all of the teachers wore egoless white and used the same script, where they sat and chanted under an altar to their guru. I was overcome by the insufficiency of my reverence. I didn't want a guru. Then, a tall beauty in capri pants and pigtails sauntered into the room and unrolled her mat. When she turned around, I saw that her lacy hot-pink tank top read, in extravagant cursive, "Dreamboat Tranny." If she could feel welcome here, so could I. If this was her spiritual community, maybe it was fabulous.

Ultimately and obviously, it is not for me to decide the fate of the t-word. But I was embraced by an expansive community that included many trans folks, and the only way I could be embraced by that community was through its expansiveness. If you look only at the surface of me, my life, my partner and my gender identity, there is nothing that qualifies me to be part of the LGBTQ+ community. Yet here I am. I have been adopted by these iconoclastic foremothers and rambunctious brothers. I think the best way forward is for us to expand, not contract. That goes for our vocabularies as well as our communities.

A while ago Heklina threw herself a birthday roast and placed ten queens on the dais, all there to do their worst. At the outset, one of the roast-esses, Jackie Beat, gave a kind of trigger warning. "Here's how this works," she said, "I'm fat," and then moving down the line she pointed out each queen's core roastable qualities: "She's old, she's a has-been, she's a slut, and she looks like a troll." The rules of the roast were implicit and held firmly in place. Then Ana Matronic said, "This is all about context, kids! Context. It's what we had before we had the Internet." Exactly.

Each queen went as far as she could without crossing the line into real cruelty while Heklina sat and feigned horror, as though she wasn't the one who had planned the whole thing.

Is a roast the S/M version of joking, pushing the limits while adhering to a strict menu of rules and boundaries? If polite conversation integrates humor in order to create a smooth ride, a roast is a rollercoaster.

A year later, I was talking with a millennial about cultural appropriation. They said it was always wrong. I said it depended on degree and context, to which they replied, "You only care about context because you're from the nineties."

♔ ♔ ♔

What are the limits of humor? Of language? Standards of acceptability fluctuate, for the culture and for me. Humor lands differently with me at different times of my life, and if I am honest, different times of the week or the day, even now. Sometimes the same words can be hurtful or healing depending on how much I've slept or how recently I've eaten. But I would rather have the option to be hurt and healed by humor than not be able to use it. Heklina's roast worked on me like therapy.

Conventional lefty wisdom and common kindness tell me if there is doubt, don't make the joke. Then a naughty little voice in me protests. I don't want to hurt anyone, but I want to make them laugh. Even better, at something they don't think they should laugh at. It's a powerful feeling.

Karl, in whose living room Queer Nation had its first meetings, offered that most of the people calling out artists on their speech are not artists themselves. Good point. "I think I stand with the clowns," he said. So do I.

By "clown" we don't mean the water-squirting flower, big shoes, scaring children cliché, but the archetype, the jester as social critic. In this sense, of course, drag queens are clowns, and much of their humor, even the basest, lays bare and tears into structures of power. Any good clown does that. But it's not as simple as refusing to "punch down." Truly good clowns evoke empathy when they invite us into the risk of laughing at the struggles of others. Punching across. Not just a "he deserved that pie in the face," but a deeper, more painful "there but for the grace of God go I." The best uses of irreverence deepen our understanding of what it is to be human.

One of the funniest things Marc ever said to me was "Hey, could you hold off on smashing the patriarchy for a little while? I'm still using it." Funnier still was when I met him to see *Black Swan*. There were a few ex-ballerina types milling around the wine bar of the fancy movie theater. "Damn," he said when I arrived. "I was kinda hoping you wouldn't show up. This place is full of hot women with low self-esteem." *Punching down, darling?*

As for drag queens, I don't know what I would do without their embodiment of women. At the clubs I came up in, though queens made incessant fun of femininity, I never felt like they were making fun of *me*. Some performances induced an initial cringe, like when a queen painted on a black eye to portray a battered woman. But it turned out that queen had endured abuse as a child, which I hadn't, so maybe experience overrides gender. I was questioning the oppressive aspects of femininity right alongside them, working it all out: body issues, privilege, whiteness, misogyny, beauty, value, sexuality, sensitivity, permission, vulnerability, authenticity. Ultimately, my feminism is big enough to hold the commonalities, intersections, and differences of drag catharsis.

The drag club was a zone in which anything could happen, and the assumption was that everyone could handle it. If it upset you, you could actually talk to someone in person about it or you could leave. The ethos was punk. *Enter the mosh pit at your own risk.* (You might not know what that is unless you're "from the nineties.") Now we use the word "problematic" as shorthand for "just plain not okay—end of story," but the reason the word was made up in the first place was to sift through complication, to ask questions—to open conversation, not shut it down.

"I want to live and I want to love. I want to catch something that I might be ashamed of," as Morrissey sang (himself oh-so-problematic). Sometimes humor is like disease, an itchy rash you can't help scratching, a mark you have to live with and warn people about. Humor is also like love. It can hurt and it can heal, and I want to be open to its potential.

REAL
LADIES

The club I joined is a unique one, open to all genders and filled with queer men flying their femme flags. The majority of the performers were cis men whose gender identity didn't correspond to what they expressed onstage as queens. There were drag kings, of course, many of whom proudly identified as dykes. There were performers who played in the genderfuck zone, who now might identify as nonbinary. There were drag queens and kings who later came out as trans, who had found kinship and safe space for their gender expression, with drag perhaps serving as a threshold into trans identity. There were trans women regulars gathered near the front of the bar to meet their devoted following of datable men. There were trans women who performed as drag queens at every stage of their transition, and there were trans women who performed in that space but never identified as drag queens.

If you walked through that cute crowd at the Stud with the bar on your right, most Tuesday nights you would see her. Just at the vestibule between the two halves of the space, perched atop that bar, was a regal redhead, the only person whom the bartenders allowed to sit in their busy work space, the bar, her throne. Veronica Klaus sat, wrapped in bias-cut charmeuse, teeming with tulle or draped in taffeta, heels on her dangling feet, gloves, veiled fascinator affixed to her head, a floral essence hovering around her. Her position in the physical space of the Stud illustrated her place in its culture, as a bridge between the community of trans women in the front of the club and the drag performers onstage in the back.

First and foremost, Veronica Klaus is a lady, a legitimate chanteuse. At the Rrazz Room or Martuni's, Veronica served her Peggy Lee voice with a veteran jazz trio, making me hoot over some forgotten gem from my mom's record collection or cry into my martini at the first line of Joni Mitchell's "For Free." But the first time I saw Veronica onstage at the Stud, as part of a cancer fundraiser for Juanita, she launched into "Movin' On Up," the theme song from the 1970s TV show *The Jeffersons*. On the tuba.

To a tongue-in-cheek description of me as a "real girl" performing drag, Veronica, in a column she wrote at the time for one of the LGBTQ papers responded, "Cut me, do I not bleed?" Her utterance contributed to a vital rising tide of voices emphasizing that trans women are women and all women are real.

In 2004 I was thrilled when the time finally rolled around again for "Imposter Night." An inside joke for which performers set aside their famous divas and turned their mimetic skills on each other, "Imposter Night" was a topsy-turvy gesture inside of that already carnivalesque space, a chance for performers to play with radical departures from their usual personas. Juanita More! went for deep cover, setting aside her elegance to don the matted fright-wig, buck teeth, and coke-bottle glasses signifying Buttlicka of Guerneville. Renttecca, who normally wigged out to hard rock, turned up as her gospel-queen drag mother Nikki Starr and raised the roof with "Long as I Got King Jesus."

I chose Veronica Klaus. Mr. David helped me out by borrowing a dress he'd made for her, a cloud of purple polka-dot tulle with a black velvet bodice. Veronica immediately knew something was up. She had never been the object of an Imposter Night escapade, and worried, reasonably in that culture of ribald humor and raucous insult (all in good fun but still . . .), that she would be ridiculed. As a trans woman, Veronica was absolutely part of the world at the 'shack, but she upheld its classiest, most classical pillar. The crude comedy that flowed through that place was not her mode.

The crass headline for my performance gesture for that show could've been "Real Girl Imitates Trans Woman on Imposter Night." The word "imposter" itself could be a trigger for a trans woman in that space. But nothing like that crossed my mind. In choosing Veronica, I upheld the adage "imitation is the sincerest form of flattery." I admired Veronica for her talent, elegance, and intelligence. We both played in the space of drag and in our different ways helped move conceptions of gender beyond the binary. I was a cisgender woman out to convince people, through performance, that I could be a drag queen. Veronica was a transgender woman who likely had to convince people that just because she performed glamorously in spaces where drag queens thrived, she was not a drag queen. My intention was to highlight our commonality in that space.

I considered "tuba-synching," but that would've been a cop-out. Veronica is a singer. I had to sing live. Besides, if I was going to cause her the anxiety of possible ridicule, I could at least take the risk of being a little bit vulnerable myself. It would be my first time singing live alone onstage—terrifying. And as Veronica, I would wear about a third of the makeup I normally wore as Fauxnique. A crimson lip, cat eye, and natural brow would replace my usual mask, exposing me further. I used drag's powers of levity to create a little bubble of self-protection. I didn't attempt a torch song or tearjerker, but backed by a bluesy instrumental, did a swinging, down-tempo version of the 'shack showtime herald, *The Muppet Show* theme.

After the performance, Veronica enveloped me in a soft, perfumy hug of genuine appreciation. Genuine as well may have been her relief that it was me, a lady as tenderhearted as she, who imitated her that night.

What I realized much later was that Veronica, by accepting my offering in the form of a song, had granted me permission to sing. After that Imposter Night I would start to find and liberate my own "real" voice.

Veronica later wrote a one-woman show called *Family Jewels: the Making of Veronica Klaus*, which addressed the subject of her transition on her own terms with candid humor. In it she mused, "Do I *feel* like a woman? What does a woman *feel* like?" As I watched her, I thought *I ask myself that question every day.* Later I wrote my show *Faux Real* which showcased my own musings: what it is to "be real," how drag was for me a practice of authenticity and liberation.

GENDERFUL

One night at the 'shack, a trans woman, tall, thin and intense, approached me with the same vibe as the villainess in *Barbarella* ("my pretty-pretty") and said in the same *eee-vil* tone, "Mmm, I get it. You're like a *woman*. Only smaller." Her calling me "small" made me giggle. In my giant platform heels I stand over six feet. Maybe she was inverting a shitty transphobic comment she might have received: "you're like a woman but taller." Was it a read, or a come-on, or both? Whatever it was, it playfully displaced my cis womanhood as the centerpiece of femininity. It was fucking great.

👑 👑 👑

In 2009, I made a one-woman show, *Faux Real*. I performed it for years, in various versions, all over the place. In it, I spend an hour and many costume and wig changes dancing, lip-synching, singing, telling stories, werqing my ass off to prove with my words, body, and fully made-up face that I'm a drag queen. I stick to the command, "show, don't tell." I don't spell it out for my audience. *They know.* It usually works. Usually.

In 2015, I performed *Faux Real* in Berkeley, where everyone is smart. Berkeley, home of Judith Butler, author of *Gender Trouble*, where I was in a play in which the name "Hegel" was uttered as a minor punchline and greeted with guffaws. "Huh-ho! Hegel! *Hi*larious!" Berkeley, where the insinuation that the audience *knows* is as delicious to them as farm-to-table produce. After my show, at this same German-philosophy-loving theater, a man approached me and said *the thing*. The thing that grates.

"Okay," he said, "wait, I don't get it."

Here it comes.

"So, you're like, a *woman* pretending to be a *man* pretending to be a *woman*?"

I think I successfully contained my eye-roll, but failed to stifle my sigh.

"I'm a drag queen."

"Wait, what?"

"You just saw my show?"

"Yeah, but . . ."

"I'm a drag queen. And also a woman. That's why I wrote that show."

"???"

"Ooh. Will you excuse me? I'm parched. So *great* talking with you. Thanks for coming!"

I could've been more generous. I usually reply to this binary-dependent confusion with some variation of "a drag queen does not have to be a man impersonating a woman, but is another creature, her own special creation, like in the song from *La Cage Aux Folles*!

I also could've been meaner. As a drag queen, shade is my birthright. But after so many versions of the same conversation over the years, I didn't have it in me.

Unsurprisingly, I have never had to explain any of this to a post-millennial. Nor to a child. The fact that anyone can do drag any way they please, makes total sense to children. In 2012 as part of a fellowship at a museum, I orchestrated an event in which teams of children devised outfits for drag queens. A blend of *Project Runway*, *Drag Race* and family craft night. Kids with all kinds of gender expression were thrilled to play with living dolls who then proudly walked the runway in their kinder-craft creations. The event reaffirmed something I've known forever: drag queens and kids are like chocolate and peanut butter. We like to play dress-up and dream ourselves into fantastical ways of being. And anyone who has spent time with both a cranky two-year-old and a messy queen can confirm that they are kindred creatures in more ways than one. As Margo Channing in *All About Eve* says of children, "they'd get drunk if they could."

Regarding my own drag queen affinity, when someone like me imports her very specific cultural location to a broader forum, she's gotta know some people may need a minute to catch up. I might roll my eyes when called upon to re-explain how any of it is possible: how I'm a cis femme drag queen, hetero-married woman living a queer life, a performance artist who can talk about it with a straight face. As I say at the beginning of my other show *The F Word*, I'm not really exhausted by educating allies. There are no dumb questions. But I prefer the smart ones.

In 2017 I engaged in a public conversation with RuPaul bestie and femme extraordinaire Michelle Visage at Stanford University. *Fancy!* The room was full of joy, with just the right amount of light reading and partial shade between me and the woman of the hour. During the Q&A, a well-spoken young person confronted us about the ways in which our work and self-presentation encouraged "compulsory femininity." I did my best to greet this staunch character with good cheer, but as a responsible elder, I had to challenge them. The fact that they framed our femme trappings as compulsory, even for ourselves, was a leap (as if I live my entire life in full face and heels. *Alas, no.*) To suggest that we could or would compel others to adopt our version of gender was simply untrue. Their line of logic revealed a painfully narrow definition of femininity. And that felt, well, femme-phobic. And dare I say, misogynistic? This possibility came flying at me like the ball I never did have any interest in learning to catch and hit me in the head in the middle of that Q&A. Had we closed the doors on our understanding of femininity? Had we let the bad people own it?

For decades I've been in the process of working, werking, *werquing* through the multiplicities of femininity. Meanwhile, I'm afraid it is being re-essentialized out from under me by well-meaning folks who don't want to wear high heels and makeup, to shave their legs and underarms, in order to be seen as women. No one needs to do that. Just because *I* do something sometimes doesn't mean I think everyone should do it. *Vive la différence!*

It has been sobering to grow up and realize that the work I thought my generation had done with our gender fuckery and riot grrrl feminism, the *reclaiming*, perhaps must always be undone, generation after generation. It is no wonder that the queer kids who came of age with Britney Spears instead of Annie Lennox, Sheila E., Madonna, Grace Jones, and Tori Amos are defining femininity in this limited way. Their most famous pop icon was a child star who grew into an auto-tuned, faux-tanned doll driven batshit crazy by the literal patriarchy. No wonder they're suspicious of the expansive possibilities of this thing we call femininity. A femme's work is never done.

I think right now the ways in which we're pinning down and defining the various expressions of gender is healthy for the culture and helpful for those expressing their genders in various or variant ways. The naming of variant gender expressions make them less "other," less alien. I also think the insistence on "this but *not* that" floods in and washes away our understanding of multiplicity and simultaneity. How can the rules and possibilities of queerness stand together? How can we?

In a 2019 public conversation with nonbinary writer-director Joey Soloway, my friend Cara posed a big, open question: "Would you like the future to be genderful or genderless?" I don't know if

Cara coined the word, but I fell instantly in love with "genderful," as if she had—an illustration of her vivid, gregarious, way of thinking. The word brings gender into conversation with those other words so often suffixed by "full"—play, wonder, beauty. I wanted it in our vocabulary. *FULL FULL FULL.* I thought. *Yes! I want more!*

"Genderless," said the creator of *Transparent.*

Sigh, said I.

I was surprised Soloway came down on the side of "less." I had always conceptualized nonbinary identity as more "yes and" than "no thank you." But then again, Soloway's years in Hollywood must have granted them a special perspective on the pernicious aspects of the gender binary. If I had spent my career bashing against the walls of sexist Hollywood instead of steeping in the small queer art pond of San Francisco, I might not feel so genderful.

For me, "genderless" connotes neutrality. I understand neutrality as part of a practice of inclusion. Neutral has its place in mediation and meditation, laws and restrooms, undergarments and formal footwear. But mostly I think "neutral" is a construct created to avoid the mess and complication and multiplicity. I live for color.

This reveals an important point about the difference between performance and personal identity, between artistic exploration and living in the world. I can conceptualize nonbinary identity, but it's not mine to define. I live in queer land; but still, I live in it as a cisgender woman. I play onstage as a drag queen.

We no longer use "real girl," a term that erases trans women and nonbinary people. All women, all girls, all people are "real." Now we cis women who do drag have a proliferation of names to call ourselves—Bio Queens, Hyper Queens, Diva Queens, AFAB Queens (acronym for Assigned Female at Birth)—which acknowledge that our drag is no less "real" than that performed by cis men. I still prefer the term, invented by Ruby Toosday in

1995, that so succinctly encapsulates the play between artifice and authenticity that forms the backbone of my own drag project: "faux queen." I dare anyone to watch me and call me a faker. I'm suspicious of authenticity. All drag is faux anyway; that's what it's about.

One night at the club Karl ran into a student of his after the show. "Wait. That was your friend up there, right?" she asked him. "I don't understand, does she just…feel that way?" Karl answered her earnest question as best as he could with a straight face and an explanation of the spectrum of drag, but couldn't wait to tell me that one. We repeat it often, with giggles every time. "Does she just feel that way?" The short answer is "yes," I just feel that way. I am talking about possibilities. The possibility ostensibly, both to imitate the thing and to be the thing that I am imitating. To reflect and analyze. I do drag as a way to reconcile that whole project. Because I just feel that way.

I loved the sisterhood of women and nonbinary folks empowering each other to do drag at the Faux Queen Pageant in 1999, building networks and culture adjacent to, but not dependent on, those dominated by male drag queens. It reminded me of the riot grrrls again, starting their own bands, festivals, record labels and 'zines instead of waiting around for the boys to let them into their club. We have worked hard to make space for everyone to play in this expanded field.

I didn't break down the barricades of a fortress that didn't want me, but ultimately I joined the boys' club. Gay men are the ones who helped me become the drag queen, and ultimately the kind of feminist, I needed to be. I've thrived and learned by *throwing* myself in the ring with them. If they hadn't welcomed me into their spaces, I would not be the artist or the person I am. And what I know about myself as an artist and a person (and a feminist) is that I am not a separatist. I persist with a stubborn desire to come together across difference.

EDIE,
THE STEVE LADY & ME

When I was a ballet-obsessed thirteen-year-old, my favorite book on the subject was *Balanchine's Ballerinas: Conversations with the Muses.* George Balanchine, creator of contemporary ballet, was *the* master choreographer and, to me, the women who danced for him were the luckiest people in the world. A muse was an ethereal being who visited the earthly realm to inspire artists and I wanted to be one. If I couldn't dance with the real "Mr. B" as his acolytes called him, I would find my own version, a great artist inspired to make dances just for me.

The documentary *Dancing for Mr. B* (1989) opens on a breathy Darci Kistler revealing that Balanchine, the titular "Mr. B," used to choose perfume for the women who worked for him. "He could tell who had been in the elevator," she marvels. *Creepy.* As I rewatch the film, the ballet stars of my youth appear as cult members under the spell of an overlord who controls their lives, tracking them by scent. Kistler's awe frames this as a romantic gesture, or perhaps an ecclesiastical one. In her footage she ramps up to the expected outburst: "We would've done anything for Mr. B. If he had asked us to stand on our heads we would have." As if standing on their heads would be anything out of the ordinary for ballerinas to do. Standing on their heads would be the least of it.

I moved to San Francisco straight out of college at twenty-one, disabused of my ballerina fantasy, but still secretly wanting to dance for someone. Not *with* but *for*. The difference was crucial. To dance *with* someone spoke of collegial sweetness and collective work. To dance *for* someone connoted romance, a top-down power dynamic in which I, not knowing what I was capable of, would be pushed, my best work pulled out of me. I may have been a freshly minted feminist, but I still believed I needed someone else to get at my best. I danced with a few choreographers in those early years, forging lasting friendships and collaborations, but never found that "master artist" to whom I could be muse. After a halting start as a choreographer, my first real works came from frustration that no one would uncover my hidden brilliance. No one would create me. I had to reach into my own soul and pull out whatever I could grab. I'm glad about that now.

After I started going to the drag club, my choreographic practice deepened. I created six short pieces between 1998 and 2003. By the time I created Fauxnique, I was already an artist. In Fauxnique, I found a way to be my own muse and my own master, and in so doing I set both of us free. My artist/creator self could put herself on display by way of a bold creature who would do anything for her, who would stand on her head and then some, and wear any perfume I chose.

When I was thirteen and in thrall to Mr. B with his pliant ballerinas, and to Edie Sedgwick with her precarious body, I also went all-in for proto-goth band Bauhaus. The *drama* of it all! Bauhaus named themselves after the German modern art and design movement that was also a scene, like the one Andy Warhol had engendered with Edie as its mascot. They were art fiends, theater nerds, high-minded poets who managed to maintain a modicum of punk swagger.

Daniel Ash, a feral creature on guitar with his wolfman hair;

Peter Murphy, hollow-chested, bug-eyed and consumptive (a truly alarming wheeze punctuating the lines of the live version of "Rose Garden Funeral of Sores"); Kevin Haskins, looming behind his drum kit like a handsome Frankenstein's monster; and David J, the bassist in his severe Caesar haircut and Lennon specs, perhaps a mad scientist posing as straight-man. I idolized Peter Murphy, but David J was the one with whom I imagined I could connect. The closest thing Bauhaus ever had to a big hit was "Bela Lugosi's Dead," a nine-minute paean to a silent film star written by David J. Dominated by Murphy's cavernous baritone vibrato and an audaciously simple bass line, the song endures as an evergreen anthem for black-clad sulkers. Find a goth who can't name that tune within two seconds of its skeleton clack drum intro and you've found yourself a poseur.

After I had grown up and outgrown goth (to the extent that anyone ever can) and had come back around to it through drag, I developed a deep friendship with Vinsantos who was, as "the macabre snob" of our drag world, the gothiest goth around. Vinsantos reminded me that the goth, the clown, and the drag queen are close kin, he being all three. In his early drag days, he was a scary ghoul, a skinny genderfuck live wire— Iggy Pop crossed with Siouxsie Sioux—with a penchant for fire performance, notorious for nearly setting the Stud ablaze in 2001 on "Punk Xmas." Really, though, like all true goths, Vinsantos wears his tender heart on his tattered sleeve. He sweetens friendly exchanges with nerdy dad humor (Me: "I'll meet you in twenty minutes after I jump in the shower." Him: "Don't ever *jump* in the shower!") or with valley girl silliness: "Oooo I love this, it's soooooo spoooooookers! It's like, the ghost of TOTALLYYYYYYYYYY!" He writes witty piano tunes about twinning with his bestie or being haunted by his grandma's restless spirit, and he loves his mother and sister. The queens who adore their sisters are always the ones I bond with best. Vinsantos introduced me to David J.

At the time I met him in 2007, David J was producing other people's music in addition to his own, Vinsantos' new album included, but had also just finished writing a play. *Silver for Gold: The Odyssey of Edie Sedgwick* consisted of a series of monologues performed by the eponymous character, interwoven with songs about her, performed by David and his band, all anchored in poetic context by a narrator. David was looking for his Edie when Vinsantos told him about me. After coming to see me perform my solo show *Crying in Public*, a love letter to sensitive souls, David asked me on the spot to play Edie. I accepted with as much professional cool as I could muster while I stepped outside my body and watched my teenage self positively lose her shit.

When I arrived in LA to begin work on the play, one of David's friends asked upon meeting me, "Is this your muse?" The comment blew a breeze of flattery over me (*Had David J from Bauhaus referred to me as his muse?*), but left a chill of ambivalence for which I immediately felt ungrateful. Here I was being exalted as a muse by someone I had exalted in my youth and now I was grumbling internally about it.

I had to remind myself that I was entering into this project as my own artist with a weighty body of work. That work had engendered this opportunity. What had prepared me to play Warhol's (and my own) waifish muse was my practice of drag. The suspension of disbelief necessary in drag made it possible for me, at that point in my life a grown-ass woman of thirty-seven, to play Edie who had died so young. I could upend the subject/object relationship and delve into the meanings of artist, muse, idol, mentor and enjoy it. Drag bestowed a kind of Warholian distance.

David J turned out to be the good guy I suspected he was. Humble, curious, and thoughtful, with a genuine desire to experiment outside his area of established expertise and a willingness to consider other points of view—all signs of a healthy artistic ego. During rehearsals, David recognized that my performance work included figuring out the intricacies of my character's movement, so he handed the role of choreographer over to me with full credit. He gave me space and trust, priceless gifts in the context of a hurried artistic process.

I think David J wrote his play to figure out a new perspective on Edie's life and times, although that life and those times had by then become classical topics of cultural study. His description of his writing process conformed perfectly to the classical muse narrative. "She perched on my desk like Tinkerbell," he said, "and the story just poured out." David's comparison of Edie to Tinkerbell was apt—Edie, a sparkling pixie in every extant photo. But it was also kind of reductive. No shade to Tinkerbell, but Edie's incandescence rivaled Marilyn Monroe's. So did her tragedy. Edie herself could have been an artist—she could dance, draw, think—but she ended up an allegory. The degree to which Edie's actual life seems inconsequential, her ghost so easily a Tinkerbell, sits uneasily with my feminism. If I were Edie's ghost, I don't know if I'd have been so generous.

I think Edie Sedgwick is as much a symbol of the hideous recklessness of the patriarchy as she is of the druggy confusion of her era. A woman trying to be free and happy but thwarted too early for that ever to be possible. A girl abused by her father, then by art-daddy Warhol and his scene's excesses. A muse. *Amuse.* There to amuse, her pain and sadness symbols never taken seriously and never transformed into anything she could use for herself.

Early in the process, when I met with David to read through the script, I brought this up. How Edie was thwarted by her era, the same as my mom's—the sexual revolution, the swinging sixties— and how sad it was that she died before she could have discovered women's lib.

"Wait, you're not a *feminist,* are you?" implored the sensitive one from the art band.

(And me, almost doing a spit take.) "Yes. I am a feminist."

"But you don't, like, hate men?"

"Of course not." *Bless.* My idol was human. Sometimes he talked like a dad.

Differing perspectives on feminism notwithstanding, David treated me respectfully, like a real artist, and this here feminist prioritizes actions over words. Besides, way back in 2008, years before Lena Dunham sashayed nude on HBO and Beyoncé put the word up in lights, only feminists brought up the word "feminist."

Upon reading *Silver for Gold*, I was struck first by the profusion of monologues I would have to learn and then by the strangeness of the only other character in the play, a wounded healer with the head of a horse whose narration contextualizes Edie as an incarnation of Persephone. This Greek mythological take was an elegant rendition of Edie's plight, reading the Factory as the underworld and Warhol as Hades. It also provided a classical context for my private critique of the concept of the muse. I saw fantastical visions of the only person who could pull off the task of playing this horse-headed guide, someone I had encountered ten years before, in the underworld of clubland.

The Steve Lady was the first queen who released the full force of my drag fandom, and she did it by looking like she was barely doing anything. I had spent much of my twenties trying to be cool and critical, to pull apart and inspect every piece of art that I saw. The Steve Lady connected me back to shameless fandom. She taught me that sometimes it all comes together in the body of a masterful diva.

The Steve Lady was a rare creature of truly gender-fluid beauty. As a man, Steven Price was breathtaking. About six-foot-four with wavy brown hair swept away from his face, olive skin, cheekbones that could slice your chest open, and a cat-eyed gaze that could magnetize your heart right out of the bloody gash. The Steve Lady was fierce. If you've ever been to the zoo and seen a wild cat, chances are, if you got even a glimpse, it wasn't doing all that much. But if that cat made a single, economical move, you were riveted and you felt the potential of its power, the depths of its reserves. She was fierce like that. And also like a supermodel: a little freakish and alien in person. Later, I met Steven's actual real-life sister and she was just as gorgeous. Like a warrior princess from *Game of Thrones*. If Mattel ever makes a fire-twirling, Burning Man Barbie, she should be the model.

The first time I saw The Steve Lady perform, she was doing David Bowie's "Rock and Roll Suicide." Her look was high genderfuck dandy, out-Bowie-ing Bowie with chiseled features under a big fedora and fashion sketch body in nipple-grazing corset trousers. All she had to do was stand there. A lot of people think drag lip-synch is just standing there and moving your lips to a song, but few can get away with that. The Steve Lady could. With a keen balance of radiance and magnetism, she put out enough energy to completely draw you in and then kept you at a distance, hovering weakly around her force field, begging for more.

I had never understood why those girls in the old concert footage of The Beatles screamed like they did. The second time I saw The Steve Lady perform, I knew. She appeared from behind the sequined curtain in a short black wig and a little hat with a mesh veil over her face, film noir style. The song was Bowie again, "Lady Grinning Soul," one of his deep cuts.

As usual, The Steve Lady barely moved. This was true of all of her numbers, even one in which she did a tango and another in which she, as a demented blue-Afro-puffed Barbie, brings a stage full of life-size toys to life with an electric shock. Now she really barely moved, every shift of her weight a meaningful punctuation. When she finally deigned to raise her veil and fix her gaze on us, there was something amiss, her gaze a ghastly pit of soulless black. I screamed. My body did it first and then my brain caught up. She reached into the audience and started making out with a boy, her fingers aggressively clawing through his hair. Then she grabbed his head and held it up over the crowd, over her head. *Aaaggghhh!* The Steve Lady was the vamp goddess of my gothic teenage dreams, and if she had been an actual vampire, I would have been hers for eternity. She would be my living end, as the song goes.

She had achieved her special effects with easy props, just as she had with her living toys number, the circuit breaker on which the action hinged just two toilet paper rolls and a potato masher attached to a Kleenex box and spray-painted silver. Here she wore those blackout sclera contact lenses that Hollywood uses to signify that someone is possessed. The "boy" she made out with was a model head used for hair styling. These days every drag queen with a set of cool contact lenses, a YouTube tutorial, and a little taste in music thinks she's an artist. I want The Steve Lady to haunt their dreams so they wake up and spend the day thinking long and hard about the mediocrity they've perpetuated, and then change their ways like drag Scrooge inspired by The Steve Lady as the Ghost of Drag Past, Present and Future.

I didn't meet The Steve Lady until the Trannyshack tenth anniversary, after I had proven myself and we recognized each other as drag royalty. When I asked how and what she was doing in LA, she replied, "*It's* an actress now. *It* does some plays. Sometimes *It* directs." The preferred pronoun "It" served The Steve Lady well, with her cold beauty of haute, hard edges. She claimed that her take on drag was based on "the absurdity of fashion" but nothing about The Steve Lady seemed absurd. Steven, in everyday conversation, did have a propensity for absurd made-up words, like when he referred to himself and his community as "fagoons" with a straight face. It was always with a straight face. A straight face was the main ingredient in The Steve Lady's beauty and humor, both mean and rotten in the best way. Gay humor that can twist a tired straight girl compliment:

"Ohmigod you're so pretty I hate you" into the perfect "You disgust me." In that spirit, The Steve Lady was cunty.

I introduced Steven to David J and he agreed; the Steve Lady would lend otherworldly glamour and acting chops to the strange role he'd written. I was relieved to have a fellow actor to bounce things off of in this process, ecstatic that that person was one of my favorite drag queens.

👑 👑 👑

I arrived at the Villa Carlotta in the pouring rain, the courtyard behind the crooked French doors in the lobby overflowing with eclectic plants as Los Angeles gardens do. Apparently, *The Day of the Locust* had been written here. Maybe in this very courtyard. The Villa Carlotta was a famous, fabulously down-at-the-heels apartment building on Franklin Avenue in Hollywood. David had arranged a funky sublet for me there from a British actor who, from the clues in his apartment, was go-to talent for audio book voiceover. Living in Hollywood for that month, I was struck by the number of people working in the film industry whom we never hear about. This offered comfort as I began my own stint in LA with a job to do and no illusions of "making it."

In the decade since I stayed at the Villa Carlotta, all of its long-term tenants have been kicked out and replaced with pricey Airbnb lodging. "Inspired by its history as a home and haunt for the artistically adventurous," its website states, "Villa Carlotta is a Hollywood residential hideaway for free spirits drawn to the iconoclastic energy of bohemian Los Angeles . . . with five-star service, the sophistication of a landmark boutique hotel, and the modern conveniences of a well-appointed condominium." I enjoyed the building's final bohemian era before greedy predators kicked the artists out and turned their ghosts into a marketing emblem.

After I settled in, David came up to my apartment with

a thoughtful little vodka cocktail proffered, to my delight, by his wife Annie, a character out of *Absolutely Fabulous*, with her sharp dyed black bob, animal prints and "sweetie-darling-sweetie-darling." The cocktail was my first in a while, my last for a while, as I was trying to watch the empty calories in an attempt to resemble Edie as closely as I possibly could. But I hadn't backslid into deprivation. I couldn't do the work required of me while starving. What had been theoretical when I signed on became real: I would carry this show, and it would be my most challenging project yet. We talked over the script in preparation for rehearsal.

The next day, David was working with the band, and I was pacing around in a corner wrestling with a monologue when Steven arrived.

"The Steve Lady!" I cried. "Miss Thing!" he answered, followed by exaggerated drag queen air kisses.

He offered to run lines with me and when I paused for a grounding breath, asked, "Does she want notes?"

"Ohmy*goddess*, queen, do I want notes?" I cried. "I'm so scared. Yes gurl, give her ALL of your notes."

I didn't know that in addition to being a drag legend, as well as an actor, Steven was also a director with a Mary Poppins bag of acting tricks and the rigor and patience to go with it. We worked that material every which way. David had his hands full with the band and didn't mind at all that Steven took the helm as my outside eye.

After the second day of rehearsal, Steven took me to Jumbo's Clown Room, the famous strip club where Courtney Love had danced once upon a time. I had only ever seen pole dancing in the context of a cabaret variety show, not in its proper context as a stripper art form, and I couldn't believe how amazing these women were, not just highly skilled, but highly trained, as if this was their calling. One dancer had a Sailor Moon vibe going on, sailor-style bikini, blondness, big anime eyes, and feigned innocence. She was really good, but when I looked over at Steven as she finished her set, he sneered disapprovingly. "I don't want to see a stripper *smiling*."

He said "smiling" as one might say "clipping her toenails on the bus." The Steve Lady's preferred femininity was not that of a nice lady, not a smiler, but a poisoner, an ensnarer, a beguiler.

When I got to know Steven as a person, I found him kind. And his disdain for smiling did not preclude outbursts of joy. One of these, which I had the pleasure of hearing often as we became friends, was the command, "Live!" As in, "Live your life!" As in:

"Should I get a double scoop of ice cream?"

"Live!"

"Should I spend three hundred dollars on pink satin pumps?"

"Live!"

"Should I strip off all my clothes and shave my head and run naked through the Scientology Celebrity Center with a steak knife?"

"LIVE!"

After tech rehearsal Steven asked if I wanted to go get dinner.

"Well, I've kind of already had my dinner," I said. (I had brought and scarfed a few pieces of sushi.)

"Oh, you *ate*?"

He looked over at my empty to-go container and then at me with big, hungry eyes, and with his long, graceful fingers and a straight face, mimed mouse-nibbling the tiniest piece of sushi in the world. An anorexic girl in-joke. Then he threw his hands in the air and cried "Live!" and we went out for platters of Mexican food at a place with red vinyl booths. That's when I knew he saw me.

What I didn't know when Steven entered into the project was that he was ill with advanced cancer. He had undergone a round of chemotherapy a week before the rehearsal process started and was still incredibly weak. The dire reality was that The Steve Lady had retired from performing long before I got to know "It." Our project would be his last.

All the while he would joke, gallows humor intact.

"You know, sometimes I just forget that my body is *riddled with cancer!*" He threw his long arms up in the air like a showgirl when he said "cancer!"

"Steve Lady!" I would say, "why am I just getting to know you *now?* Why couldn't we have been friends ten years ago?"

"It's for the best. *It* wasn't very nice back then. *It* was, well, a real cunt."

The Steve Lady I knew was not a cunt. *It* saved my ass. I could not have done that show without *It*.

On the second to last night, as I came backstage to prepare for Act II, in which I drag myself across stage in a stupor as strung out, post-Ciao! Manhattan Edie, Steven looked at me with soft eyes and scooped me up in a big hug. "Girl, you *transformed* tonight. You *became* her. I *live!*" All I wanted at that point was to make The Steve Lady live.

Near the end of the run, David J came into my dressing room with a furrowed brow and a pursed lip, looked at me in the mirror as I was doing my face, as I had done for the last six shows, and said, in his thoughtful way, "Are you sure you need that much makeup? I wonder if it might be good to tone down the drag a little bit." *Wait. WHAT?* The makeup was the intersection between me and Edie. The makeup *was* Edie. It was her mask; she said it herself in recordings I had researched. Edie was, in that sense, a drag queen. And the only reason I was there was that I was a drag queen. David would never have cast me in that role at my age unless he had seen me as a drag queen. Drag was my way in, the only way I could play my old self's thin-spiration role model without succumbing to that self's habits of body hatred. I talked David out of his concern, got into full face, and gave my best performance yet, liberated by the mask.

The process of playing Edie helped me to rediscover the drag queen superpower, that the mask *is* the thing. That mask, my drag, gave me permission to play at being ten years younger, four inches shorter, thirty pounds lighter. And from behind that mask lies a special potential to connect personally with an audience, to show real vulnerability.

After the run was over and I was back home, my first priority was to treat myself to a milkshake, my second, to finally read the reviews. Whenever I'm in a show, I never read any reviews until it's over, a practice I share with many and which I cannot recommend enough. *Silver for Gold* was no exception. David J, a heartier soul than I, considered it his duty as director to read every single word about his play as soon as he could. I dug up the reason for David's eleventh-hour second thoughts about my Edie drag on the *Los Angeles Times* "Reader Review Blog," which bore the *LA Times* logo and looked deceptively official. A naïve, pre-Twitter moment of democratization. The writer who had sown David's doubts was not a hired reviewer, but a layperson. His piece started, "Edie Sedgwick was twenty-seven years old when she died . . ." *Spill the tea, Mary,* ". . . but this actress looks like Roy Scheider after a binge session at Sephora." *Hahahahahahahaha! HA!* And the last remnants of the anorexic fourteen-year-old in me thought, *Roy Scheider. So sinewy! At least he didn't call me fat.* I can't imagine how hated I would be for having the audacity to play Edie Sedgwick at the advanced age of thirty-seven if this play had happened in our golden age of social media discourse.

As the years march on, I will only look more like Roy Scheider in drag. An ugly bitch on my own commode. (Pardon me while I go watch *All That Jazz* again.) In lieu of eternal youth and beauty, I'll spend what little time I have left working to expand those concepts. I would rather *live* and create a world that welcomes the beauty of wisdom, that congratulates women on their achievements—for living lives—instead of shaming them for looking like they've stayed around too long and gotten tired. I want to celebrate women for contributing something valuable, not for being beautiful, dying young, and reinforcing our fantasy of the tragic artist's muse.

On Steven's last visit to San Francisco, late summer 2008, the same year the play had happened, Juanita threw a small dinner for him at her apartment with scrumptious food and a bunch of friends gathered around, most of them from the earliest days of the 'shack, before I was involved, and many of whom I was seeing out of drag for the first time. We had come to pay our respects, but the vibe felt relaxed and festive. Maybe this was because a lot of people in that room had lived through the worst era of AIDS. Death was an estranged cousin from the old days.

Steven stretched his supermodel limbs out on Juanita's bed and received us all, looking exhausted but still stunning. Something awful had happened to one of his eyes, either from radiation or the cancer itself, so Putanesca had bedazzled a pirate eye-patch with black jewels so Steven could still be in full command of his glamour. With one eye The Steve Lady held the room.

Steven died that September. Soon after, generations of friends and family came together for a big memorial drag show. Among us were many drag children who didn't actually know Steven, only the legend of The Steve Lady. It seems weird to go to the memorial of someone you didn't know at all, but that's what people do with stars. I performed and, without imitating It, tried my best to embody the principles of The Steve Lady, the main one being suspenseful stillness. To "Out of the Blue" by Roxy Music, I stood in front of an electric fan, as still as I possibly could for as long as I could before putting my hand on my hip, and then again before turning my head. I tried, on the cellular level, to transform into the kind of magnetic creature that The Steve Lady was. I forged a few friendships there, as I've learned one sometimes does at memorials. I hugged my new friend, his old friend Jessica, and I said, "I just got to know him. I wasn't done! We were just getting started." And she said, "I knew him a long time and *I* wasn't done. I wasn't done."

We just kept hugging each other saying that: "I wasn't done."

The Steve Lady left us wanting more.

NOT NOW,
VOYAGER

I. Wrecking Reykjavík

"Fauuux . . . NIQUE!"

That is always how Heklina said my name.

"Faux . . . nique! I got invited to go to Gay Pride in Iceland, but I don't wanna go alone. Too boring. I was gonna bring Princess Kennedy and Putanesca. Wanna come along?"

"Do I? Omigod Hekles, of course I do. Do you think we'll get to meet Björk?"

"Hahahahahahahaha-HA."

I took that to mean "fat chance."

I was excited to be going to Iceland, especially with these queens. Putanesca is like one of those Hollywood actresses with a penchant for multiple adoptions, a collector of drag children. She is a selfless pragmatist who will give you the shirt off her back, and if you throw in some tulle, tinfoil, and fake flowers, she can make you look like a deity from another planet. Putanesca was one of the art-damaged queens who really stood behind me and always championed my ideas, however cuckoo. Though she could be prickly, I knew she would probably be a good travel companion, as she always insisted on taking care of people. I loved Kennedy but guessed we might get into a little bit of trouble. Kennedy was a party queen whose parents were high up in the Mormon church. Long-legged, blonde, and spray-tanned, her drag persona was akin to Paris Hilton, but *so much* prettier, a party girl with a heart of gold. A few years ago she moved back to Salt Lake City and transitioned to become the fabulous woman she was always meant to be. In addition to creating glamour as a highly skilled hairstylist, she also spent time as a journalist, works generously on behalf of homeless youth, and is now perhaps Salt Lake City's most ardent trans activist.

Back then, however, in 2004, Kennedy's main role was not as an activist but a kind of activator. Right after the Miss Trannyshack pageant, I went out to hear Juanita DJ at a holiday party. I met Kevin at Vertigo on Polk Street and after having waited forever for the bus, I really had to pee. The club had a situation in which the door to the bathrooms opened right onto the dance floor, so I shimmied straight over to it, only to have Kennedy and two of her twink friends cut me off at the pass, run right in, and slam the door. *Oh, she did NOT.* I banged on the door.

"Kennedy! Kennedy! I actually have to PEE!"

"Oh, hello, Fauxnique. Won't you please come in?"

"Thanks. You don't mind if I pee in front of you do you?"

"I don't if you don't."

Kennedy and her friends were having a "meeting in the ladies' room."

Vertigo's ladies' room was blessedly clean, well-lighted and spacious, perfect for a "meeting," but I did wipe down the seat and put a strip of toilet paper on either side of it before sitting down "because you're a lady," Kennedy said. *Thank you, yes I am.* No sooner had I sat down to pee than Kennedy turned around from her business meeting and stuck a key piled high with snowy coke right under my nose.

"Fauxnique?"

What the hell? I hoovered it up, "just to be neighborly," as Glamamore is fond of saying. She says it about drinking whiskey on a Monday, and I thought it now, as if Mister Rogers and not a sexy blonde drag queen was the one proffering expensive drugs while I sat on a toilet in a gay bar. But really, the distance between Mister Rogers and Kennedy is not so extreme. She would never nearly kick someone who actually had to pee out of the ladies' without offering her some of the reason for having nearly kicked her out. The good Mormon kid survives in the party girl. Indeed, I have on one occasion seen Kennedy drop everything to literally help an old lady cross the street. She's a good egg.

And speaking of good, that bump might still remain the only truly good cocaine I've ever done, so Kennedy's etiquette was fortified with real generosity. I can count on one (and a half) hand(s) the number of times I've done that drug, and vow never to do it again unless three conditions are present: first, it is out in the open for everyone to share, no hiding in the bathroom business; second, after doing it, I can jump into a pool with my high heels on; and finally and most important, no one was harmed in the process of its production and procurement. This last condition is the impossible one, and the reason I'll never do it again. There is no such thing as fair-trade cocaine, my darlings. Also, it's just not that great. I'm talkative enough, and really, if I'm gonna bother to do drugs, I want to see some shit. And yes, my attitude toward drugs shifted dramatically between my mid and late twenties, a huge leap from the straight-edge kid I was. But still, this memoir is about drag, not drugs. My drug exploits could barely fill a four-page 'zine. That night, though, it was good fun.

Kevin and I danced and talked and talked and danced and talked and talked and talked. Then at 2 a.m., I followed Juanita and her gaggle of fashionable young acolytes to the Grubstake, the tiny Polk Street diner immortalized in "The Golden Age of

Hustlers," trans legend Bambi Lake's ballad of the San Francisco demimonde. I ordered what Juanita always ordered, The Nugget, a cheeseburger with a fried egg on it. Juanita's boys were agog as I proceeded to actually eat the whole thing.

"I thought dancers didn't eat."

"Gurl. Who do you think I am, Ann Reinking?"

"???"

"Gay card revoked! I'm hungry from all that dancing and I only did the one bump of coke."

"Wait, what? You did one bump? Who does one bump? Omigod Fauxnique, you're so cuuute."

I've been pretty lucky all my life that my substance use has remained at a level that's quaint to the serious party people.

In Iceland it wasn't so quaint though. We landed in the treeless mist at around nine in the morning to the accompaniment of a flight attendant who partially satisfied my desire to meet Björk by sounding exactly like her. "We arrre staerrrting ourrr des-sent int-to Rrrekjavik." We picked up the duty-free booze we had been told to bring as a hostess gift—booze, like almost everything in Iceland being prohibitively expensive—and headed to Heklina's friend Coco's house. Robust, half-Icelandic Heklina, impervious to jet lag, set her bags down and immediately prepared to leave for a swim in one of the tiny city's copious public pools. I, never one to resist the opportunity to get into water, joined her despite the fact that at this point I was practically hallucinating from lack of sleep. Though the swim did me almost as much good as a nap, I struggled to stay awake through the delightful dinner our host made: salad and salmon, perfectly cooked, one of the few edibles that Iceland doesn't have to import. The next morning we wasted no time, waking up before any drag queen ought to so we could pile into a rental car for a tour of some geysers (which Icelanders pronounce "geezers") and a soak in the steamy, divine, alien waters of the Blue Lagoon.

Wrung out, steamed out and still pretty jet-lagged, we

headed back to Coco's house to get ready for our show that same evening. After eating half a piece of leftover salmon with some salad and neglecting to drink enough water, I proceeded to get into drag. Our show was not at a gay bar at all but at a small, stark theater, more like a meeting hall. Puta and I did "America" from West Side Story (her idea). Puta placed me in the role that Lady Sergio usually assumed, that of Rosalia pining for Puerto Rico. Puta cast herself in the role of Anita (as sung by its originator, Chita Rivera), making her pro-NYC argument with sardonic comebacks and high kicks. The song's instrumental break trumpeted a climactic fake fight consisting of faux slaps and wig-pulling and much gnashing of teeth and shaking of crinolines. The mixed crowd loved all of us, but of course after the show it was Princess Kennedy who landed a spot on Iceland's version of *Good Morning America*. She was the prettiest. Within the hour she began proclaiming "I'm huuuuuge in Iceland!" The ice bucket full of free beer in the dressing room was a lovely unexpected postshow perk, and, knowing how expensive even a beer would be in the club we were headed to after the show, I drank one and then another in quick succession. I was thirsty.

After heading back to our host's to drop off our drag bags and switch gears, Kennedy made a couple of screwdrivers with the vodka she had brought and handed one to me.

"Fauxnique?"

"Kennedy! You think of everything. Geez, I haven't had a screwdriver since high school."

Puta and Heklina abstained.

No sooner had I finished my screwdriver (*that juice really goes down easy, and I'm so thirsty*) than Kennedy poured me another over the ice of the last one.

"Oh, I . . ."

"Drinks are so expensive here."

"Right." I drank half and gave the rest to Kennedy.

"Fauxnique, I didn't know you were such a lightweight."

"You didn't? Oh."

We walked to the club, which, like everything in Reykjavík it seemed, was two blocks away. It was all blond wood and clean surfaces.

This will be a cute place to spend the . . . oh no. On the heels of the sudden realization that I am drunk is that feeling: *Oh NO. Nonononononono.* I run out of the bar just in time to puke in the adorable cobblestone gutter in front of the adorable bar in adorable Reykjavík. I kneel there for a while on the cool stones, thinking *now that the poison is out of my body, maybe I can go back to the bar. What would Kennedy do?* For her, this would be a minor setback in an otherwise lovely evening. Then I remember how little water I have had to drink, how much I must have sweated and steamed out in the hot spring earlier that day without realizing it, how dehydrated I must be. Then I remember *"beer before liquor . . ." Oh, how could I have forgotten?* Even just thinking the words "never sicker" brings the next wave. Kennedy and Puta come out of the bar.

"Oh. That was fast, Fauxnique," says Kennedy.

"Gurl. What the fuck? We gotta get you home," says Putanesca.

"Well, then I'm going back into the bar! See you later, queens!" says Kennedy.

I steady myself enough to walk, but Puta insists on propping me up the whole way back to the house, which feels too intimate. I really just want to be by myself with my head down and my tail between my legs, five paces back in case I need to throw up again. Which of course I do in seconds, and when I do, Puta insists on actually holding my hair, or rather my wig, back.

"I can . . . (blugh) . . . you don't have to . . . (blugh)."

"Gurl, please. You're. A mess."

When we get to the house, Puta literally carries me up the stairs. I really, really could have just stayed on the comfortable floor. It would have been perfect just to curl up like a dog by the door, and periodically open it to take in the fresh Icelandic air. And puke.

After my harrowing spin through that poisoned night, Puta never taking her eyes off of me for a second (in the bathroom even, so I didn't die on her watch I imagine, but still, really? The bathroom?), I finally fall asleep. Or pass out. Somehow, I remember to set an alarm to wake me up in time to prepare for our gig the next day: queen-waving from a parade float and then performing on the main stage in Reykjavík's LGBTQ Pride. *Ugggghhhhh.*

Princess Kennedy, who was out until 6 a.m. is already back from filming her Icelandic TV spot looking as fresh as any Miss Utah ever did. I drag my bedraggled, hungover ass downstairs to gulp down a few glasses of water and find Puta at the dining room table already starting to get into face in front of her portable makeup mirror.

"Good morning, Puta," I venture.

"_____"

"Hey, Puts, thank you so much for taking care of me."

"_____"

"I'm sorry I was such a mess."

"My back. Is killing me."

"I'm so sorry."

"You know I have a bad back."

"Thank you so much for doing it, but you didn't have to carry me up the . . ."

"_____"

"I'm sorry."

"I'm so sick of dealing with drunks."

I gave Puta a wide berth until we had to be onstage together to do "America" again. I feared our fake fight during the number would transform Puta's annoyance at me into the true rage she held for every other drunk who had ransacked her life and that she, as Anita, would haul off and actually punch me in the face.

That was the first and only time I have been called "a drunk." If she hadn't been so mad and I hadn't been such a pitiful excuse for one, I might have taken it as a compliment, let it make me feel like Bette Davis as Margo Channing in *All About Eve* for a moment, but I couldn't. I just felt like the kind of silly drunk straight girl who invades the gay club and makes it all about her: lightweight as dead weight.

I tried not to dwell on it, but I felt badly. I apologized to Kennedy, who, though she wasn't the one to carry me up the stairs, was the only one I could talk to. She handled it with party girl, big sister wisdom.

"Oh Fauxnique. Don't worry, honey. Sometimes we drink too much. Everyone's had to have someone hold her hair back at some point. Once, I was in the middle of being introduced to a Japanese princess and I had to turn around and puke into my purse."

Princess Kennedy's story may have been apocryphal, as it is too similar to the 1992 incident in which the first President Bush threw up on the Prime Minister of Japan, but hers is more fun, and the spirit in which she relayed it meant a lot to me.

I managed, in a tenuous triumph over my hungover haze, to get myself together, having applied a decent drag face, laced myself up in the royal purple chiffon goddess gown Mr. David had handed down to me, and grabbed my long velvet coat in case the Icelandic August breeze cast a chill over our Pride float ride. It was not until we arrived at the outdoor stage in the designated roped-off zone of street that I noticed my drag bag felt eerily light. *No.* I had forgotten that fucking crinoline! All the drama of my duet with Putanesca depended on that stupid pile of fluff. My throat sank into my stomach. Heklina greeted me just then.

"Fauxnique. Good. You're here. I'll go tell the stage manager."

"Hekles, I just realized. I forgot my crinoline." Tears threatened to ruin my face as my negligence threatened to ruin the performance.

"Ugh. Fauxnique, if you start to cry, I swear I'll kill you!" Heklina only half joked.

"I know. I'm so sorry. I'm so sorry. Is there a way we can avoid telling Puta?"

"Ha! No! Well, whaddyagonnado? Let's send Donni back to get it. He just left the house."

Thank the Gods of Drag for Donni, Heklina's sweet, even-keeled friend. I was glad it was him being sent to do this errand and not Coco, with whom I was sure I was also on thin ice after having spent all night in his house expressing my loud and frightening bout of alcohol poisoning.

Puta's cloud lifted when our performance was greeted by one of the biggest and most enthusiastic crowds for whom we had ever performed, and it was during the day, which is usually an obstacle for Drag. The weirdest thing was the hysterical volume and number of teenage girls screaming for our performance. The sweetest thing was the number of families, mostly of the hetero type, toddlers on their parents' shoulders waving rainbow flags. It appeared that all citizens of Reykjavík loved drag queens. They were far ahead of the cultural curve in their typical Scandinavian way.

Later, while we were waiting in line to pee at a neighborhood bar, we were approached by a cute blonde girl of about seven or eight, and her little brother, around five. She walked over to me, little brother in tow and looked up.

"Arrre you a boy or a girrrel?"

"I'm a girl."

"Do you want to be a boy?"

"No."

"Do you ... want to be a girrrel?"

"Yes. Yes, I like being a girl."

"Arrre you a lesbian?"

"Well, I mean, I've visited Lesbos once or twice, and I might visit again, but I didn't like, need to rent a U-Haul and move there or anything."

"???"

She proceeded down the line of drag queens.

To Kennedy: "Arrre you a boy or a girrrel?"

To Puta: "Arrre you a boy or a girrrel?"

And then when she got to Heklina, she studied her for a moment and said, "You. Arrre a boy."

Every time Heklina brings up how much of a mess I was in Iceland (it was over fifteen years ago and she still brings it up): "Haha. Fauxnique! Remember when you tried to keep up with Princess Kennedy in Iceland?"—as if I could forget—I just reply, "You. Arrre a boy."

II. A Lady in London

A couple of years after Iceland, we went to London. A group of queens had opened a club there called Trannyshack, and after her cease-and-desist letter failed to do its job due to some international loophole, Heklina, ever the businesswoman, figured if she couldn't beat 'em, she would join 'em, and parlayed it into a gig. Because I happened to be standing in the room when the invitation came in, Heklina asked me if I wanted to go. That is often how it works with Heklina. She wants to get the gig booked and move forward. Not a lot of hemming and hawing with her, which often works in one's favor if one is in the right place at the right time. With me on board, she had checked one queen off the list and had three to go. The other three were Kiddie, Putanesca, and Holy McGrail. I hoped Puta knew I planned to drink lots of water and not much booze. No one would be holding my hair back this trip.

Holy McGrail was another faux-hyper-cis-bio-AFAB-femme queen. A champion crafter, she specialized in debilitatingly long nails, always encrusted with jewels, and gravity-defying wigs, always at least four at once. In all of her finery, it was impossible to tell what gender she had been assigned at birth.

Our first gig was at the Soho Revue Bar for Trannyshack, the club that stole our name. The booker, the main name-stealing culprit, wore a necktie that said "FEMINIST" down its length in big block letters. I took this as a good sign. But as soon as I settled in, the clucking and chattering began. I was putting the finishing touches on what to me was a super draggy face for my Madonna number when one of the London queens walked in. I introduced myself as any decent person does backstage, and instead of a "nice to meet you" she made a stink face and replied "You're a *woman*? Well, that's kind of false advertising, innit?" And then she literally pretended I wasn't there for the rest of the evening. Heklina came over a few minutes after the exchange and said, "Can you try to look a little less fishy? The English queens are mad!" I wondered why she cared about the opinions of these catty queens who had stolen her club name instead of sticking up for me like she had in the past. Probably because they held the purse strings in that situation. On our way out, the promoter said to Heklina, "We'd love to have you back, but next time don't bring any women." Feminist indeed.

Our next London gig was at the Royal Vauxhall Tavern (RVT) for a club night called Mister Sister, which was the total opposite. There I met people whom I would recognize as London branches of my nightlife family tree. The historic RVT was kind of an analogue to our home bar the Stud. Everyone was welcome and accepted in the same way they were back in San Francisco. It was a queer bar, not a boys only club. The fact that we encountered such radically different spaces illustrates the complexity and simultaneity of drag and nightlife microcultures that can exist in any city. The Mister Sisterhood was powerful and supported my return to London several times in the future to perform solo shows. Now both the RVT and the Stud are at the forefront of the movement to preserve queer bars as historic spaces with a mixed crowd at the core of their nightlife ecosystem—women, men, trans and nonbinary folks mixing and making vital art at a time when money and real estate threaten to squash the vibrancy of queer culture.

III. Ciao, Fauxnique!

In 2013 I was invited to Rome by a collective of Italian drag kings and faux queens calling themselves Eyes Wild Drag for their "Genderotica Festival," a week of performances, talks, and workshops around gender. All of the events happened at two "occupied" venues, a massive Brutalist cinema and a baroque eighteenth-century opera house. The idea of a group of artists just occupying a building to keep it from being torn down— artist squatters' rights—was inconceivable to me as an American, and one from San Francisco no less, where forcing artists out of their homes and studios may as well be the official pastime. I thought immediately of all of the decommissioned cinemas in my city that had become bougie gyms, all of the multimillion-dollar artists' lofts occupied by code-writing "creatives" and all of the artists and arts organizations needing space. *Why couldn't we be like Italy?* Of course, Italy was at the time surviving its own political turmoil. It doesn't feel like the utopia of funding and arts support that a lot of Northern Europe feels like, but these spaces and the cultures created there provide an inspiring model for what it is to fight the powers that be. The DIY pluck of the festival reminded me a little of nineties San Francisco.

Italy is one of those cultural locations in which traditional binary gender roles and their compulsory performance hold strong. This complicated my presentation as a feminist cis woman drag queen in ways I had not experienced in the US. Some of the feminists I spoke to in Italy met my reclamation of feminine drag as a liberatory practice with skepticism. In the talk I gave at Genderotica, I attempted to drive home my point that high heels can be fierce and feminist by telling one of my favorite stories, a borrowed one, from my fashion-forward trans femme friend Chloé. She was once walking down the street in Rome and saw a woman standing outside a church, coiffed and made up for filth. Fendi sunglasses, nails done, gold jewelry sparkling, silk Versace blouse, pencil skirt. The *pièce de résistance* of the outfit: crutches and cast. On the leg that wasn't in a cast was a perfect stiletto heel. I would have died to see this fabulous creature in person. In my home city, yoga pants and Ugg boots clothe the uninjured horde, but this woman was out and about ruling and owning it with a cast on her leg! *Werq.*

My femme fortitude was tested when the group brought me with them to perform at Pride in Catania, Sicily, which turned out to be one of those places where the necessity of LGBTQ+ Pride resonates deeply. Along with the compulsoriness of gender roles often comes a less than friendly attitude toward out queerness. If Rome reminded me of nineties San Francisco, Sicily was a little like the American South. The tight-knit queer community in Catania really seemed to need each other.

Upon our arrival, I checked in with the appointed stage manager as soon as I could to figure out the performance conditions, which had been difficult to determine during the rest of the trip. With her halting English, and me trying to ask questions in the best Italian I could muster, which was pretty much just me speaking Spanish and switching the ending vowels, I determined that the charming outdoor stage that existed in my mind, with its backdrop of fairy lights and bougainvillea, did not exist; or rather, the fairy lights and climbing flowers would manifest, but to quote said stage manager:

"Ah, there is, ah, no stage."

"Ah. Ok. Ehm. *Y el piso es?*" I answered in Spanish "*¿Que es "piso" en Italiano?*"

"*??? Ah. Il pavimento?*"

"*Si si. Il pavimento.* Ah. Pavement? I'll be dancing on . . .

pavement?" I'll be dancing on pavement . . .

"*Il pavimento è pietra.*"

"*Pietra* . . . Oh. Cobblestones?"

"*Sì!*"

Gurl. I had my black swan number planned. The one with all of the echappés and hops en pointe. By this point in my life's journey I was no little swan, no spring cygnet, so dancing en pointe at all was pushing it, and on cobblestones I would court career-ending tragedy. In light of this, I was gunning to see the performance area at least, to work out which parts of the cobblestone ground might be danceable, to rework my number to meet its limitations.

"It is time for lunch."

"But I need to go look at the performance space and figure—"

"We will see the stage later. Now we eat." *Of course we do.*

And honey, did we ever! We sat at an outdoor table on the volcanic rock patio of the town gay bar. In Catania, it seemed, every place had somewhere to sit outside; apparently better to risk exposure to open homophobia than to waste one possible warm moment under a trellis of orange blossoms. I respect that fully. Course after course: the freshest seafood I'd ever encountered, perfect cheese, vibrant salad, vegetables Alice Waters would envy, pasta as a side dish, which Italian restaurants in the US pretend happens here, but really, *pasta as a side dish*. And then *affogato* for dessert—ice cream with espresso poured over it (which, by the way, they also have at breakfast). I realized then that although Italy struggles with arts funding and LGBTQ+ rights in some of the ways that the US does, and Sicily even more so, their major currency is luscious, abundant food. The cliché holds. If nothing else, Italians will always feed you. Italy had been an adventure in eating, but the food in Sicily was something special. With my teenage torture around food a distant memory, I could enjoy it fully.

Over that beautiful lunch, ugly issues were being discussed.

It seemed that the Pride producers were scrambling to find lighting because the tech crew they had hired, on discovering that the gig was gay, had pulled out at the last minute. It was unclear as to whether the hired crew knew all along and decided to strike as a deliberate tactic, to screw over the queer folks and make them have to scramble for another solution. So, with scant resources to begin with, the hardworking organizers of Catania Pride were forced to spend time and money searching for someone to light the show that evening. For me, this threw light onto the privilege my friends and I enjoyed as members of the San Francisco LGBTQ+ community, the luxury of the problems we discussed around our Pride: whether our Grand Marshall was properly politicized, or our floats too commercial, while the Catania queers were dealing with open hostility, and in this case, possible attempts at sabotage.

After lunch, while I waited for the performance space to open for a surface-check, I popped into a class that one of the drag kings in my cohort was teaching as part of the schedule of Pride activities—a masculinity workshop: how to use movement to prepare the body for male drag. I rarely perform as a drag king. In fact, one Morrissey imitation aside (*so nelly!*) the masculine space has been the site of all my drag failures. I really bit the dust when I performed as a butch bike messenger for a Bike to Work Week benefit. I even brought my bike to the club and put it onstage. What I thought would be an easy two-minute song ("Take Stuff from Work" by King Missile) was a tricky spoken word piece, always the hardest to lip-synch—once you lose your place, forget about it. The same had happened when I attempted "A Boy Named Sue" by Johnny Cash. I tried to forget them both and move forward.

However, in Italy the body-based performer part of me is curious about what is on offer. The workshop starts with standing, grounding, placing our weight to cultivate stability and strength. This feels good. Then we start to move, careful not to torque the neck or head too much when we turn to look, careful not to give away too much as we pretend to greet each other. Then we walk, not swinging our arms too much, not bending our legs too much, moving our hips as little as possible. It is a trip, and for me, profoundly uncomfortable. I feel suddenly trapped and stiff. I begin to feel sad. I exchange worried glances with Alessandro, the adorable twenty-year-old gay boy who is one of the organizers of Catania Pride and who had helped me get settled earlier in the day. Our exchange of glances says, *Gurl. This shit is hard core. I don't think I can keep it up.* Then we share a bemused little giggle. We shake it off and sashay our separate ways, Alessandro to help the rest of the crew set up the show, and I to my hotel room. I text Marc and tell him about my experience, how sad it made me to be prevented from moving my hips. "Yeah," he writes back, "masculinity can be a real bummer."

When I arrive at the square where I am to perform, a gaggle of about fifteen baby queers are doing a sort of flash mob gesture dance in chairs to none other than "Let's Have a Kiki," the Scissor Sisters song written by and featuring my fabulous friend Ana Matronic. It is the queer anthem of the summer and seeing these kids "werque and serve" as Ana commands in the lyrics gets me giddy. I beg them to teach me a few of their moves, and soon I am fully revved up to give Catania Pride the Fauxnique Experience.

I perform my ballerina number with gladness in my heart for my hip-sway and the femme family tree of which I am a part, and with a picture in my mind's eye of that dignified and unstoppable Italian lady soldiering on with her crutches and her flawless outfit. I channel my best Super Femme on those cobblestones in my pointe shoes. After the show, Alessandro comes backstage with an elegant lady, not quite as done up as Chloé's wounded warrior queen, but chic and perfumed, with a silk scarf and gold earrings. Both are dabbing at tears.

"Fauxnique!" says Alessandro. "This is my mama."

Alessandro's mama opens her silk-clad arms with a very Italian "Ah!" and wraps me up in them and of course I start to cry too, trying not to get makeup on her pretty scarf. It is a big deal for a Sicilian mama to show up at Gay Pride, even one as fabulous as Alessandro's. I tell her that I think her boy is wonderful. She says she knows. The greeting my friends and I throw around at home every June with a twinge of irony really means something here: "Happy Pride."

PAGEANT IV:
BUTTERFLIES ARE FREE

Pageant day arrived. Everything was in order. I had enlisted four stellar professional dancers from that part of my world, two men, two women, who had nailed the choreography and backup lip-synch in five short rehearsals. We gathered all of the props and costumes just in time for dress rehearsal at the venue. A drag dress rehearsal is one of my favorite things to behold: a parade of muscular men in T-shirts, cargo shorts and high heels, wielding cardboard props. The sight of a queen lip-synching sans wig or lipstick calls up drag's vulnerability, its dependence on the drama of the mask to work its real magic.

Thanks to my tightly organized group of dancers, we had time to run through the number twice, enough to encounter the glitches we would need to avoid in performance. I was as ready as I could possibly be, and as calm, though my nerves were zinging. All I could do was visualize embracing and being embraced by this audience. I had been in their place many times, but now I was on the other side. Bigger than any I had ever encountered from the stage, this audience was a monster I couldn't wait to meet.

Backstage was the madhouse you would picture, to rival the backstage at the Muppet Show: feathers flying, headdresses knocking things over, clouds of hairspray, clucking and cackling.

I had to find a good corner in which to prepare, but finding space for my usual fifty preshow jumping jacks, a great warmup, and now an obsessive superstition, along with my vintage *Interview* magazine T-shirt, proved a challenge. "One, two, three, four, five—oof, so sorry—six, seven, shit, sorry—eight, nine . . ."

The swimsuit competition went supremely, lots of cheers on the reveal and a hilarious comment about my "fierce tuck" from Heklina.

The video plays to more laughter than I expect, its final lines intoned by my narrator-turned-emcee in his refined English accent: "Here she is, dragging the last of her dignity onto the stage for you, Ladies & Gentlemen, Fauxnique!"

I enter, trailed by the four dancers, who sprinkle fake snow. In my huge, white gauze cocoon gown, I look like Magenta from Rocky Horror playing the French Lieutenant's Woman in a snowstorm. "When I think of those East End lights, muggy nights/The curtains drawn in the little room downstairs."

The four dancers surround me and strip me of my gauze gown, to reveal me en pointe, wrapped in yards of wide white ribbon, a body-conscious dress that references the Herve Leger bandage dresses of that moment's fashion, another layer of cocoon. Meanwhile, the original gown has transformed into a giant butterfly net—yards of loose-knit gauze flowing from a hula-hoop. I bourrée across the stage, away from them. When they catch me, each dancer takes the end of a ribbon from my dress and unwinds me as I turn like a top; this action reveals a delicate lilac chiffon faerie dress. With each reveal, the crowd cheers. My backup girls and boys become ribbon-dancers as they leap through the air with the remains of dress number two flowing behind them. They drop to the floor and lift their arms, fluid movements that become the current of a river that I step into, and then as a team they lift me off the ground. The dancers toss me back and forth between them, pick me up, and carry me on their shoulders. The lifts get grander and the crowd cheers more. Oh, just wait, people! Wait for this one!

The final lift maneuver hoists me up over the dancers' heads, making me look as if I am swimming through the air like a mermaid through water. This gets a huge vocal surge from the crowd. Then, as the first notes of the last refrain of the chorus begin: "Someone saved, someone saved, someone saved my life tonight (someone saved my life, to-night)," I lie down on the floor upstage for a brief moment, and as I rise, so do my enormous chiffon butterfly wings, expanding to a twenty-foot span. I swan my arms with joy as the backup dancers flap and flutter the enormous wings: my own drag flags. A blizzard of butterfly-shaped confetti blows through the air. A thousand new fans go wild.

In all of my years of performing, I have never experienced anything like this moment. Whether I win or not, this is the fulfillment of everything I have always wanted. All of the hard layers of adult cynicism, the art rules, and second guesses that have built up around my childhood fantasies of being a ballerina, of being a faerie, crack apart like an old cocoon. I'm a butterfly! My dancers wrap me up in the huge wings and escort me offstage on the fade-out of the song, which none of us can hear through the noise of the still-roaring audience.

After a gleefully dazed backstage costume change I emerge in my final look: the hat and the muff that completed the swimsuit ensemble with a black satin dress from the late 1920s handed down from my paternal grandmother. She was a Polish-Czech farm girl raised outside of Spokane, Washington, and this dress is one of a few fancy things she owned, a surprising abundance of snazzy dresses for someone who milked cows. Grandma Katherene was an adorable flapper with a pretty soprano voice and, according to family legend, she had worn the dress to audition for the Metropolitan Opera when they held an open call in Seattle. I asked her about this shortly before she died at the age of ninety-eight. "Oh, heavens! I never did audition for the Met. I wanted to, but I got too scared and I never went." My heart broke for her and all of the other girls of her generation whose talent fell into the hole where their confidence should have been. She didn't seem too bothered by it eighty years later, and my dad refuses to believe her, maintaining the legend that she at least gave it a try.

Tonight I would reinfuse that dress with magic. The gown would get into the game, if not for the gatekeepers of the Met, then for the judges of the drag queen competition. Adorning the dress were ribbons and brooches and a tangle of pearls. I wanted to look like I had escaped the Fauxqueenistan Revolution with all of the jewels I could carry on my body. On one ribbon I had pinned a cameo bearing a photo of Julie Andrews from Victor/Victoria, a talis(wo)man only I would see, but powerful nonetheless. Someone teased me about how ballsy it was for me to work a look that already featured a sash, as if I expected to win. I hadn't even thought of that. I did not expect to win. There was no way.

"Second runner up—Buttlicka of Guerneville!"

As I stood onstage looking out at the crowd, I was calm. I was where I belonged. I was in my place, even if I didn't place, and all was right with the world. This rightness was uncanny, as it came from my doing something I never dreamed I would do: perform as a drag queen in front of a thousand people. And yet it was absolutely right.

"First runner up, Mercy Fuque."

Well, there you go. I hadn't placed. It was okay. Even though faux queens and drag kings always competed, everyone knew the only people who ever won this thing had been born boys.

Then I looked down, and right there in the front row of the audience, at the edge of the stage, was Miss Gina La Divina. Miss Gina is a classic showgirl. A trans woman and a trailblazer and more femme than any of us will ever be. A wig stylist extraordinaire, Miss Gina can make you look like you just stepped off the stage at the legendary Finnocchio's circa 1967. I loved Miss Gina, but I was a little afraid of what she thought of me. If ever there was a queen who might disapprove, it would be this drag traditionalist, wouldn't it? She met my eyes and silently mouthed, "You. Go. Girl." My werq was done.

"Well, history has been made tonight, Ladies and Gentlemen, here at Trannyshack. It's been a long time coming. We'd like to introduce to you, Miss Trannyshack 2003. Fauxnique!"

I won. I've never won anything (except for that conciliatory curling iron in 1999)! I immediately burst into tears. I won Miss Trannyshack! 2002 winner Suppositori Spelling places the sash across my body and tries to wedge the crown on my head of teased-out polyester yaki hair. I cry some more. I give a short speech in which I remember to thank everyone, except, like Hilary Swank when she won the Oscar for *Boys Don't Cry*, my helpful, supportive, beloved husband. I float backstage on a cloud and meet more people in an hour than I have met my entire life. A crew from *VH1* is there for some reason, and I realize they probably won't use the interview footage as my lower right eyelash has fallen down onto my cheek and tears of joy have ruined my makeup—and not in a cute Hollywood way.

I have made herstory. People tell me my number made them cry, which makes me cry again. It seems the only person mad at me is Buttlicka. There's chatter about controversy, but no one reads me to my face. The final reveal is how uncontroversial it is.

After hundreds of goodbyes Marc and I shove my hula-hoop gown, chiffon wings, and giant muff into a taxi and head home where I sit in bed and remove the clusters of weave hair from my own while I replay everything over the phone with Precious Moments between bites of Oreos.

The next morning I bounce out of bed after five hours of sleep, ready to rule. Inspired, I get on my bike and go take a dance class, after which my phone is full of congratulatory messages. When I see Mr. David a few days later, he scoops his beautiful hands under mine, curls his beautiful fingers over mine, looks into my eyes and says: "This is the most feminist thing you've ever done."

ACKNOWLEDGMENTS

I am full of gratitude for everyone who had a big or small part in bringing this to life. Sometimes small things do big things, Miss Thing.

To everyone who met "I'm writing a book!" with "I can't *wait* to read it!"

To everyone who taught me to dance and write.

Marc, for everything always. Husband, I do not know what I'd do without your eye, your ear, your mind, your hand, your shoulder. You are my acerbic, accurate comma-chameleon and the love of my life. I know how lucky I am.

Mitzi & Tom, my parents, for *literally giving me LIFE*. For taking me so many places and supporting my cross-country launch at seventeen. For always saying "tell me about that" instead of "what is that?"—a great way to approach life and art.

Kevin Clarke for bringing me to that damn club and spending so much time tied to me in so many ways. You've got a friend (for life).

Karl Soehnlein for wisdom and woo and artist dates. For giving me the deluxe MFA treatment and being there right when I needed you.

Michael Nava for trusting my work and believing in my story. I can't tell you how much your swift affirmation meant to me. Of *course* you and Mitzi share a birthday.

Salem West & Bywater Books for beautiful, clear, gracious support. And Ann McMan for the fabulous design.

Matthew Davison for kikis and good counsel and the best email introduction I've ever seen.

Evan James for seeing my work so clearly so many years ago and circling back to it with your discerning eye and beautiful mind.

Chad Lott for swooping in and punching it up. You're a mensch and a detail queen of the fiercest order.

Selby Schwartz for being one of the first people to ask "Hey, have you ever thought of writing a book?" For seeing her *as* a book before she was one and knowing just what she needed.

Michelle Tea for getting her started. Everyone knows you're the coolest cool girl, but you're also the nicest cheerleader.

Philip Huang, my naughty cheerleader, my faerie clown, my *A.C.S.* I could *never* have done this without you.

Beth Pickens, I *would* never have done this without you. Your work has saved my life and transformed it.

Jennifer Baumgardner for telling me it was a memoir.

Stephen Petronio for making it seem urgent.

Rick/Rohona/Bogina for telling me to call Matthew and making me laugh 'til I cry.

Glamamore & Juanita for bringing me into the fold. I love you *more*! See?

Heklina for creating the 'shack, that magical space, and defending my honor.

Everyone I wrote about. You and your work have made me who I am: Kevin, Glamamore, Juanita More!, Ana Matronic, Vivian Bond, Veronica Klaus, Heklina, Vinsantos, Jim Winters, Putanesca, Princess Kennedy, Timmy Spence, Peaches Christ, Precious Moments, Miguel Gutierrez, Suppositori Spelling, Bea Dazzler, Ruby Toosday, Mercy Fuque, Rusty Hips, Eyes Wild Drag, Judith Butler, Michelle Visage, David J, Leigh Crow,

Renttecca, Lady Sergio, Kay White, Chloé, Alessandro, Jason, Susan, Michi, Missy and Jessica Tanzer-Conroy.

All the people who gave me places to read: Michelle Tea, Julián Delgado-Lopera, & Virgie Tovar at Radar Reading Series; Jennifer Lewis at Red Light Lit; Juli & the Poetry Center at San Francisco State University; Peaches Christ & Out Loud and Heklina & D'arcy at Oasis; Jack Davis & Jess Curtis/Gravity at CounterPulse; Eric Bloom, Rob Bailis & Red Hen Press Poetry Hour at Broad Stage; Gregory Gajus at Saints & Sinners/ Tennessee Williams Festival; Siobhán Cronin & Carl Tashian; James Carroll Fleming & Mica Sigourney/A Bar of One's Own at the Stud; and Juanita/The House of More! podcast.

To the people and places where I first developed the cabaret shows and talks that seeded these chapters: Jessica Heidt at Climate Theater, D'Arcy Drollinger at Oasis, Dawn Amber Harvey at Hackney Attic, Maysoun Wazwaz at SFMOMA

All the boys and butch queens up in pumps who made lists, remembered cues, reminded me to do my jumping jacks, calmed my nerves, rotated mirrors, brought me sandwiches, ran my fan, put eyelash glue on confetti and picked up my sweaty Spanx: Ryan Darley, Mica Sigourney, Kegan Marling, Jesse Hewit, Brian Knecht, Travis Santell-Rowland, Stanley Frank, Kevin Hoskins, Matthew Benedict and Joaquin Castillo-Arana.

Liam Passmore—who came here to judge, but participates so beautifully and gave me one of the best lines in the book.

Jessica for walks in the woods, for reminding me that I *will* be misunderstood and for being there when I am.

Lawrence for driving me around in that powder blue Rabbit and still being my friend.

Molly D. More to come, more to share. I'm *lichen* it!

Gregory Stock for reminding me I already had a real foundation.

Jim Winters for art nerd lineage, queer-only-child vulner-ability and listening to me read super early drafts.

Long live Shindig!

To all the people who sat and listened while I read to them: Marc, Mom & Foxy, Dad & Marie, Karl, Kevin, Pickles, Matt, Jesse, Larry, Keith, Seth, Brontez, Lawrence, Chrystal, Matthew, Gregory, Molly, Jim, Joshua and Lambert (who saw my deep relationship to "werq" and work).

Arisa White for publishing the seeds of the intro on *Her Kind*.

Headlands Center for the Arts for the gift of time and space.

The Stud: its collective, its former owners, its bartenders and its denizens. Long live the Stud!

Fontaine Weyman, Arturo Cosenza, Kegan Marling, Robbie Sweeny, Gareth Gooch, Robert Takahashi Crouch, Reverend Michel and Eric "Shutterslut" Stein for capturing the ineffable with their cameras.

To the ones we've lost: Phatima Rude, Peggy L'eggs, Nikki Starr, The Steve Lady, Miss Mike Finn, Gregory Nelson and Augusta Moore. Rest in peace, power and glamour.

ABOUT
THE AUTHOR

M onique Jenkinson is an artist, choreographer, performer and writer who dwells joyously at the intersection of contemporary dance and cabaret, and considers the performance of femininity as a powerful, vulnerable and subversive act. In the guise of her drag persona Fauxnique, she made herstory as the first cis woman to win a major drag queen pageant. Her solo performance works have toured nationally and internationally in wide-ranging contexts from nightclubs to theaters to museums, for screaming fans and discerning critics. *Faux Queen* is her first book.

Amble Press, an imprint of Bywater Books, publishes fiction and narrative nonfiction by LGBTQ writers, with a primary, though not exclusive, focus on LGBTQ writers of color. For more information on our titles, authors, and mission, please visit our website.

www.amblepressbooks.com